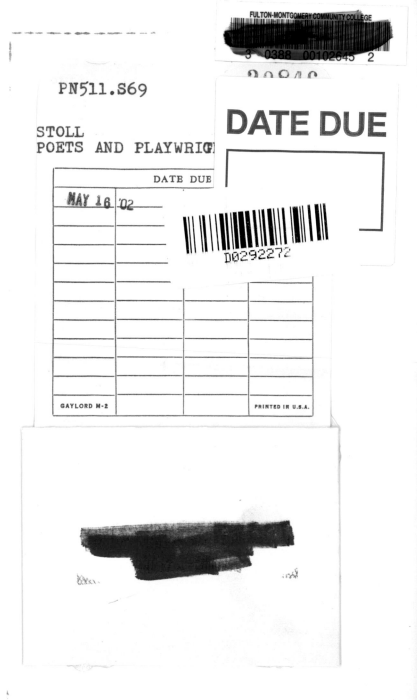

POETS AND PLAYWRIGHTS

Shakespeare
Jonson
Spenser
Milton

POETS AND PLAYWRIGHTS

SHAKESPEARE · JONSON · SPENSER · MILTON

Elmer Edgar Stoll

UNIVERSITY OF MINNESOTA PRESS, Minneapolis

PRINTED IN THE UNITED STATES OF AMERICA AT THE
NORTH CENTRAL PUBLISHING CO., ST. PAUL

Library of Congress Catalog Card Number: 30-8126

Published as Minnesota Paperback No. 1 in 1967

PUBLISHED IN GREAT BRITAIN, INDIA, AND PAKISTAN BY THE OXFORD
UNIVERSITY PRESS, LONDON, BOMBAY, AND KARACHI, AND IN CANADA
BY THE COPP CLARK PUBLISHING CO. LIMITED, TORONTO

Preface

Four[1] of these essays — among them, the longest — are quite new or have not before been printed. The others have appeared at various times in the last ten years. On the first page of the three of these which have in part been read in public, the place and time are indicated, as well as (quite summarily) the sort of changes which may have since been made. The three others, "Cleopatra," "The Old Drama and the New," and "Was Paradise Well Lost?" are, little changed, reprinted by permission from the *Modern Language Review* and *Modern Language Publications*.

The essays are very unequal in length; but to facilitate the reading of numbers III and IX, I have, besides the division into sections, added a few captions to the Table of Contents and to the text.

There is some repetition of ideas, and even of phrases, in the essays on the drama. But one play or character presents problems somewhat akin to those of the others; and every time I approach anew the subject of Elizabethan art in general, I cannot but in some measure traverse ground which I have covered before. In the most recent and extensive of the studies, "Shakespeare and the Moderns," there is, along with new matter, something of a

[1] Numbers III, V, VI, and IX.

review of Shakespeare as I conceive of him, in order the better to compare him with those who in some respect or other are his peers.

I hope that my indebtedness to other writers has been sufficiently indicated. In the interest of the general reader I have intentionally ignored the matter where it was obvious or unimportant.

E. E. S.

[1930]

Contents

POETS AND PLAYWRIGHTS

Shakespeare
Jonson
Spenser
Milton

I

Cleopatra

CLEOPATRA — the name itself works a spell. It wakens memories, renews vibrations; a name that has, I suppose, at no time been forgotten during two thousand years. Ever since the age of woman-worship and chivalry the Egyptian queen has been one of love's martyrs. She is a Good Woman to Chaucer, and figures in his *Legend*. Being all save dull and stupid that a loving woman ought not to have been, she then became all that for her own delight and her lovers' she ought to have been, having loved and been loved unto death. That was the medieval cardinal virtue; without warrant in holy writ, it was the saving grace:

Ne shal no trewe lover com in helle.

And though intellectually we do not accept that dogma, imaginatively we do.

Poets, from Horace to Hérédia, have sung of her; but since Shakespeare put her into a play she has been his; and Swinburne and Heine have chosen to write, not of the person but of the character, not poems but rapturous prose. Shakespeare himself keeps his head. No creature of his pen is so many-colored — so romantic and yet so real. Most of Shakespeare's women are less real than romantic, the creatures of his dreams. They are highly individualized, have their own unmistakable tone and accent, but are not presented fully, in the round, and have few connections with the world as we know it. They are encompassed and enshrined in a penumbra of poetry — we know their emotions but not their everyday thoughts and ways. Shakespeare's Cleopatra, too, is enveloped in poetry, but through it we see her from every side, and are dazzled by her many facets. She is treated sympathetically, yet austerely, in a drier light than Juliet or Rosalind. She is made more interesting and bewitching than lovable, is loved more than she loves. The medieval virtue the poet does not accept at par: he looks upon Cleopatra both as what she ought to be and as what she ought not to be, a very vulnerable heroine, a quite mingled blessing unto her lord, though saved and saving at the last.

1

Though no character of Shakespeare's is more of an imaginative success, there is difficulty and disagreement about the interpretation. Professor Schücking has of late declared that as a whole the character is inconsistent, with a great cleft in the middle, being that of a vulgar, hysterical harlot at first and of a sublimely devoted lover at the end. And discussion of all sorts has arisen about Cleopatra's intentions in her flight from Actium, in her dealings with Thyreus, and in her attempt to cheat Caesar out of her treasure before her death. Did she think of betraying Antony? Did she conceal the treasure to deck herself out for her final triumphal exit, or was it all a little game with Seleucus, and her rage a mere feint to make Caesar think she intended to live? All these questions are interesting to us not only for their own sakes but also because of their involving Shakespeare's methods of presentation in general. But are we not then considering too curiously? We treat Shakespeare as if he were Browning; and the critic who perhaps best knew Browning and Shakespeare both, Mr. Arthur Symons, wrote, more than forty years ago, much to the point:

The dramatic poet, in the ordinary sense, in the sense in which we apply it to Shakespeare and the Elizabethans, aims at showing, by means of action, the development of character as it manifests itself to the world in deeds. His study is character, but it is character in action, considered only in connection with a particular grouping of events, and only so far as it produces or operates upon these. The processes are concealed from us, we see the result. In the very highest realisations of this dramatic power, and always in intention, we are presented with a perfect picture, in which every actor lives, and every word is audible; perfect, complete in itself, without explanation, without comment; a dogma incarnate, which we must accept as it is given us, and explain and illustrate for ourselves. If we wish to know what this character or that thought or felt in his very soul, we may perhaps have data from which to construct a more or less probable hypothesis; but that is all. We are told nothing, we care to know nothing of what is going on in the thought; of the infinitely subtle meshes of motive or emotion which will perhaps find no direct outcome in speech, no direct manifestation in action, but by which the soul's life in reality subsists. This is not the intention: it is a spectacle of life we are beholding; and life is action.[1]

When, however, he says we "care to know nothing" of what is going on in the thought, Mr. Symons is thinking of the Elizabethan or of the whole-souled spectator today, not of the reader or critic, who cares much. And the "drama of the interior," such as Browning's, does not leave such obstinate questionings of our modern spirit unanswered. It analyzes the motives. It presents the character's point of view. Indeed, in large part, the point of view — the character's intellectual structure and anatomy, his opinions of himself and others, in particular his attitude to some special question or issue in the play as contrasted with that of others, together with his purposes, both open and hidden, and the mental processes involved — all this is the character itself. The character lies in the psychology, and actions and the manner and turn of the speech are less important. But in Shakespeare these are more important,

[1] *Introduction to the Study of Browning* (1906), pp. 4–5.

point of view being slightly and not clearly and explicitly presented; and consequently, since the character can be only what Shakespeare made it, point of view should be less important to us.

With him the main thing is action, says Mr. Symons above, what the characters do. But Shakespeare's characters have, above all, much to say. Yet it is not the internal organism that concerns him but the man as he appears — as he acts and speaks, and as (in a sense) he externally thinks and feels. The speeches are not so long as in Browning, but they are much longer than in the stage plays of our time, and are far more developed than the action requires. They present the thoughts and emotions, the fancies and imaginations, of the moment, and serve both to reveal character and to give the action significance and force. In a fashion, of course, the characters give their point of view fully and clearly enough — in respect of others, themselves, or the question in hand. Hamlet is an example — so are Iago, Brutus, and Macbeth. But yet they do this very inadequately for our present-day interest in soul states. Hamlet never tells why he delays; Iago tells why he acts, but with apparent falsity; Macbeth, instead, gives every reason why he should not act; and Brutus produces reasons for action which are fairly incomprehensible. Often, indeed, anything like a really psychological interpretation is forestalled by the dramatist's construction, which in true dramatic and Aristotelian fashion is concerned primarily with plot and situation, and depends on conspiracy or feigning, disguise or mistaken identity, slander or deception, and the unmotivated acceptance of these, in so far that we are often at a loss to tell when the characters are quite themselves, when merely playing a rôle or being played with. Hamlet, one of the poet's most vivid characters, plays a part through four acts, and the only psychology that can be made out for him is the (to me) absurd one of a double consciousness.[2] And when they do speak of their motives, often the point of view is not strictly their

[2] Posited by Mr. Clutton Brock.

own. The bad men, in particular, like Iago and Richard, consider themselves bad, as Browning's and Dostoevsky's and the criminals of real life do not. Even the great issue, upon which, according to some conceptions of the drama, it necessarily hinges, is never clearly faced and debated as it is in Browning and in most French plays. As in so many of these, in the play before us that issue would be between love and honor, between Cleopatra and the empire of the world. It is involved in the story, but never clearly propounded or considered; and Antony returns to Cleopatra without weighing her in the balance against the world, without consciously and deliberately choosing between them, as Dryden's hero does. *All for Love* is the Laureate's well-chosen title.[3]

It is in a sense from the exterior, therefore, that Shakespeare, as compared with Browning, presents characters. The opinions, the point of view expressed, are, though important in them too, less vitally and essentially important. Are Shakespeare's characters therefore less noble works of art? A question not to be asked. Though intellectually less consistent, emotionally they are more consistent; though less carefully analyzed and perfectly articulated, they are more vivid imaginative wholes. How can this be? As I have often said, mainly through their speech, both the substance and the form of it.[4] In the place of psychology, with its analyses and subtleties, the poet had an infinite tact, the artist's delicate, plastic, life-giving touch. "The Shakespearean delineation of character owes all its magic," says Mr. Shaw, "to the turn of the line, which lets you into the secret of its utterer's mood and temperament, not by its commonplace meaning, but by some subtle exaltation, or stultification, or shyness, or delicacy, or hesitation, or what not in the sound of it." Browning, too, of course, has something of this touch to his hand, as in Pompilia and Caponsacchi — else he would not have been a great dramatic poet — though he

---

[3] The ideas in this paragraph are for the most part reproduced from my *Shakespeare Studies* (1927), by permission of the Macmillan Company.

[4] See *op. cit.*, pp. 115–116, and my *Othello* (1915), pp. 63–70.

has less than Shakespeare; just as Shakespeare has at moments, and in simpler form, something of Browning's analysis. The touch, however, the simple but mysterious act of external, imaginative formation, is the chief thing of all.

2

Critics, brought up on Browning, Ibsen, and the French drama, nowadays forget this; and one wonders whether they find vital characters in Æschylus and Sophocles, in whom, of course, they can find no psychology. But if the sculptor has clay or marble, and the painter lines and colors, to fashion into the semblance of a man, what has the dramatist? Speech, primarily; it is speech that he has to mold and form. Like an architect, to be sure, he has various material at command. Action, too, as we have seen, and the relation of the character to the other characters are important; and mere speech in itself, of course, is not much, and the deeper he can go into the thought of the character the better, if without losing his hold upon the imagination of the audience. But there is a region of simple thought, in which most men live and move, devoid of subtleties, and requiring little analysis, which suffices — nay, is preferable — for the purpose. Such is the thought of the characters in Greek drama, and of many in novelists such as Fielding and Scott, Dickens and Jane Austen. And the greatness of a dramatist or novelist as a creator of character lies, not in going deeper, but in making much of this and giving it reality. For it is essential, not that the character himself should be a thinker, or even that he should be thought about, but that he should take shape and live. And as with other works of art, it is in the special medium of expression — speech in this instance — that he lives or fails to do so. It is always in the appeal to the eye or ear that the artist's power lies — a painter must know how to paint, a dramatist how to write. For art proceeds from sense to sense, from imagination to imagination, rather than from intellect to intellect.

Even in recent times this is so — essentially, art has not changed. Analysis and psychology, now more practiced, are far less immediate, less powerful means of presentation. They are like a knowledge of anatomy in sculptor and painter, important but not all-important. Nothing counts like ordinary speech, formed, transformed, by the creative, imaginative touch. It is the method of Dickens [5] and Thackeray, page after page. Micawber and Pecksniff, Sairey Gamp and the Wellers, Major Pendennis and Beatrix, one and all they live, not by virtue of the analysis — not by their ideas and opinions or point of view, nor even by the vividness of their manners or picturesqueness of their eccentricities, though certainly these have a part in their make-up — but like Juliet and her nurse, like king and clown and the whole immortal company, by their accents and intonation, their unmistakable voice and utterance, by the turn of the thought rather than the thought, and by their vocabulary and the form and rhythm of the phrase. All things belong together — but the ear, rather than the reason, is the judge. All things belong together (though no one else would have put them together), as they do in Shakespeare; and though there is, of course, a spirit or thought pervading the volume of words, it is only with glimpses of the innermost soul — its secret motives, its self-deceptions and masked movements. And so it is even in Hardy

[5] The present essay, though for some time in mind, has been immediately prompted by a desire to demonstrate more fully what is meant by characterization without psychology, particularly by the differentiation of the speech. In the last pages (63–70) of *Othello* I have sketched it, and in *Shakespeare Studies* I frequently illustrate it, but at least one reviewer of the latter regrets that I have not made it clearer. It is not an idea peculiar to Mr. Shaw, or a practice peculiar to Shakespeare. Since finishing the essay I have come upon Professor Elton's discussion of Dickens (*Survey of English Literature*, 1830–1880) and find the following: "The best of his creatures . . . whether Pecksniffs or Gargerys, are triumphs of style rather than of character-drawing . . . the word-craft of Dickens, the energy and keeping, the resource and wit, with which he fabricates the right style for them all, is the wonderful thing. It is never quite the language of this earth, but something better, which he has caught up and sublimed out of what he has actually heard." The words, as I think Professor Elton would agree, apply well to Shakespeare; though the best of his creatures are triumphs of character-drawing, also — which is not quite psychology.

and George Eliot, Meredith and James, who deal with these. The analytic turn of the last three makes and keeps their characters logically (or illogically) consistent and distinct, but it is not what makes them real to us, or makes them effectively known. And it is this plastic power that in the best creations of Meredith and James overrides and overwhelms their authors' own personal idiosyncrasies of speech, as indeed it does Browning's and Shakespeare's. Then the voice of the puppet is no longer the right voice of the showman, even as its gesture is not the proper gesture of his hand. Of James's characters, indeed, Mr. Chesterton says: "We cannot but admire the figures that walk about in his afternoon drawing-rooms; but we have a certain sense that they are figures that have no faces." Shakespeare's figures, though not psychologized, are more realized and embodied. They have voices and (though he hardly ever describes them) we have the certain sense that they have faces too.

Of the foreigners one has to speak more warily[6] — with them one's ear is a treacherous guide. But certainly of the psychologists Proust and Thomas Mann the same holds true. Character after character in the *Buddenbrooks* speaks with his own particular tongue: and many of the characters of Tolstoy and Dostoevsky seem to us to do so even in translation. And whether our own ear perceive it or not, the great foreigners, of course, cannot be far apart from Shakespeare. They mold speech as cunningly as others of their nation do clay or color. Only, as is obvious, it is a power that is more apparent and easily perceptible in prose than in verse, in the romantic writers than in the classical, in the Teutonic and Slavic than in the Latin.

[6] And the foreigner, in turn, of us! So fine a poet and critic as Chateaubriand complains that Shakespeare's young women are all alike — the same smile, look, and tone of voice. Evidently what he misses is the analysis, the Racinian psychology. And his ear is not sufficiently attuned to perceive the exquisite differentiation in tone between Rosalind and Beatrice, Viola and Julia, Perdita and Miranda.

Even the action, to Shakespeare more important than any psychology, is often important for its own sake, for the effect of plot and situation, rather than for its bearing on character. We have not the right at every turn to interpret it as owing to character. This, as has been recognized by Sir Walter Raleigh and others, is the case especially at the beginning of the play, as in *King Lear* and the *Merchant of Venice*; and we must not come to the conclusion that Cordelia cherishes her own pride more than her father's happiness or safety, or that Bassanio in his dealings with Shylock is deplorably careless or obtuse and in the choice of caskets exceedingly clear-sighted. And as is universally recognized, this is the case in the *dénouement* of the comedies. But it is so even in the body of the play. The wager on a wife's chastity, as in *Cymbeline*; the woman's substitution of herself for another, as in *All's Well* and *Measure for Measure*;[7] the sovereign deposed or lurking in disguise, as in *As You Like It, Measure for Measure*, and the *Tempest*; and the avenger biding his time, with insufficient reason, until the last scene of the play, as in *Hamlet* and other Elizabethan tragedies: one and all, these situations are not to be reckoned to the discredit of the principal persons concerned. They are traditional and conventional, and are made use of because of the situations they afford, or because of the ingenious solutions to complications, or (and here they affect character most nearly) because of the opportunity for contrasts. They display character, but often they do not spring out of character. They are to be taken for granted, not to be interpreted, analyzed, or motived. Posthumus is not meant to be a cad; nor Helena and Mariana, to be man-hunters; nor the three dukes (in the above-mentioned comedies), to be replicas of Richard II or Henry VI; nor Hamlet,

---

[7] In his articles in the *Publications of the Modern Language Association of America* Professor W. W. Lawrence has shown how traditional, familiar, and unquestionable these situations were in Shakespeare's time.

to be an insidious procrastinator. Plot came first with the poet, not, as the critics often say and continually imply, the inner nature of the hero. The action gave birth to the character, not the character to the action. The story, in its essentials, was not invented but borrowed, and the characters then fitted to it; and often the plot was so ingenious and improbable that they could not well be fitted to it and remain — in themselves considered — romantically engaging. Indirect conclusions and inferences, particularly, are unjustifiable. In a learned and enlightened essay that recently met my eye, I find the Duke in *Measure for Measure* taken to task for being "shifty, timid, and inclined to intrigue," in part responsible for Angelo's fall whose hypocrisy he had a little suspected, and therefore not worthy of Isabella. But as for inclination to intrigue — yes, and as for shiftiness, if the action is to be the evidence — is he not then getting, in her, a kindred spirit? And as for the mere inclination, is that a flaw or defect (save where it is explicitly made out to be such) in all Shakespeare or Elizabethan drama, or all the drama of the Renaissance, French, Spanish, or Italian?[8]

In Ibsen, in Alfieri, in Racine, the action and character are pretty much one and the same. So far at least as the hero is concerned, every detail of the action implies character or has a bearing upon it, although action is not the only means of revealing it. But as Sir Robert Bridges and others have shown, Shakespeare's characters are much larger than the business in which they engage, often are superior to it, sometimes, like Macbeth and Othello (as we shall see), are in a sense contrasted with it. Helena, Mariana, and the three dukes, certainly, are superior and somewhat external to it. They have better natures, and bigger thoughts, than their conduct betrays. But that is not all. We have a more vivid and intimate impression of their personality (though in many other

---

[8] Mr. Masefield, who exquisitely and poetically misreads Shakespeare, dwells on the evils of conspiracy and treachery as if these were the themes of the plays, instead of an element of their structure. See my *Shakespeare Studies*, p. 101.

Shakespearean characters it is more vivid and intimate still) than in the case of other dramatists. This is produced, not indirectly, by the action, but by means quite direct and immediate. And that, I think, is, above all, by this abundant and (so far as the requirements of the action are concerned) somewhat superfluous speech. The characters are "oversize," are (though intended to serve the action) in the upshot presented somewhat for their own sake, and are so real that they project from the scene, stand out upon the page. Or rather, they seem so real because they do that.

4

Now this plastic power is the decisive thing, as it seems to me, in the question regarding Cleopatra. Not that I accept Professor Schücking's opinion that Cleopatra is artistically inconsistent. On the stage, as in life, a character has a right to change — in Cleopatra's case, to cease from changing — under stress of love and in the presence of death; and of this Shakespeare takes due account when the mercurial lady cries,

> now from head to foot
> I am marble-constant; now the fleeting moon
> No planet is of mine.

As so many of us do, Professor Schücking exaggerates, to make his point. She is no Doll Tearsheet or Doll Common in the early scenes, nor a sublime queen — "Thusnelda in chains" — in the later ones. She is vain and voluptuous, cunning and intriguing, wrangling and voluble, humorous and vindictive, to the end. Her petulance and violence when she gets the news of Antony's marriage is not her then prevailing mood, and yet it reappears when she rails against fate and fortune at Antony's death and against Seleucus in his treason. She had been elegant and queenly enough before the news, and she is so afterwards; in a moment she recovers herself and makes amends; and she had but used the license — exercised the divine right — of a queen. She is a monarch, a maker of manners, after the similitude of Elizabeth, who raged and stormed on occasion, but did that, like everything else, with an air. Shakespeare keeps "decorum," but not like Corneille and Racine; his kings and queens are given greater range and latitude, and are such by what they do rather than by what they do not. They are human nature enlarged, not enchained. And her caprice, why, it is the premise with which the poet, as in Enobarbus' and Antony's own description of her "infinite variety," begins. Caprice, conscious and unconscious, is her nature, as to be queen and coquette is her station in life. *La donna è mobile*, and she is quintessential woman. It is so that she lives — that she delights and attracts the men. In her inconsistency she is consistent. But the chief means by which the dramatist makes her so is the identity, through all her changes, of her tone and manner. She changes as a vivacious, amorous, designing woman changes, not so as to lose her identity, like Proteus.

5

When she first appears she is languishing:

Cleo. If it be lóve indéed, téll me hów mùch.
Ant. There's beggary in the love that can be reckon'd.
Cleo. I'll set a bourn how far to be beloved.
Ant. Then must thou needs find out new heaven, new
earth.

And these first words in the delectable colloquy are like her, time and again. It is love, but also "the love of love and her soft hours." This phrase is Antony's, who for the moment is in her mood; but it is she who is most settled in it, as at the nucleus or center of her emotional vortex. The voluptuous invitation of the first line — as if to coax the very soul out of his body — is, in both sentiment and rhythm, in keeping with the beginning of a later scene, when Antony is gone:

> Give me some music; music, moody food
> Of us that trade in love.

That is the sensuous murmur of one who in retrospect or in prospect tells the moments over and over, and whose ample discontent craves music or "mandragora" to soothe it, rather than a fire flickering on the hearth or a flowing stream. Yet a lover's imagination is necessarily dramatic in form, though wholly lyrical in substance. *He* now is murmuring —

> He's speaking now,
> Or murmuring, 'Where's my Serpent of old Nile?'
> For so he calls me: now I feed myself
> With most delicious poison.

The last phrase, with its figure, is it not exactly — poetically — fitted to her lips? They know every pulse of passion, but no touch of restraint, every refinement save that of propriety. She is the serpent, which twines and charms, lovelier than lamb or dove.

And in the same audacious, sensuous key, for all her exaltation, she expresses herself on her deathbed. She is tenderer with her women, and stronger and more constant, than she has ever been; but her thoughts of Antony, though now an inviolable shade, are not celestial or Platonic. They are steeped in amorousness, and she is waiting, coiled on her couch. She loves him more than at the beginning; but neither now nor at his death is she, as Professor Schücking declares, "all tenderness, all passionate devotion and unselfish love"; nor does she quit life because it is not worth the living. On life she really never loosens her greedy grip. Her beauty she clutches to her dying bosom as the miser does his gold. Her robe and jewels are, even in death, assumed to heighten the impression of it upon Caesar — though only to show him what he has missed. She hears Antony mock him now, from over the bitter wave; and at the beginning of the scene she cried,

> go fetch
> My best attires; I am again for Cydnus —

as one who, to please both him and herself, and vex their rival, would fain die at her best, reviving all the glories of that triumph.

To an ugly death she could scarcely have brought herself; and it is
an admirable example of the dramatic touch and tact and mere
instinctive choice of what belongs together (of which we have been
speaking) that a little before she should have vowed to Proculeius,
as she spoke of going to Rome:

> Rather a ditch in Egypt
> Be gentle grave unto me! rather on Nilus' mud
> Lay me stark-nak'd, and let the waterflies
> Blow me into abhorring.

Not to be like that is the death which even then she is choosing
and devising, but an event, a scene, well-nigh an amour. And now
that she sees Iras fall and pass away so quietly, she thinks the stroke
of death is as a lover's pinch, which hurts and is desired. What is it
that nerves her up to make haste and apply the asp? Pride, fear to
be made a show of at Rome, and — something deeper. "Love is
enough," but not enough for her.

> If she first meet the curlèd Antony,
> He'll make demand of her and spend
>   that kiss
> Which is my heaven to have.

Without kissing what would heaven be — nay, without jealousy?
The vanity and coquetry of her lightly clear the grave. Of all these,
her truly "immortal longings," Plutarch, the philosopher, however, says nothing, and makes her apply the cobra, as if it were a
leech in a clinic, to her *arm*.

> Peace, Peace!
> Dost thou not see my baby at my breast
> That sucks the nurse asleep?
> *Charmian* . . .
> *Cleo.* As sweet as balm, as soft as air, as gentle —
> O Antony — Nay, I will take thee too;
> What should I stay —
>   [*Dies*]

No Freudian is needed to defend the change. For a woman this in itself is a sensation, turning the poison all to balm; and she is wrapped and folded up in sensuous imaginations to the end.

This indication of her vanity and amorous indulgence is the nearest approach in the character to what we should call psychology. But this is simple, concrete, for the popular stage. Not analyzed, it is variously, abundantly presented, and, with the phrase "of us that trade in love," is plainly labeled. And it is in harmony with her luxurious, coquetting spirit throughout. She lives for pleasure and neglects the state. She deals affably with Caesar's ambassador, Thyreus, and vouchsafes him her hand; and is demure, and complaisant, even apologetic, with Caesar himself when she meets him, and when, long before that, she begs good news of the Messenger, who has none but that of Antony's marriage. As his supreme reward, she proffers him her bluest veins to kiss, a hand (quoth she) that kings have lipp'd and trembled kissing. And continually she is dreaming of conquests past, of triumphs yet to be. She compares her lovers and her love for them, and herself as a prize, in her "green and salad days" and now:

> Think on me
> That am with Phœbus' amorous pinches black
> And wrinkled deep in time? Broad-fronted Cæsar,
> When thou wast here above the ground, I was
> A morsel for a monarch; and great Pompey,
>
> .   .   .   .
>
> Ink and paper, Charmian,
> Welcome, my good Alexas. Did I, Charmian,
> Ever love Cæsar so?

If she is swarthy, why, Phœbus himself was enamored of her! The same figure, we have seen, she has at the end, for the touch of death; and every now and then her language is tinged with erotic notions, although, as we are yet to see, the poet here restrains himself. This coquetry and eroticism, Professor Schücking thinks, is vulgar, but the point is that it continues to the last. She makes eyes at Caesar and Thyreus, and though uplifted by the situation, she speaks when facing death in the same unedifying vein. If this be a sign that she is a harlot, she is ever one. But again Professor Schücking exaggerates, ignoring the nature of the sex. Few women who have had more lovers than one can easily forget the circumstance; and Cleopatra is not so much boasting as (out of her extensive experience) making comparisons, and declaring that Antony overtops them all and their mutual love is greater than any other she has shared. He is her "man of men."

6

The death scene, then, though queenly and elevated through Cleopatra's dignity and tenderness, is quite true to her earlier self; and though glorified by the poetry shed upon it, is not sublime. She is no Thusnelda, whether in chains or out of them. Indeed, she now shows still other traits of her earlier self — her jealousy of Octavia as well as of Iras, her pride of place and achievement, her spirit of intrigue and emulation, her *camaraderie* with her maids, her sense of humor. To Octavia she had paid her compliments (and not for the first time, either) the moment before, as she vowed she would not go to Rome:

> Nor once be chastised with the sober eye
> Of dull Octavia.

Now, at the supreme moment, she even assumes her empty title. "*Husband,* I come!" She would have everything, not only fame but name — the despoiler. She has always remembered that she was a queen; she remembers it still, with robe and crown; but by virtue of her more than conjugal courage puts in the yet higher claim. And with Iras and Charmian she is mellower but not different. It is like her inconsistent, inconsiderate spirit to be tart with them when they cross her, and yet make them companions, and kiss them both before they die. She does not sentimentalize; they are even now not foremost in her heart:

> Come, then, and take the last warmth of my lips.
> Farewell, kind Charmian; Iras, long farewell.

For Iras this is just in time; and it is a vivid moment as Cleopatra looks down upon her, who is already what she herself will in another moment be.

> Have I the aspic in my lips? Dost fall?

. . . .

> Dost thou lie still?

There we see "in Venus' eyes the gaze of Proserpine." She is startled, is full of curiosity, of admiration or the spirit of emulation, but not of tenderness and gratitude. She thinks of death, not of the dead. She thinks of herself, as she did even when Antony was dying — "Hast thou no care of me?" — and as she railed at the world, Fortune, and the gods. Her love is never "unselfish" — never unlike her.

But the preëminently felicitous touch, I think, which links her most unmistakably with all her earlier self, and thus effectually contradicts any impression of sublimity, is in her sense of humor. Seldom does a tragic character — even in Shakespeare — keep this faculty to the last. Mercutio does, and Edmund, the cynical bastard; Juliet shows a single faint flicker of her earlier gaiety;[9] but Cleopatra, the tameless and reckless, keeps more of hers. Juliet, speaking to Romeo, though dead before her, cannot help doing it — out of the simple fullness of her love — a little as she had always done, as if he were alive. Cleopatra is not so lost in love or sorrow either; but she is still less concerned to preserve propriety and decorum. Even as they are about to lift up Antony into the monument, she cries, with something like mirth, out of her excitement and rebelliousness:

> Here's sport indeed! How heavy weighs my lord!
> Our strength is all gone into heaviness,

[9] O churl, drunk all, and left no friendly drop
To help me after?

That makes the weight: had I great Juno's power,
The strong-wing'd Mercury should fetch thee up,
And set thee by Jove's side. Yet come a little,—
Wishes were ever fools — O, come, come, come.

[*They heave Antony aloft to Cleopatra*]

And when, afterwards, she receives the country-fellow with the basket, she draws him out, and then, for the curious fun of it, asks him abruptly, upon his praying her to give the asp nothing because it is not worth the feeding, "Will it eat me?" She is playing with her thought, as with her man. But though it takes nerve to do this, she strikes no heroical attitude; and just before that she asks him, like the very woman, the coquette and coward that she really is, who fled from Actium,

Hast thou the pretty worm of Nilus there
That kills and pains not?

For she would do it prettily, painlessly, by a poisoned bouquet if she could. And she is half in jest with Charmian when she utters her fears of Iras stealing a march upon her in the purlieus of Paradise. And then, at the moment that she is nerving herself up, and gritting her own teeth, as the sound of the verse betrays —

Come, thou mortal wretch,
With thy sharp teeth this knot intrinsicate
Of life at once untie —

she laughs out, as one who has played cleverly and won:

O could'st thou speak
That I might hear thee call great Cæsar ass
Unpolicied.

There, perhaps, is a bit of the pluck and spunk of Thusnelda, but a lighter spirit. Apostrophes generally seem rhetorical and artificial, but they have a root in nature, and never was there one more appropriate and dramatic than this. The contrast between "great Cæsar" and the worm, which scorns him — a feeling which is but her own playfully transferred, the boast of the creature rebounding delightfully as a compliment upon herself! All her life has been a game, the asp is her last little unexpected trump, and even though now Caesar cannot hear her, she cannot but cry, "Ah, ha!" It has been *another* game, for the most part:

> Give me mine angle; we'll to the river: there,
> My music playing far off, I will betray
> Tawny-finned fishes; my bended hook shall pierce
> Their slimy jaws; and, as I draw them up,
> I'll think them every one an Antony,
> And say, 'Ah, ha! you're caught.'

But it is much in the same spirit, whether she wins an Antony or beats a Caesar and his sister. And the bold, insulting language of the apostrophe is in keeping with that used earlier, in her amorous rage against her lover —

> none our parts so poor
> But was a race of heaven: they are so still,
> Or thou, the greatest soldier of the world,
> Art turn'd the greatest liar; —

or in her retort to Dolabella, when he denies there was ever such a man as the Antony she has pictured — "You lie, up to the hearing of the gods"; or in her threat when Iras is praising the great Julius at Antony's expense — "By Isis, I will give thee bloody teeth"; or in her railing against the messenger and Seleucus, and against the world as a "sty" and Fortune as a "hussy"; and in her jesting with the eunuch Mardian. Hers is not the language of Windsor or Versailles, then or since; but nature's and her own. And these words to the worm, almost her last, how felicitously *un*sublime! For in a drama, as in life, the most poetic death is the most natural — Sir Thomas More's, Charles the Second's, or the Emperor Vespasian's, who jested when fairly *in extremis*; and Cleopatra, though dying, and doing it like a queen, is unmistakably the same old girl.

Her vivacity and volubility, another trait which she never loses, it would take pages to illustrate. When in the earlier scenes Antony is trying to break to her his purpose of setting out for Rome she

will not permit him more than a word at a time, and she catches
him up and twits him, rallies and teases him, without mercy or remorse. So with the messenger of his marriage — she interrupts and
anticipates, wheedles and deprecates, bullies and cajoles. And
when baffled by Fate at Antony's death, and by Seleucus in the
presence of Caesar, she rails almost as volubly as ever. Once the
excitement holds over and appears in connection with another
subject. The monument has been scaled and she has been thwarted
in an attempt at suicide; then Dolabella appears; and into his
kindly but unheeding ear she pours a eulogy of Antony. Again and
again Dolabella, who has something to tell her, and is as little interested in her amorous recital as she herself would have been in
one of his, endeavors to distract her, but in vain. And in such excitement, in joy and in grief, but not in anger, she is given to repetition, in a way not quite like any other Shakespearean character.
"Note him," she says of Antony to Charmian in the first act; "Note
him, good Charmian, 'tis the man; but note him." It is the language
of exuberant glee. And nothing so much gives us an impression of
the identity of her character as the appearance of this trait in the
midst of her grief:

> What, what, good cheer! Why, how now, Charmian,
> My noble girls! Ah! women, women, look,
> Our lamp is spent.
>
> Ah! women, women! come; we have no friend
> But resolution and the briefest end.
>
> He words me, girls, he words me, that I should not
> Be noble to myself.

Here it is really not the language of grief but of her bearing up
against grief — or rather it is the essential utterance of Cleopatra.
For she is alive, every inch of her, to her finger-tips; and her speech
has the undulation of a bird's flight, or of a thoroughbred woman's
gait of her own happy time, ere woman had heard of heels. Only it
is not a walk, but a dance — or rather, a flight, which, for one who

is equal to it, is, no doubt, more satisfying and exhilarating than
either.

7

Surely, then, this character holds together, as a living thing.
There are matters left unexplained, but none that cannot be explained — which is Shakespeare's method. Why did Cleopatra conceal the treasure and pretend that she had given a full account? It
may have been to make use of this for her supreme and ultimate
toilet, or it may even have been in order to be detected in the
fraud and convince Caesar that she had no thought of death. Either
explanation would be in keeping with her sinuous, elusive nature,
but neither (without some hint to the audience) with Shakespeare's
unelusive art. What fits both his art and the character is that she
should have endeavored to deceive and defraud Caesar for the
game's own sake, without material profit, as indeed she presently
does again, with her asp. Jonathan Wild, on the scaffold, applied
his hands to the parson's pocket, and emptied it of his bottle-screw,
which he carried out of this world in his hand. Carmen picked the
pockets of her friends.

However it be, her conduct at this juncture — her lie and her
rage against Seleucus for not bearing her out in it — is, though
quite like her, unbecoming; this is vulgar, though Professor
Schücking does not call it so. But her vulgarity here, where she is
supposed to be a sublime queen, like the other vulgarity where she
is only the harlot, should not offend us, whether artistically or
morally. Vulgarity has a place in great art; and we suffer, Professor
Schücking and some others of us, from a Victorian, or a petty
French, decorum. No lady, no Cornelian or Racinian queen,
would act so: but neither the one nor the other could interest us
so much. It is too late to apologize for human nature as it is — for
the art of Shakespeare or Dostoevsky. How many of Shakespeare's
greatest gentlemen are on occasion vulgar — Hamlet, Othello,

Mercutio, Brutus — and his ladies, too — Beatrice, Portia, Rosalind! And there is the wonderful Lisa, in Dostoevsky's *Possessed*,
who slaps Stavrogin's face in the presence of the whole company!
The Gipsy aches to do it, to the greatest soldier of the world —

> I would I had thy inches; thou shouldst know
> There were a heart in Egypt!

Scott's Elizabeth is of the same spirited, irresponsible family, drag-
ging Amy Robsart from her hiding-place "in a fit of vindictive
humiliation and Amazonian fury." In all these writers, including
Shakespeare himself, decorum, too, plays a part — that it may, with
fullest effect, be flung aside. At the great moments, in art as in
life, it often proves to be but a mantle. And taste in an author
and taste in the character are, of course, not altogether one and
the same.

8

Morally, too, the vulgarity, and above all the voluptuousness,
need not touch us nearly. The dramatist has despite his sympathy
"held the balance even." He has secured our interest without
prejudicing the moral cause. He takes care, indeed, that the virtuous woman, Octavia, should be kept in the background, and that
the simple beauty of the homely and civic virtues should not enter
into competition with the dark and dubious beauty of an abandoned passion. But he shrewdly remembers its illicit basis, its suspicions, jealousies, and resentments; and at her best Cleopatra is
fain to call herself a wife. Here is no glorification, in medieval
style, of illicit love at the expense of the married state, whether
on the part of the lovers or their friends. These are no Lancelot
and Guenevere, Tristram and Iseult. For that matter, there are
none such in Shakespeare.[10]

[10] He must have known something of the medieval romances and their chivalric code of morals; at any rate he knew Elizabethan dramatists, like Chapman,
who reflect it. But nowhere does he take up this point of view. Antony and
Cleopatra are his nearest approach to this type of lover.

And, most remarkable of all, the poet restrains himself in the matter of voluptuousness and erotic coloring. This is suggested rather than presented and expressed. We are made to see that Cleopatra and Antony indulge their sensuous imaginations but we are not told them: Cleopatra feeds herself on most delicious poison but pours very little of it into our ear.[11] How much more reticent and restrained is the expression of their sensations than that of Browning's Sebald and Ottima, of Meredith's Richard and Bella, creations of proper Victorians; and our contemporaries I forbear to cite. Though real enough, these Egyptian passions are not near and nude, but keep the cool, serene distance of art. They are as if in a picture or a song, not as if seen or heard through a cranny in a bedroom wall. And Cleopatra's words are sweet as her woman's lips, soft as her breast, sharp on occasion as her teeth and nails, but in the lines her alluring person or Antony's overmastering one scarcely appears, and troubles no innocent spirit. Only her hand appears. "Eternity was in our lips and eyes, bliss in our brows' bent," but there she is twitting him. And his "playfellow," "plighter of high hearts," we see it only when (as here) it has been playing false with Caesar, or when (before that) with its bluest veins to kiss, it is offered as a bribe to the Messenger. He is soon to feel it, after another sort.

But the main reason we are not troubled is — that this man and woman love each other. There is more in it all than mere body and beauty. Their imaginations are fired, even their hearts are touched. There can be no question of this at the end — the words

[11] Others have remarked upon this, as Mr. Arthur Symons, Professor Tucker Brooke, and best of all, Mr. Granville Barker. Of the elaborate technique of enticement, as found in the *Ars Amatoria* (which Shakespeare surely knew), there is almost no trace in his plays. The lovers' lies and perjuries, stratagems and deceits, the various devices to keep the lover guessing — when he is anxious, to thwart him, and when he is cooling, to lead him on — which we find in Chapman and Fletcher, as in Spanish and Italian comedy, are here almost unknown. His lovers are of the frank idyllic tradition, which came down from Greene; and the coquetry the young women have in them is of the innocuous sort which we see in Rosalind.

of Antony and Cleopatra at his death are among the immortal
utterances of sexual tenderness. But this appears also elsewhere,
particularly after Actium, in the quarrel about Thyreus, and at
the time of Cleopatra's birthday, as well as at the beginning of
the play. In Cleopatra it is another vein of unity and continuity
in her nature. Though afterwards deepened through trial, her
feeling at the outset is more than mere vanity and sense. She knows
Antony and has with him a community of tastes. Like the truest
lovers they *like* each other, and that is partly because they like the
same things. They are comrades and companions. Not on the highest level, to be sure — they do not spend their evenings talking
philosophy or reading verse. But not all good or respectable people do, married or unmarried. They are given to sport and merry-
making. They have a taste for billiards, considerably before their
time. They go fishing, and play huge pranks upon one another.
They roam the streets together incognito and note the qualities
of people — in the alien crowd they but feel more keenly their own
companionship. They feast and carouse and — most delicious inti-
macy (read Anacreon, the Greek or the Scotch) — once fairly get
drunk together. Vulgar, again, there is no denying, but wine and
women, the pair of them, have longer been known to poetry than
daisies and daffodils; and next to being one soul (which but seldom
comes to pass) is the having of the same sensation. On this occasion, as Cleopatra recalls — for *meminerunt omnia amantes* — they
played the true lovers' game of changing places, and she put "her
tires and mantles on him, whilst she wore his sword Philippan."
So they once did, the man fondly remembers, in Browning's *Lovers'
Quarrel*. And while in the former case it was more the woman's
doing than the man's, and like Bella's dressing up as a dandy in
Richard Feverel, designed (by a contrast less feasible nowadays)
to heighten the effect of her feminine charms, it was for the fun
of it as well. And not for long can two people have so much fun together without being fond of one another too. Sense craves and

cries out for spirit as its consummation, even as spirit does for
sense.

9

Yet they betray each other. Antony marries; Cleopatra coquets
with Caesar through his emissary, and is agreeable enough with
him to his face. And she flees from Actium, and possibly (though
not probably) is to blame for the conduct of her fleet at Alexandria.
Heine explains it all to his own satisfaction. "For Cleopatra is a
woman. She loves and betrays at the same time. It is a mistake to
believe that women when they betray us have ceased to love."
There is Manon Lescaut! But there is Antony! It is a mistake, also,
to believe that *men*, when they betray us *others*, have ceased to
love. And that is nearer the truth. Richard Feverel certainly loved
Lucy, and there is many another hero like him, whether in romance
or in reality. Our monogamous logic is quite too narrow and absolute; and we practically contradict it ourselves by our approval
of second marriages, which are not supposed *ipso facto* to declare
the love for the first wife or husband to be as dead as they are.

But was this Shakespeare's opinion? He was not given to gen-
eralization or to abstract thinking of any sort. He presented situations truly, but without premises or conclusions, and apparently
without full consciousness of them. He was no Browning, Meredith, or Balzac. Indeed, he was conventional in his notions and
opinions, and such premises or conclusions he might even have
abhorred. Though not at all a Puritan, he was in this respect like
Tolstoy; his presentation of character was far wider than his intellectual scope. He saw farther or deeper than he undertook to think.
And very likely, if called upon, he would have explained the
treason as it seems that he would have us understand the jealousy
— the fact, like the suspicion of the fact — as owing to their illegiti-
mate relation.

Here again he holds the balance even. He disapproves of their relation and yet does not refuse it love's title or prerogative. He makes the lovers jealous and suspicious, and yet glorifies them with poetry and elicits our sympathy. This is not a contradiction save as it is a contradiction in life (as we have seen) and as it must be (still more) in art. A character in a drama or a novel is not quite the same as in reality, and far more than in life must we be made to sympathize as we disapprove. Macbeth and Lady Macbeth are unjustifiable traitors and murderers. But an all-encompassing cloud of poetry, and various devices of mediation and conciliation, such as the "supernatural soliciting" and the love of the woman and the pride of the man, engage and secure our interest and sympathy despite the heinous crime. Painters like Velazquez shed the glory of color and chiaroscuro upon the meanest and most ignoble of objects. Poets do the same. All art is a compromise, an accommodation; all art, even the noblest and truest, must needs please or interest, must in a measure sacrifice truth to effect. It regards less the proportions of nature than the limitations of the medium — of the readers' or spectators' minds. Sculptors peremptorily continue the line instead of breaking it; and in marble thicken the ladies' necks, wrists, and ankles, and (if it be bas-relief) flatten the round muscles. Painters, like stage-managers, turn, however animated the group, the faces of nearly all the figures towards us. And seldom can a character in a drama or even in a novel bear the full stark light of common day. It is the product of a fine labor of simplification and intensification, of projection or subordination, of parallel or contrast. So the love of Antony and Cleopatra is in a sense incompatible with their lives and their natures. The poet puts words of censure in the mouths of Antony's friends and respectable enemies at the beginning; but more and more suppresses these, and instead makes much of their servants' devotion, as he seeks to elicit our sympathy towards the end. He is careful to put Octavia and her children, and the legitimate claims of society, in the play (indeed) but in the background; and to touch on no note of pathos in connection with hearth and home. And the paramours' physical relations "he lifts" says Mr. Barker, "to a plane where he can cope with them, upon terms of poetry, of humour, of enfranchised wit." Whether it was (as Mr. Barker thinks) because, on his stage, Cleopatra must be a boy, or because such was his and the other Elizabethans' loftier notion of dramatic art, in either case this is not nature quite as they one and all must certainly have known it, or as Shakespeare himself in *Venus and Adonis* knew how to paint it, or Marlowe in *Hero and Leander*, or Spenser at Acrasia's Bower. As with most people, the love of the famous paramours is the noblest thing about them: but by the license of exaggeration in art their love is made greater than they. That license we instinctively allow; all this paltering with the truth we warrant. Yet here, and here only, as it seems to me, is there cause to cavil at the unity of Cleopatra's character — as we carelessly forget that she is a figure in a drama and look upon her as but a bit of life.

II

Henry V

SHAKESPEARE'S *Henry V* is the last of his English "histories," which cover the line of kings from Richard II to Richard III. Though itself not one of his greatest plays, it was written, in 1599, when Shakespeare had entered into the plenitude of his powers, had almost finished his series of comedies, and was about to touch the pinnacle of his art in *Hamlet, Othello, King Lear,* and *Macbeth.* That — from 1602 to about 1607 — was the period of tragedy; this, of history and comedy; that, the period of gloom and terror; this, of love and joy and "high, heroic things." Not that the prevailing mood of either period is necessarily to be taken for the mood of Shakespeare the man. A man who writes tragedy may himself be not uncheerful, just as one has been known to write jokes for the newspapers at a time when his heart was breaking. But so far as the plays themselves are concerned, the period which ends with *Henry V* and *Twelfth Night* reflects a joy in life and

NOTE. This essay, originally the introduction to an edition of the play published by Messrs. Henry Holt and Co., in their *English Readings*, is here reprinted by their kind permission. There is no material change save at pp. 43–46; but here and there certain adjustments and allusions were introduced for a special occasion, a reading before the Shakespeare Association, at Kings College, London, in 1921, shortly after the settlement of the Irish troubles under Mr. Lloyd George.

an exuberance of spirits, which then, for some reason, suddenly pass away. This is true not only of the substance but of the style. The expression now is highly colored, lavish of poetry and the beauty of phrase and figure. In the great tragedies ornament seems to be disdained, and the sweetness of the master's style is sometimes almost lost in its Titanic strength.

To this more human and genial period *Henry V* wholly belongs. In it are mingled the serious and the comic, as in *Henry IV*, and the shadow of Fate nowhere appears. Shakespeare is here following the older tradition of the English "history," though much improving upon it. Marlowe, in his *Edward II* (*ca.* 1592), had eliminated the comic element; and Shakespeare, in *Richard III* and *Richard II*, had followed suit. These "histories" are really tragedies; and both have the pomp and (the earlier, at least) the horror of the older Elizabethan tragic manner. There is the supernatural machinery of the plot, inherited from the tragic poet Seneca — Fate lowering in the background, ghosts shrieking in the foreground, and omens and premonitions, prophecies and curses, fulfilled to the last jot and tittle. And there are atrocious crimes and deeds of violence, and fierce men and comparatively fiercer women, with long high-flown speeches in their mouths, passionate, declamatory, full of introspection and self-consciousness, and often not very closely fitted to the business in hand.

In *Henry IV* and *Henry V*, then, Shakespeare turned back somewhat from the Marlowesque history to the earlier popular tragi-comedy, but he pretty much abandoned the Senecan tragic machinery to be found in both. There were no doubt several reasons for this. In the first place, he must have felt that this tragic manner was too stiff and heavy for some of the material in English history which he wished to present. Henry IV was too business-like, Hotspur too high-souled and eccentric, to lend himself to such a style. In the second place, he inclined to hearken to the popular cry. Before Marlowe English audiences had delighted in tragedy (or history) blended with comedy, just as they had done in the Middle Ages; such had always been the popular dramatic taste; and Shakespeare instinctively knew that only by satisfying this deep-seated craving could the artistic miracle be wrought — when, as with an electric shock, artist and public come vitally in contact. How then could he meet the popular demand without stooping to it? One of the readiest ways was to drop the portentous and atrocious old tragic manner and adopt one that more nearly accommodated itself to the sobriety and simplicity of life as we know it. Titans and ogres and men heroically mounted on stilts do not mingle readily with jolly good fellows and clowns: you cannot always be sure which set you are meant to laugh at. In *Henry IV* the serious part blends with the comic much more readily than in *Titus Andronicus* or *King John*, if for no other reason, simply because it is more within human reach and compass. And, in the third place, he now wished to treat a subject which demanded this blending of the comic and the serious, of low life and high life, by its very nature. Henry V combined the two elements in his single self. The hero of Agincourt had in life, as in Shakespeare's previous play, been a madcap and boon companion. To the popular heart this was the most interesting thing about his character — on the popular stage it was the one thing that could not be omitted or ignored. In these plays, then, in which he appears, *Henry IV* and *Henry V*, comedy was essential; and to harmonize with the comedy, as well as to fit the historical subject, the serious part must step down a bit to a more human level.

The greatest success in "history" that Shakespeare attained was in the *First Part of Henry IV*. Here is to be found his liveliest and most richly-colored picture of tavern and country; here is to be found Falstaff, and Falstaff at his best; and here, in Hotspur, and in young Harry roused to emulation, are to be found a pair of Shakespeare's most radiant figures of English youth and chivalry. But the main thing is that the two elements, serious and comic,

hold together better here than in *Henry V*. The Prince of Wales
still belongs to both worlds; and both worlds, that is, the court
and the Boar's Head in Eastcheap, are made to reflect or echo one
another. At court, for instance, Henry IV complains of his son's
debauchery and takes him to task; at the Boar's Head, the actual
scene between them is enacted by the Prince and Falstaff in burlesque; and then the alarm of war breaks in upon that haunt of
jollity, and brings it and the court together, driving the droll and
motley crew to Shrewsbury, not in quest of honor, to be sure,
though young Harry — roused from his indifference — is in quest
of nothing else.

1

In *Henry V* the hero has already forsaken Eastcheap for ever;
Falstaff and his companions he has banished from his sight; and
though after Falstaff's death his scurvy cronies follow the army
into France, they do not enter the King's presence or indeed have
much to do with his story. They are in the play, not so much because they belong there, as because, having been in the play preceding, they might be expected to be in this — the audience craving,
like the clientèle of the present-day newspaper, the comic characters it already knows; and because the introduction of new comic
characters, more closely connected with the King, had been made
difficult by his reformation.

Plot, indeed, is not the strong point of this "history." *Henry V*
is, as has been said, rather a series of tableaux. The choruses, which
not only effect the transitions but also introduce glowing descriptions, elsewhere out of place, indicate as much. Pictures of life,
interspersed with poetry and eloquence — these make up the story.
A drama, of course, requires a struggle; and the King, by his re-
form, is past that. His career is simply a triumphal progress from
Harfleur to Agincourt, and from Agincourt on to the French crown
and the French princess' hand. There is even no external struggle,

because there must be, in this patriotic drama, no enemy able to withstand him.

Wherein, then, lies the value of the drama? In the quality of the pictures of life and character, on the one hand; and in the quality of the eloquence and poetry — the patriotic passion which runs through the play — on the other. It is the latter, the patriotic fervor, along with the dominant figure of the King, that gives the play unity of effect. Nowhere else in Shakespeare is there so much of it as here. John of Gaunt's great speech in *Richard II* — and that is no more than a speech — is the only thing to compare with it. Shakespeare in general was not so patriotic, or at least not so imperialistic, as his contemporaries Sidney, Raleigh, Spenser, Daniel, and Drayton; he was not interested in America, or "Virginia," as they were, or in the greatness of England there, or in Europe, or on the sea. He had nothing to say, as they had, of the Queen, and the glory of her arms, the vast empire that then was making. He was not highly patriotic, just as he was not a partisan, whether in matters of state or of church. He loved men, loved Englishmen, more than England. But, as he always did, he rose to the occasion: he was enough in love with everything to do that. The choruses and the King's speeches to his soldiers stir and quicken your blood, and ring in your memory, after the book has been laid down:

> Once more unto the breach, dear friends, once more,
> Or close the wall up with our English dead.
> .   .   .   .   .   And you, good yeomen,
> Whose limbs were made in England, show us here
> The mettle of your pasture.

The words thrill us, who in these years have but sat at home, now more than ever, for we know that they were read and uttered of late by thousands of Englishmen on French soil, facing this time, happily, a different foe. Like the words of the Prayer-book and of the devotional parts of the Bible, they have been made sacred by the lips, now silent, which repeated them. Like those, they have become part of the litany of the nation, and of her daughter nations too.

2

Apart from this, the play interests us most as a picture of life and character. The patriotism, though ardent, is not highly enlightened. The war is for no good cause; Henry's claim to the throne is, for all that he believes in it, unfounded. And the ideal of the English is, so far as it is expressed, honor and glory, not love of country, or liberty, or devotion to one's faith. It is a feudal, chivalric war, waged, not for a cause like a crusade, but like a tournament for a victor's crown. Henry, before the action, rejoices that Englishmen are not there in greater numbers, partly indeed, because "if we are mark'd to die we are enow to do our country loss"; but much more because "the fewer men, the greater share of honour." Henry has the mind of a king but the soul of a paladin. He speaks for the moment the language of knight-errantry — the language of Sidney, Raleigh, and Drake, to be sure, and all very noble and glorious, but in these days, when bloodshed is of itself more abhorrent, exceedingly remote. For the ethics of statecraft and warfare were, in Shakespeare's time, not so clearly and soundly established as today. English rulers then were a little like some Continental ones of late, and apart from the motive of honor, they were for war from motives of calculating expediency. Henry IV is made by Shakespeare twice to express the opinion of the poet's friend, the Earl of Essex, that peace and unity at home were to be secured by waging foreign wars. In *Henry V* even the Archbishop advises waging one in order to save the endowments of the Church. Like some of the political leaders and writers of late, war they thought the great domestic curative and tonic. And like these, Englishmen then, as well as other Europeans, believed in waging a war of terror. The historical Henry V was no lamb, though he was not quite the lion that Shakespeare makes of him, roaring before the gates of Harfleur:

> If I begin the battery once again,
> I will not leave the half-achieved Harfleur
> Till in her ashes she lies burièd.
> The gates of mercy shall be all shut up,
> And the flesh'd soldier, rough and hard of heart,
> In liberty of bloody hand shall range
> With conscience wide as hell, mowing like grass
> Your fresh fair virgins and your flow'ring infants.
>
> (Act III, iii, 7–14.)

His bark is worse than his bite, we trust; but even so his words are not out of keeping with the gentle poet Edmund Spenser's views on the subjugation of Ireland; or with the Spanish ways in Holland — and the Catholic ways in France — of stamping out heresy and dissent; or with the policy of the strong arm and violence as taught by the teacher and mentor of our contemporary Professor Treitschke and General Bernhardi — Niccolò Machiavelli — less than a century before Shakespeare's day.

But Shakespeare was not a political or moral theorist. He was not a theorist at all, not even, in any abstract or analytic sense of the word, a thinker. He was an artist, which is something widely different. His morals and his politics, his science and his history, were those of his time or one still earlier; but his art was for the ages. He was not a philosopher, a seer, an oracle, as some worshippers have taken him to be; he was not, of course, a prophet living in spirit in the nineteenth century while working in the sixteenth; but he was a man and dramatist as others were — Sophocles, Molière, Lope de Vega — and as such he was not very different from a great painter, sculptor, or musician. Like theirs, his work was to reveal not truth but beauty, to imitate and ennoble life, not analyze or expound it. Plot and situation, dialogue and character, style and meter — these are the elements of his art in which he wrought as he strove to produce the illusion of life upon the stage. These are the things that we should attend to as we, in turn, strive to discover how far he succeeded in producing the illusion of life upon the stage. And in this particular play, as we have seen, plot and situation count for little, dialogue and characters for nearly all.

3

Chief of the characters is, of course, the King. He is, on the whole, done according to historical and popular tradition; he is the Hal of *Henry IV*, reclaimed and sobered. He has the manliness, the physical strength and ability, the personal courage, the generalship, the ruthlessness (as well as the mercifulness toward the poor and the weak), the piety (though not the bigotry and intolerance), and the exalted patriotic temper, which the chronicler Holinshed had attributed to the great popular hero of the land. But the mere transcription of traits will not go far towards making a character; and Shakespeare gave him many other features, and put in his nostrils the breath of life besides.

The most remarkable thing about him is the way that Shakespeare reforms him and yet contrives to keep him human and recognizable. Reformations are ticklish things to handle on the stage; edifying, but alienating, they ordinarily lead beyond the province of art and poetry into the dry and sterile air of morals or the dank atmosphere of sentimentality. This on the whole the royal reformation does not do. Henry is a knight and a hero, a king and a wise ruler, and a general who has put almost all petty personal considerations under his feet; but he is still a friendly good fellow, has his joke before battle and in the midst of battle, and woos the French princess in no silken terms of gallantry, but more like a captain of cavalry than a king, though more like a king than a suitor, with fire in his heart though with a twinkle in his eye. Wine, at times, is still a bit too good for him; like his princely younger self, he has now and then a longing for the poor creature, small beer. Bardolph, Pistol, and Falstaff himself, risen from the dead, would have known him, though to recall him and what he had been to them, both in purse and in person, would now have cost them a pang. There is in the hero of Agincourt that mixture of the serious and the humorous, of the dignified and the simple and naïve, which was impossible in French tragedy until it came, in the nineteenth century, under Shakespeare's own influence, but which, in some form, is to be found in many of his best characters and is one of the most authentic signs of their reality. They are not mere rôles — not wraiths which the moon shines through.

Some readers may object a little to Henry's obtrusive morality and his familiarity with the Most High. They may be reminded of later czars and kaisers, likewise engaged in wars of aggression, and be inclined to call it all hypocrisy or official cant. Shakespeare surely did not mean it so; the Elizabethans would not have taken it so; and such monarchs, again, like their parties, are specimens of times and manners, now long out of date, but not out of date in the age of Elizabeth. In any case, Shakespeare has deliberately brushed away much of the piety clinging to him in Holinshed. He has added, to be sure, the prayer the night before the battle, in which he speaks of King Richard's death. But that really is a relief; Henry is not so pious as penitent, and would make amends for his father's wrong, by which he profits. And a striking positive change is made when the action is about to begin. The speech he now utters (IV, iii, 18–67), part of which has been quoted above, is all of honor; but the corresponding passage in Holinshed has something of the twang and snuffle of a Puritan preacher's cant:

But if we should fight in trust of multitude of men, and so get the victorie (our minds being prone to pride), we should thereupon peradventure ascribe the victorie not so much to the gift of God, as to our owne puissance, and thereby provoke his high indignation and displeasure against us.

That, for a man of action, at such a moment, is not in Shakespeare's vein. Piety and humility for the night-time; but "amid

the clang of arms," as Mr. Stone says, he would have his hero
"speak in a rapture of martial ardor which sweeps every other
thought from his mind." Now he must think only of battle and
drink delight of battle. Instead of preaching in such an hour or
praying, Shakespeare would have him assert himself, let himself
go a bit, like, say, George Washington, another hero who sometimes seemed something of a prig and (in popular legend at least)
was always the pink of propriety, but who in battle went so far as
to break out spontaneously into oaths. "God's will!" cries King
Henry, "I pray thee, wish not one man more . . . God's peace!
I would not lose so great an honour." Like Nelson at Copenhagen,
he "would not be elsewhere for thousands." Like Roland of old,
he would not have wound his horn. "The game's afoot," as he
cried to his men before Harfleur; his blood is up; and the name
of God rises to his lips only in oaths or in the war-cry, "God for
Harry, England, and St. George." Like every man of action, when
the time of action arrives he thinks of nothing — feels the need of
nothing — save to get into it. And in that hour he has no religion
but that of the old English adage, "God helps him who helps
himself."

Was Henry, then, as some have thought, Shakespeare's ideal?
Gervinus and other German critics have declared he was, being
the antithesis of Richard II and Hamlet. Some of them have even
gone so far as to say that Henry is Shakespeare himself, with his
practical genius and well-balanced nature, his taste for the low as
well as the lofty, and his sense of humor in the midst of duty — his
liking for play when at work. Mr. W. B. Yeats holds just the contrary. Poet of the Celtic twilight, of them that went forth to battle
but always fell, he thinks that Shakespeare infinitely preferred
Richard; and that Henry is given the "gross vices and coarse
nerves," and "the resounding rhetoric, as of a leading article,"
which befit a man who succeeds, though his success was really
failure. "Shakespeare watched Henry V, not indeed as he watched

the greater souls in the visionary procession, but cheerfully, as one watches some handsome spirited horse, and he spoke his tale, as he spoke all tales, with tragic irony." But when Shakespeare — when any popular dramatist — is ironical, we the people must needs know it; or else his popular art has failed him and missed the mark. Here is no evidence of either. Instead of being sly, or insinuating, or pregnant of innuendo, he is more exuberant and enthusiastic than usual; the choruses, which are the authentic voice of the poet himself, put that beyond the peradventure of a doubt. And the likelihood is that Professor Dowden is nearer the truth; Henry V, at least in some measure, approaches Shakespeare's ideal of the practical man, which is not his highest ideal. Shakespeare, no doubt, admired success, though without worshipping it; he himself succeeded, not inconsiderably in his brief two score and ten; but the men he admired most, I daresay, were the finer spirits such as Hamlet, Brutus, or Prospero, whether they succeeded or failed. It was their devotion and gallantry that he admired, not (pessimistically or sentimentally) their devotion and gallantry foiled or thrown away.

It is more to the point to say that Henry is the ideal of England, not Shakespeare's but his country's notion of their hero-king. He is the king that audiences at the Globe would have him be. This is particularly true as regards what we nowadays consider his bragging, his priggishness and cant. The obtrusive morality and piety were expected; for that matter they are like the sort of thing you find in a Speech from the Throne or our American Presidential Thanksgiving proclamations at the present day. Officially, piety has been ever in favor; even in ungodly America ceremonies so diverse as the laying of a corner stone and the conferring of the German degree of Ph.D. are performed in the name of the Father, the Son, and the Holy Ghost; and in the new Assembly of Southern Ireland, I notice, the order is given by the Speaker to "call the roll in the name of God."

And on the Elizabethan stage piety and morality are as inseparable from the ideal king as the crown on his head, the royal "we" in his mouth, or the "strut" (lingering down to the eighteenth century to be admired by Sir Roger de Coverley) with which his royal legs must tread the stage. There is in all Elizabethan dramatic art something naïve — something self-descriptive — in the lines, which in the three centuries of evolution towards the more purely and strictly dramatic has nearly disappeared. The wicked, like Richard III in his first soliloquy, know that they are wicked; the good, that they are good; heroes like Julius Caesar boast and vaunt their prowess; and a king, like a god on the stage, must every minute remember, and make us remember too, that he is nothing less. Henry's preaching, swaggering, and swinging of the scepter may repel us a bit today; but that is because as we read we democratically take him for no more than a man, as people at the Globe did not nor were expected to do. Even we, at the theater, are perhaps not so different and enlightened as we think. King Edward VII, not emulating the ceremoniousness of his ancestors, walked and talked like other people; but on the stage, not more than a score of years ago, Richard Mansfield, as Henry V, found it expedient to strut and swagger a bit again, in the fashion that pleased Sir Roger.

Or if Henry's blatant piety still offend us, surely we should find relief from it in his bragging and swearing. For these efface any impression of sanctimoniousness — these are royal, too, in the genuine antique style. Fancy William the Conqueror, Richard the Lion-hearted, or a king of Henry of Lancaster's kidney, shorn of all these high privileges and immunities of utterance, particularly on the stage. A medieval king can hardly be expected to talk like a gentleman in top hat and gaiters. The lion must not speak small — leviathan must not speak soft words unto thee — but have his roar. Despite our enlightenment, most of us, I suppose, have a sneaking notion of a king as one who talks and does, with a super-

latively grand air, pretty much as he pleases. At the theater — at
the Elizabethan theater far more than at ours — many, for the time
being, have hardly any other notion of him at all. "We are the
makers of manners," says Henry himself. And something of this
loftiness and liberty of utterance must be granted him even in his
morality and piety.

For through it all the man appears. Like Shakespeare's other
characters Henry has an individual tone, his own voice, not just
anybody's, and one unmistakably human. It swells and subsides,
pulses and undulates, alive as a limb in a Rubens or a Raphael.
Here are both man and king, both individual and Englishman,
in Henry's mingled downrightness and moderation, as he flings
his cards upon the table, though ready enough for all that to play
on:

> There's for thy labour, Montjoy.
> Go bid thy master well advise himself,
> If we may pass, we will; if we be hind'red,
> We shall your tawny ground with your red blood
> Discolour; and so, Montjoy, fare you well.
> The sum of all our answer is but this:
> We would not seek a battle, as we are;
> Nor as we are, we say we will not shun it.
> So tell your master.

That's the voice of a king, a man, an Englishman, and yet not
quite that of any other that I know.

As a king, Henry is made to suit the Globe; as a man, to suit
the English people. How English he is — so practical, sportsman-
like, moral and pious; so manly and stalwart, and yet free and
easy; so self-assertive and yet modest and generous; so fierce against
his enemies, and yet merciful towards women and the weak; so
serious, and yet simple and humorous; and so bluff and downright,
and hearty and genuine, in the avowal of his love. And how instinctively an English audience must have taken to him! His wild-
ness in youth gave him an added flavor, as it did to Richard the

Lion-hearted before him and to Edward VII since; and his skill
at leapfrog — a game which had not yet passed over into the hands
of boys any more than had hopscotch, played, in their wigs, by
Hogarth and his middle-aged friends, in the eighteenth century —
fitted him even then to be a hero in this land of sport. The wooing
scene itself, in which he refers to this and other accomplishments,
must have been enough to float the play. If there is anything that
the English take to, it is the unconventional and plain-spoken,
especially when combined with humor and genuine affection at
the core. "A character" the combination is called, as you find it
throughout English literature, from Dekker down to Fielding and
Dickens. And this character has the further charm of a king and
soldier trying — and yet scorning — to be a suitor; unconventional
in part because he cannot help it, in part because he would not
help it if he could; wooing, and overruling, a conventional and
coquettish princess, in a language that he cannot speak and she
will not understand. All that is simple and English, all that is
affected and French, and all that is mannish and womanish, too,
comes out in the lively encounter between them; and how hugely
an English audience must have been tickled with the contrast!

4

I am well aware that this interpretation of Henry's character
is not that of some eminent recent critics. Like Mr. Yeats, they too
think him coarse, hard, cruel, or calculating; and they have the
same idealistic contempt for the vulgarity of success, and are likewise addicted to the Celtic cult of failure (though so far as a
stranger in these British isles can discover, the Celts themselves, as
in America, now worship at a different altar, and their prayers are
heard). My interpretation, based upon that of Mr. Stone, is led
and regulated by historical considerations of Shakespeare's intention and the prepossessions of his audience; theirs is pretty much
as if the play were *not* a popular patriotic spectacle in the days of

Elizabeth and the Armada, but came from the pen of Browning, say, or Mr. Drinkwater. They in my opinion thrust Shakespeare out of his play, who in his own person, in the second chorus, calls Henry the mirror of all Christian kings — words which only echo those of his author Holinshed: "a maiestie was he that both lived and died a paterne in princehood, a lodestarre in honour, and mirror of magnificence, the more highlie exalted in his life, the more deeplie lamented at his death, and famous to the world alwaie." How else, pray, could on an Elizabethan stage the victor of Agincourt have been presented?

The author's intention, here so manifest, is the prime thing for the reader to consider. Even in modern dramas and novels it is; and the writers themselves have often to complain of misapprehension, and in order to forestall it some of them, like Shaw, Barker, and Bataille, take pains to expound their purposes and methods in prefaces or other comments of their own. How much more necessary it is to know and appreciate the purposes and methods of dramatists three centuries old, and to consider whether in our personal judgment of them we are swayed by those prevalent today!

Not that the purpose of the author is everything — he may have failed. And Shakespeare's opinion of Henry may not be borne out by the words and conduct he devises for him in the text. This evidently is the opinion of the critics; or else that Shakespeare really intended him to be coarse, politic, a merely efficient and successful man of the world. Whichever it be, Professor Cunliffe has rightly objected, and has shown that it is owing to our present-day prepossessions — our insensibility to the divinity that doth hedge a king, and our aversion to Henry's religiosity, to his type of coarse sally and practical joke, and to his avowal in soliloquy, of earlier days, in *Henry IV*, that he consorts with his wild companions only as a pastime, in order that he may shine in his virtue the brighter on the throne. But Mr. Cunliffe in turn himself proceeds to interpret him as efficient, though in a better sense. Negatively, Mr. Cunliffe seems to me to be in the right; positively, not wholly so. His quarrel with the contemporary critics appears to be only that they are not favorable. He really takes much the same point of view, uses much the same words, only he blunts their edge. And this is inevitable, because of the position that he has assumed at the outset. "Let us try," he says, "to make out as far as we can how Shakespeare himself conceived [his characters]; but after all the one great question for us is the impression they make on our minds." In fact, Mr. Cunliffe has, whether implicity or explicitly, stood by Shakespeare's conception in criticizing the opinion of the critics; but wholly by the "impression" in establishing his own.

Both Mr. Cunliffe and the critics have insufficiently considered the conception of the dramatist and his technique, as well as the ethics of the age. The royal strut we have considered above. That, as well as Henry's religiosity and his practical joking, is necessary to the poet's purpose in presenting a truly popular English hero-king: and the expectations of the audience are here at one with earlier dramatic practice and the Renaissance critical principle of "decorum." The "efficiency" is another matter. It is an unpleasant word even as Mr. Cunliffe uses it, something of a euphemism. And this impression that he and the other critics receive is mainly owing to two things: the soliloquy already referred to —

I know you all, and I will awhile uphold . . . (*I Henry IV*, I, ii.)

and Henry's treatment of Falstaff. The soliloquy all the critics take psychologically, and rightly they then object to the Prince's sowing wild oats so consciously and cunningly, in order to make his reformation the more telling. That would be unendurable. But really it is only the old-fashioned self-descriptive method that we have spoken of above, which Shakespeare in soliloquy employs both with heroes and with villains. It enlightens and reassures his audience. And if that be so, the other charge, of treason to Falstaff, collapses of itself. Mr. Bradley says that the Prince "should have given Sir John clearly to understand that they must say goodbye on the day of his accession." Then it would have been part of the character, beyond a doubt. And Mr. Cunliffe, in defence of Henry's casting him off, can find nothing better to say for him than that it was "a political necessity and a fore-ordained part of Henry's plan." But in the soliloquy there is no avowal of such a purpose, and when the thing comes about, whether in the play or in Holinshed before that, it is not as a matter of expediency at all but only of morals. To Shakespeare, moreover, Falstaff is not the wholly amiable, well-nigh estimable character that he has since become. The King casts him off with a regrettable priggishness, but not in the spirit of expediency or policy. The King casts him off, but morally, officially it is to his credit. The poet's hand here is a bit too heavy, but he would simply convey to the audience that as King of England Henry has broken with the past.

5

In *Henry V* the supreme comic figure does not appear; that was a risk not to be taken. The reformed young king could not decorously permit of him in his presence; and, in his presence or out of it, he would have upset the balance, and broken the unity, of the play. So, like Cervantes with Don Quixote, and Addison with Sir Roger de Coverley, he kills him off to keep him from falling into weaker hands. His death is reported, not presented; and that too is well ordered, for the death of a comic character should not touch us too nearly. Here it does not: as it is told by Mrs. Quickly, the pathetic and the comic were never better blended by mortal pen. And the whole little scene is the best thing in the play — whether it be for Falstaff's cronies as they comment and engage in reminiscences, or for the fat knight himself as his shade is thus summoned up before our eyes again.

It is a scene that might easily have become sentimental or maudlin. But sullen and dogged Bardolph is still himself, even in this the one exalted moment of his life: "Would I were with him, wheresome'er he is, either in heaven or in hell!" And motherly, consolatory Quickly, who had always looked on the bright side, and called shady things by fair names, is still herself as she smoothes Sir John's pillow and bids him " 'a should not think of God, — I hoped there was no need to trouble himself with any such thoughts yet." The "fine *end*," she thinks, is all that matters, hell or heaven. And now that he has got to one or the other, she will not have it that he is in hell, but in Arthur's bosom, if ever man went to Arthur's bosom. That British bosom for Abraham's, and not troubling oneself with God till the very pinch of death is at one's throat, are typical of her simple heathen soul. Her own legendary king is more to her than your alien patriarch; superstition is deeper rooted in her heart than the Christian faith; and the blossoming there is the kindliness of naked and benighted human nature, not of piety. She knows and notes the immemorially ominous signs and seasons — the hour just between twelve and one — even at the turning of the tide — and his fumbling with the sheets, playing with flowers, and smiling upon his fingers' ends. All that she noticed; and still, woman and heathen that she was, she comforted him by bidding him not yet think of God. But the fine end he made justified her — "an it had been any christom child," she said of it — for not having put him to that sore "trouble." For he, a heathen too, who had avoided trouble and endeavored to be "o' good cheer" all his life long, took her comfort readily and thought of God no more. Even the fat knight, though now his nose be sharp as a pen, seems still himself. "Peace, good Doll!" he had said in his latter heyday, "do not speak like a death's-head; do not bid me remember mine end."

6

Quickly is a study both of the consolatory sex and of a stratum of human culture; English enough, she is not labeled English; but there are in this play national types as well — numerous Frenchmen and some Frenchwomen, a Welshman, an Irishman, and a Scot. And like all the foreigners on the stage (unless the scene be laid in a foreign land) they are, even as at the present day, made comical, if not contemptible and silly. The stage, at least the comic stage, is beyond the reach of internationalism. The French here are presented for patriotic purposes and in keeping with patriotic prejudice; the French are written down that the English may be written up. They are made vain, frivolous, boastful, courageous, indeed, in a fantastic and high-flying way, but some of them cowardly and dastardly to the point of failing to observe the primary laws of arms. Shakespeare would, for the moment, seem not to know French character, or not to make use of his knowledge if he have it. And yet the Princess Katharine is, as has been observed by Mr. Stone, a charming sketch of a *jeune fille*. True to type, she expects to marry only according to her father's desire and choice. True to type, Shakespeare's English maidens enjoy their liberty and follow the dictates of their hearts. Yet her rigorous training in the proprieties has made her, not as it might have done, a prude, but a coquette. She is demure, coy, properly tantalizing. She does not fling wide the gates of her heart like Juliet, Rosalind, or Miranda, but peers and parleys through the lattice. She does not, like them, "avouch the thoughts of her heart with the looks of an empress," and frankly and freely say, "I am thine"; but, glancing down or sidelong up, she murmurs: "Is it possible dat I sould love de enemy of France?" — "I cannot tell" — "dat is as it sall please de roy mon pere." But with her eyes and her blushes she contradicts her tongue. She is, since his earliest comedies, the only innocent coquette in Shakespeare; and apparently Shakespeare is here presenting a social or racial characteristic, as he no doubt had discovered it in French and Continental literature, or from travelers' reports or possibly from an acquaintance with French life itself. Or it may have been owing merely to coincidence, as he framed a contrast to the frank Englishman, for of racial characteristics on the Continent Shakespeare must have known little; but if with so few opportunities as he had had in England he succeeded so well as he did with the Jew, he might easily have learned this much about the young women across the Channel.

7

The representatives of the three British nations, presently to be allied with the English, are treated more sympathetically than the French, though comically and according to popular tradition. The Scot is cool and canny, but intrepid. The Irishman is touchy, boastful, and "spoiling for a fight." But the pedantic and punctilious Welshman, Fluellen, is for fighting only when provoked, and not even then unless the time be fit and proper. He will not quarrel with MacMorris till the battle be over, then he will. He does not openly resent Pistol's bringing him bread and salt to his leek "because it was in a place where I could breed no contention with him." "There is occasions and causes, why and wherefore," he avers, "in all things." He is all for soldierly discipline and etiquette, for the proprieties, whether in military science, in military conduct, in history, or even in the use of an allusion or a figure of speech. But he keeps a rod in pickle, and when the "occasion" comes applies it with no little zest. Not that he is vindictive. He gives Williams a shilling as the quarrel ends, and Pistol a groat to heal his pate; and in the former case at least he does not understand why the fellow will not take it. *He* would have taken it.

For he is a pedant — a schoolmaster — out in the world, and, as the profession nearly always is, comically out of place in it. It is because he is a schoolmaster, not a politician, that he exhibits the blandness, indeed, but not that flexibility and knowledge of othei peoples which would be expected of him in England today if we were to justify Shakespeare's knowledge of his race. A schoolmaster is a schoolmaster the world over. "He feels it his mission," as Mr.

Stone has said, "to set people right"; and whether by instruction or admonition, by encouragement or chastisement, he does this to everybody, scolding a bit as he does it, but keeping on the whole unimpaired the good-humor of the virtuous. Those who are right need never be ruffled. He gives money after blows as the old-fashioned teacher did rock-candy or a catechism; and he mingles blessings with his scoldings, "Got pless you, Aunchient Pistol! you scurvy, lousy knave, Got pless you,"[1] in much the same spirit. He is comical most of all because he is so mistaken in human character — like many teachers, he helps those who care not to be helped, and would enlighten those who are but too happy to sit in darkness. Pistol he took at first to be as valiant a man as Mark Antony, because of his "prave words." So, casting pearls before him, Captain Fluellen takes time and pains to expound to him the inner and moral meaning of the classical myth of Fortune, whereas Ancient Pistol, if he knew it, cares for neither meanings nor morals. He condescends even to his King; and in the glow of his loyal and patriotic pride as a Welshman declares that he need not be ashamed of your majesty (who as Harry of Monmouth also passes for a Welshman), praised be God, so long as your majesty is an honest man. To be a Welshman, as only a Welshman can know, is to be more than any king. Who dared to say that Shakespeare wasn't a seer and prophet, and did not, in the spirit, see these closing days of the year 1921?

Fluellen is a full-length portrait; the Scot or the Irishman, the merest sketch. Shakespeare had seen schoolmasters of his tribe, no doubt, in Stratford, which is, of course, near the Border; and he drew another and similar one in Evans, the parson and school-master in *The Merry Wives of Windsor*. Even Shakespeare in a sense drew best what was nearest at hand and most familiar; and in those days when travel was difficult and the vast majority of people

---

[1] The Welsh and the Irish in Elizabethan drama speak an English not recognizable as theirs today, but it is undoubtedly true to life. It is owing to the fact that at home they were still speaking the Celtic tongue.

died like plants where they grew, he had seen little of the distant Irish or Scots or French. He could not see them as the angels see them, or (which often comes to the same thing) as they see themselves. Even Shakespeare was a citizen, not of the world, but of Stratford. And from afar he looked at these foreigners through the spectacles of comic tradition, with tolerant, not unkindly, though thoroughly English eyes.

III

Shakespeare and the Moderns

SHAKESPEARE, by common consent the greatest name in drama, is on the stage a name and little more. How seldom does he look down from the wall or ceiling of the theater, where as the patron saint he hangs enshrined, upon his creatures treading that little space to which he likened, and which he made, the world! Like many another in the calendar, he is rarely invoked, little frequented. Is it because of the difficulty of his language? In part, for in Germany, where he is still played, he speaks the modern tongue. But there is a better reason — the form in which his plays are cast. It is not that which is now prevalent: it is not so essentially, so rigorously dramatic. And this fact counts for somewhat less in Germany, where the audience comes less simply and openheartedly to be entertained. There the theater is a school, if it be not a temple — and *Hamlet* may well be still in favor where the populace flocks to *Faust*. But in England during the seventeenth and eighteenth centuries the greatest of dramatists was freely adapted, frankly rewritten; and in the twentieth he is read, taught, and continually written about, not played.

1

What is drama, as we now practice or conceive it? From narrative or epic it differs chiefly, of course, in the matter of direct presentation. It does not so much tell a story as enact it, and the less there is told the better drama it is. In that regard the method is indirect. Information or comment coming to light incidentally, and falling naturally from the lips of the character, is no longer narrative or description but drama itself. It is of the action, of the character, whether the person speaking or spoken of. And as far as possible nothing is told at all. Contrast or parallel, repeated or varied, saves words and turns mere narrative to deed and demonstration.[1] Seeing the thing done is better than hearing that it has been done, as Horace noted long ago; and as the art developed, it has more and more abandoned words for deeds and gestures, for sights and sounds. There have, of late, been successful plays without words, as there have been plays without printed words upon the screen. The situation rightly handled is of itself eloquent and immediately so; and situation is the essence and soul of drama. It furnishes the accumulation and compression needed, the long, thin series of events (as it is in life and in narrative) being rolled or telescoped together. A situation, a complication, is better than a mere story; two persons acting and reacting upon each other is better than one acting alone; and other things being equal, four is better than two, with all their colored and conflicting opinions and judgments, attractions or aversions. And therefore even in the earliest effective performances on a stage there has ordinarily been some sort of observance of the unities. Drama is troubled, or languishes, when the action is stretched out over years and is trundled about from place to place, requiring continual readjustment upon the part of the spectator; but above all when the action itself has no unity — is not given depth as well as breadth, volume as well as extension.

---

[1] See below, p. 92, note, for my acknowledgment of indebtedness to Mr. Lubbock. The figure of *volume* for drama as contrasted with *surface* for narrative, which I use freely, is also his.

Most of these qualities, of course, Shakespeare also exhibits, and generally to a far greater degree than his contemporaries or successors. But since his time drama has become more essentially and exclusively dramatic, as painting has become more pictorial, sculpture more sculpturesque. The unities, now commonly observed, he for the most part ignores; he tells the tale from the beginning, not merely from the third act. And while he keeps, of course, the unity of action — otherwise he would not be a great dramatist — he seldom keeps it like the Greeks, the French, and the moderns, or attains to that compression, concentration, or intensification which arises from enacting only the last stage of a single story, whether it be in one place and within the twenty-four hours or not. On the other hand, he commonly has an underplot, which diminishes, indeed, the effect of compression, but serves to complete the illusion of reality, in a story told from the outset, by filling the necessary interstices of time. The web of his art is, in general, far wider than the modern or the ancient, but looser — thinner, even — in a sense.

There remain in it many elements of narration and description. In both Shakespeare and the French classical drama, as in the Greek before them, words abound. In words, indeed, is vested the drama, but not in all of these. The speeches are often long, and the style is not only too elevated but too complicated, whether for the illusion of life or for the most telling effect upon the stage. There are soliloquies, with which drama has since dispensed. And in these and the other speeches is to be found much that today has been relegated to the italics of stage-directions — looks and gestures, sights and sounds, time and circumstances, scenery and local color. As thus presented, these matters are often finely poetical, above all in Shakespeare; and, what is more, the garden of the Capulets, "pleasant" Inverness castle with the martins fluttering about it, and bare, tempest-swept Gloucester heath, enter in a way into the dramatic fabric, its warp and woof. Shakespeare's scenes are not, like the neo-classical, enacted *in vacuo.* At the end of one scene, between the royal murderers, "light thickens," without as it does within; in the next, which is that of the murder plotted,

> The west yet glimmers with some streaks of day.

Such touches not only mark the time but create an atmosphere, and furnish a fitting background for the horror. They raise it up under the firmament, plant it and root it in the earth. Yet they are words, deficient in action, and often words not so natural and incidental as these — description sometimes not wholly motivated, apostrophe such as would never have been uttered. Though they are much better reading than our stage-directions, they are sometimes a little out of place, not for the characters' own lips or ears. They are for the audience, and, as in the exposition between Tranio and Lucentio in the *Taming of the Shrew,* inform a person on the stage where he is and what he is doing, which he sufficiently knows himself. Or they tell what the author knows. The Archbishop of Canterbury, called upon by King Henry to justify his invasion of France, expounds the Salic Law; Jaques descants on all the world's a stage, Mercutio on Queen Mab, Gonzalo on the Ideal State or Commonwealth; and Hamlet, on the eve of his all-absorbing enterprise, impersonally and imperturbably holds forth in a little lecture on the right and proper way of acting. Meanwhile, they keep their eyes on the spectators. They step down center, into the glare of the footlights, fairly turning their backs upon their friends. What is less obvious, and yet more difficult for the dramatist to avoid, is the character's omniscient, unblushing description of himself, his vices and virtues, his talents and tastes. The author speaks, and to the audience, which in the drama is not supposed to be present. The point of view of the audience is taken rather than of the stage, of life itself. Or else (which surely cannot be) the character himself is here taking a pose. He should be portrayed in focus, with eyes bent upon his friend or on the way before him, not rolling inward or upward. But the virtuous in Shakespeare know at times how virtuous they are, the vicious how vicious; and both good and bad are often aware of their moods and passions, even nurse and cherish them, and are not unmindful of their own beauty or greatness.[2] The wicked but not utterly abandoned find it in their hearts to desire the right stage-effects, like King John, who (as Sir Walter Raleigh notices) would fain have the present nefarious scene, with Hubert,[3] laid in the churchyard, when midnight is striking; and like Macbeth, who bids the earth not hear his steps, for fear the stones prate of his whereabout and take the present horror from the time, which now suits with it. To some candid critics this seems really meant for self-consciousness; but it is the author addressing the audience, comment misplaced, description or narrative, not drama at all. And yet, nevertheless, despite these and other drawbacks, Shakespeare is the greatest of dramatists, his characters are the most vivid array of portraits in literature, and many of his scenes are the most captivating or enthralling ever on the boards. That this is no paradox we shall see.

His dramatic procedure first concerns us. Shakespeare has no mysteries, or has them not for long. For a scene or an act he may keep a secret — as with Othello's purpose of suicide and the fact that Hamlet's uncle is the murderer — but oftener he does not keep it at all. And in drama, as not in the novel, this is often a good

[2] To this method of self-description, it seems to me, is to be attributed Othello's and Hamlet's, Brutus' and Coriolanus', Antony's and Cleopatra's remembering their greatness at the end. Othello should be thinking of Desdemona, Hamlet of Ophelia or the distracted State. Mr. T. S. Eliot (*Shakespeare and the Stoicism of Seneca*, 1927) takes it that this is a *bovarysme*, an endeavor to escape reality. There may be a little of this, or of that influence of Senecan Stoicism which he discovers; but drama is influenced by philosophy less than by dramatic tradition and technique. To Seneca the dramatist is owing much of this technique of self-description, although, since this is really drama undeveloped, something of the sort there would have been without him. And like him Shakespeare and all the Renaissance demand at the great and final moments an heroic attitude; and this attitude, like everything else, they put directly and explicitly into words.

[3] *King John*, III, iii.

method for plot or action, though less good for characterization. The latter we take up below; the former we approach at once.[4]

2

SUSPENSE IN SHAKESPEARE AND IN THE MODERNS

As many critics have noted, anticipation of tragic or comic outcome may be more effective than surprise — it is always more effective, to be sure, than surprise without due preparation — and Shakespeare's method in *Macbeth* is that of the *Œdipus Tyrannus*. Since drama is meant to be presented, not read, and depends on imagination and immediate effect, rather than on reflection and memory, there is an advantage for the audience, when its attention is rightly directed and focussed, in knowing more than do the characters on the stage; and here already, in a sort, is that compression which we have spoken of. Out of this irony a kind of situation arises — the material is presented in relief, becomes two-sided and casts a shadow, does not lie flat and thin. Moreover, the tragic or comic effect is thus prolonged and deepened. The expectation of the ultimate unmasking of Fate before the eyes of Macbeth and Œdipus well-nigh furnishes forth the play. This is the clearer, calmer, more monumental method, and Shakespeare and the ancients have it in common.

And yet, as the critics[5] have not noted, this method is a good one mainly for the behoof of contrived and artificial complications, usual in ancient and Elizabethan drama but unusual today. I

---

[4] I would not be understood to think that I am here covering the ground of the differences between Shakespeare's art and the modern, whether in plot or in characterization. There is much left unsaid because it has been said already, by Dr. Bradley, Sir Walter Raleigh, and others. And this essay, like that on Cleopatra, is intended to be supplementary to my larger discussion in *Shakespeare Studies* (1927).

[5] Lessing in his *Hamburgische Dramaturgie* (No. 48 *et seq.*) speaks contemptuously of the method of surprise, affected by the French and the Italians. He forgets that it is sometimes employed by Shakespeare. And what he says is true of the momentary, empty surprise, really without suspense, without preparation or a thickening cloud of trouble in the air. See below, p. 74.

mean, to give place and scope to the ironies of disguise or mistaken identity, of deception or slander, of playing a part or overhearing, or of prophecies or oracles coming true upon the stage. The audience ought to know (as it does) that the youth whom Orlando is wooing is Rosalind, and that Lady Teazle is behind the screen; and, despite Jonson's superb tour de force, ought to know (as it doesn't) that the Silent Woman is really a young man. When, on the other hand, the situation comes about less peremptorily, more naturally, as in the first act of *Hamlet* and the last scene of *Othello*, and as nowadays it is always expected to do, there is an advantage in keeping the secret (of fratricide, in one case, as of suicide, in the other) until it can be naturally divulged. The situation having come about as in life itself, so should come the disclosure. Thus it is in keeping with, and indeed depends upon, that indirect and gradual disclosure of character, preferred by modern drama, which we discuss below. Yet the advantage is not chiefly that of verisimilitude. It is rather that of stimulation and provocation, of satisfaction or surprise. The audience are led to participate (not left superior and aloof), and to live and learn even as do the persons in the play. They must bestir their wits somewhat as the author has done before them, if they are to feel the full force of the outcome. And they profitably and cheerfully surrender the advantage, which really is a disadvantage, of being *told*.[6] How much they would lose if they knew of the crime before Hamlet knew of it, of Othello's purpose as soon as he did!

But in either case, whether the dramatist keep the secret from the audience or disclose it, proceed according to the method of mystery or that of anticipation, there should be something of suspense, though the word is more appropriately used (as I shall use it) of the former. And in either case, there should be a process of preparation, an effect of expectation — or if of surprise alone, it should be after preparation all the greater. The surprise should

[6] See below, p. 92, note.

die away only in satisfaction and approval. In both cases alike there should be the effect of compression, a duplicity of impression, in the one case perfectly clear to the audience from the beginning, in the other not clear before the end. Any deficiency in the method of mystery as regards the prospect would, other things being equal, be more than made up for to the audience, at the moment of disclosure, in the retrospect, and by their being put on a level with the characters on the boards. There would be less of anticipation, more of stimulation.

3

Of still another and also a right effect of suspense Shakespeare gives us little. I mean not only that which springs out of the tantalizing concealment and thrilling disclosure of the inner character, discussed below, and to be found in Ibsen; but also that effect of oscillation in the dramatic movement, which we find not only in Ibsen but in Corneille and Racine, Lope and Calderón. This latter Mr. Bradley,[7] indeed, finds characteristic of Shakespeare — the swaying of fortune or of the hero's decision from one side to the other, highly favorable to both a spectator's and a reader's interest.

There is in him something of it, to be sure, but far less, whether in the succession of scenes or in the scene itself, than in the great Frenchmen and Spaniards or even Beaumont and Fletcher. There the scenes are all a-quiver, and they follow one upon another like the waves — and troughs — of the sea. In the first scene of *Andromaque* we learn that it is a question with Pyrrhus whether to marry the heroine, who does not love him, or Hermione, who does; and that the life of Andromache's son, which has been demanded by Hermione's father, is at stake. In scene two he refuses to give him up. In scene three he tells his confidant that for all he cares Hermione may go her way to Sparta. In scene four, repulsed again by Andromache, he utters a threat against young Astyanax. In the

[7] *Shakespearean Tragedy* (1908), p. 50.

next, Hermione, in her jealousy, is disposed to lend an ear to Orestes, her rejected suitor; in the next after that she is ready to follow him if Pyrrhus refuse to surrender the boy. Then Orestes rejoices, confident of success; then Pyrrhus desperately vows that he will hand the boy over and marry Hermione after all. So the action oscillates, as it progresses, throughout the play, and in one play after another; and while the process at times tends to become somewhat mechanical and arbitrary, so tireless as to be tiresome, it is essentially dramatic. But Macbeth, and Lear, and Othello fall, though swiftly, almost steadily deeper into the toils of fate. Macbeth hesitates only in a single brief scene, the seventh of Act I, in which his lady upbraids him for it; and Othello, though he has two or three momentary revulsions of feeling, can hardly be said to hesitate at all.

This difference in the movement is owing somewhat to a difference in the total conception. The Elizabethan drama is still a story on the stage; the Bourbon is mainly an emotional debate. The Elizabethan action is more external and consecutive; the Bourbon more concentrated — centered and revolving in the soul. Decisions continually hang in the balance, from scene to scene, almost from speech to speech. That compression and condensation of which we have taken notice here assumes especially the form of a struggle between emotion and emotion, purpose and purpose, will and will. This of necessity involves suspense; but even of the mere wavering of fortune there is not much in Shakespeare. In *Hamlet* and *Coriolanus* there is more than in most of the other great plays, as the "mighty opposites," in their struggle, win or lose; or as circumstances thwart their purposes, which do not change. The drama of Beaumont and Fletcher, however, of Calderón and Lope de Vega, is not a debate; and yet it enjoys an oscillation and fluctuation almost as marked as the French.

Taken, then, as a whole, Shakespeare is less logically and consistently dramatic. He is less intellectualized and argumentative, to be sure — virtues which have their drawbacks — but he has kept more of the narrative and descriptive methods; he has less completely translated his material out of the language of the one art into that of the other, or (slightly to change the figure) less completely transposed it from one medium to the other, from picture and canvas, so to speak, to sculpture and the round. And yet — how can it be? — Shakespeare, at his best, is more telling and captivating, whether on the page or on the stage.

4
SHAKESPEARE'S PARTICULAR ACHIEVEMENT

What above all he captures, and keeps and fixes for us, is the illusion of life. Despite the frequently exalted and fantastical turn of his speech, despite the frequently contrived and unplausible nature of his plots, Shakespeare attains to this the dramatist's chief end more happily than does any ancient or any modern. What he bestows on us less frequently is the pleasurable sense of the most expert and consistent use of his special medium — drama and nothing but drama, the peculiar and exquisite effect of the most masterly and economical handling of his art. Indeed, he is careless of his medium, lacking apparently esthetic principle and program; he "wanted arte," said Ben Jonson truly; and what he is chiefly intent upon is not craftsmanship but reality, not the manner but the matter. But somehow, we know not how, he masters both. His characters talk like real people, as the great Frenchmen's characters do not. His scenes are like real life, as the great Frenchmen's scenes are not. In short, Shakespeare has less of structure and specifically dramatic method; he proceeds less abstractly and logically, rigorously and consistently, and less cunningly provides for compactness, for effects of suspense and oscillation; and yet at his best, though irregularly and loosely, he grasps the scene as a whole.

The murder scene in *Macbeth* is an example. Here is little

struggle or debate, oscillation or suspense, and no artful withhold-
ing and disclosure, at least in the stricter meaning of the words.
Corneille, Racine, and their priest and apostle Brunetière, might
have caviled; but nevertheless and despite all, here is drama, or a
better thing. It is the thing itself — it is murder — in its whole
tremendous import and impact. The situation is seized and comprehended, rather than fashioned and projected; is given life
rather than force, is presented rather than worked up or wrought
out, poised or cunningly constituted; but certainly here for once
a pair of lost souls look out fearfully upon one another, their crime,
and the world. Save for the contrasts, the scene depends for its effect upon the individuality of the speech, and the full and vivid
realization both of the circumstances and of such thoughts and
notions, feelings and reactions, as these circumstances would
arouse. The scene is realized — and by the characters themselves.
It is not an abstract, logical, structural, but an immediate and
imaginative method, easy to recognize, difficult to analyze or explain. Be it what it may, the imagination flashes from pole to pole,
from this world to the next. "What hands are here?" — as if they
were not his own. "Wake Duncan with thy knocking — I would
thou couldst!"

It may seem scarcely relevant to speak of style; but what is drama
too if not writing, and I am reminded of that definition framed by
Stendhal and reaffirmed by Mr. Middleton Murry: "Style consists
in adding to a thought all the circumstances calculated to produce
the whole effect that the thought ought to produce." Here are all
such circumstances, clinging as if to a magnet — the misgivings and
trepidations, the starting at sounds and imagining of sounds that
are not, the questions asked but left unanswered, the concern of
the characters for themselves and for one another, and, above all,
that tragic terror which finds its proper and most penetrating voice
in habitual commonplace utterances, as when, upon Macbeth's
staggering in with the blood on his hands, the lady cries, "My hus-

band!" which he is, indeed, still. He is hers, she may think, now more than ever, the blood having made them one; but all that they have been in the past is by her homely outcry flung into contrast with what they are at this moment. And thus, as well as in other ways, the very heart and core, the form and feature, of the situation are set before us, though not heightened by mystery or given the added force and effect of suspense.

And I am reminded also of Mr. Murry's quotation from Chekhov's words to Gorky: "You are an artist. You feel superbly, you are plastic; that is, when you describe a thing you see and touch it with your hands. That is real writing." And this is real writing, in a still higher degree; these things are, to even finer effect, both seen and touched. The situation is felt superbly, and therefore we feel it; it is felt by the characters themselves. Even to the uttermost limits they traverse the tragic passion, and then the spectators (sometimes, as we shall see, they are on the stage, as well) do this by sympathy and contagion. They weep with them that weep. But on the French stage, and still more on the modern, there is frequently less of tragic or comic effect, less of tears or laughter, than in the audience. The method of analysis and debate, of suspense and subsequent disclosure — all the various devices which produce emphasis and climax — cause the upshot itself, the desire, purpose, or deed disclosed, to loom larger before the spectators' eyes. By the art of preparations the dramatist leads up to great, but in themselves simple, unheightened, and outwardly unemotional, utterances — like the *qu'il mourût* of Old Horace when asked what his remaining son should have done, alone against the three; or the words of Curiace, friend of one of the Horatii already designated for the combat, and lover of their sister, when informed that he has been chosen for the opposite side. "Are you displeased?"

Non, mais il me surprend:
Je m'estimois trop peu pour un honneur si grand.

There the French dramatist does not linger, or lavish the store of passion or poetry at his command. At the great moments his characters often do not betray so much feeling as do Othello, Macbeth, or King Lear; nor do the other characters on the stage so fully and amply reflect this as do Othello's wife and his friends, the Fool, Kent, Gloster, Edgar, and Cordelia, the Doctor and the Waiting-woman in the sleep-walking scene, or (for that matter) as does the Greek Chorus. They do not need to. The situation in itself is potent. The tragic cause sufficiently appears and asserts itself upon the boards; the effect, somewhat more immediately and independently than Shakespeare produces it, in the house. And so with laughter. The house rings with it, in Paris as in London; but there is comparatively little of it on the stage of Molière. To this, however, we must return below.[8]

Though so different, Shakespeare, of course, is, in the murder scene, not even technically undramatic. He uses contrast, for instance, as between Macbeth and his wife, more variously and poignantly than the Frenchmen; and contrast is a fundamental dramatic device. And in the matter of making the talk simple and real, and of seizing and catching up in his magic net all the circumstances of the situation — of sights and sounds, imagined and (if not imagined) magnified, like the blood and the knocking — he pens drama itself. It is not too elevated and eloquent, rhetorical and antithetical, as the French frequently is. What is more, it is given a time and a place, is embodied, costumed, and lighted — the hour is past midnight, the chambers are above and the knocking is at the south gate, and there is wine in the murderers' veins, blood on their hands. Above all, here as elsewhere, the picturesque and significant moment is chosen, an unforgettable attitude is struck, and the author's imagination has scope, and play, and range. The positive, not the negative, is what counts in art; what is there, not what isn't there, is what we feel; and of the positive

[8] See p. 70 f.

there is far more in Shakespeare. Macbeth meeting his lady before and after the murder; the Weird Sisters on the heath, and Banquo's Ghost at the supper; Lady Macbeth welcoming the great news at the beginning, but walking in her sleep and wringing her hands at the end — these, and others like them in tragedy after tragedy, are audacious and sublime conceptions and inventions, beyond the reach of dramatic logic, beyond the compass of any other pen.

This is a matter of story; and a story on the stage, when it is from a master-hand, certainly has its virtues, not only in point of reality as compared with the emotional debate but in that of stage interest. As Shakespeare practices the art, there is, then, less suspense, less oscillation than in Corneille and Ibsen, but there is often greater interest, whether in character and circumstances or in the action itself. There is more striking incident; and without any real secret being kept or much swaying of fortune's favor or of the hero's or villain's resolution, the audience is held, and led, from point to point. It is so in *Hamlet* and *King Lear*, in *Othello* and *Macbeth*. Will Hamlet succeed in revenging his father and how? What will become of Macbeth now that he has the crown, or of Lear now that he has surrendered it? What will happen to Othello now that Iago has caught the scent and is hotfoot on his trail? We are so interested in them, their situations are so striking and poignant, Othello and Desdemona have so completely won our hearts and the plot against them is so devilish, that we follow it, all absorbed, though the course taken is fairly straight, with nothing to throw Iago off the track or to save his victims from his fangs. This is dramatic too.

As we have seen, Shakespeare realizes the circumstances: he is equally gifted in framing the scene to fit the circumstances given. No one has such an instinctive differentiating sense for various shades of the same passion, for various attitudes of the same person, as time tells and Fortune turns her wheel. He has a genius for seasons and occasions, for the character in its phases, for the

situation not as structure but as a unique though indubitable
moment in this particular person's life. Othello before the Senate,
stately and serene, gracious and chivalrous, is still himself at the
end, although this be but the wreck of him, by passion now certainly shaken, by the dart of chance now pierced. Mercutio,
wounded, is game to the last gasp, the same wit who had made
merry over Romeo's sentiment, the same fighting-cock who had
irritated Tybalt; but though he dies jesting, without a touch of
sentiment or solemnity, he scolds a bit, and the mirth ebbs out of
his words even as does the blood out of his veins. And Lear, the
proud and passionate king, groping his way like a child out of the
darkness of his madness to the light — his daughter Cordelia, with
her heart melting within her, bent over him — where shall we find
the like discrimination of rightness and reality among the ancients,
the Spanish, or the French? Shakespeare is dramatic less structurally and economically, less from principle and by profession;
but surely these his daring creations, and (as it were) natural variations, are what is prime and fundamental in dramatic art. And it
is a lesser glory, though it be no little one, to attain rather to outward and technical perfection, to continuity and consistency of
form, like the authors of *Horace* and *Phèdre*. Their form is
rounded and perfect, right but a little tight, like that of Mozart
and Haydn; Shakespeare's is like Beethoven's.

5

The particular bent of their genius, in both the Englishman
and the Frenchmen, appears when their dialogue condescends to
the level, and contracts to the dimensions, of common life. By
penning long tirades, as we have seen, both the one and the others
often transgress the bounds of probability and on the stage now
somewhat bore us. But when Shakespeare is simple he is conversational and gives the illusion of real people talking as they will
and do; when Corneille and Racine are simple they still retain

dramatic structure and give the effect of suspense. Pauline, who, thinking her lover long dead, has married another, receives from her father some news (which Shakespeare in the same circumstances would, as like as not, have imparted in the lump) in its full effect, bit by bit.

Pauline. Quelle subite alarme vous peut toucher?
Félix.   Sévère n'est point mort.
Pauline.   Quel mal nous fait sa vie?
Félix.   Il est le favori de l'empereur Décie.
Pauline. Après l'avoir sauvé des mains des ennemis,
            L'espoir d'un si haut rang lui devenoit permis;
            Le destin, aux grands coeurs si souvent mal propice,
            Se résout quelquefois à leur faire justice.
Félix.   Il vient ici lui-même.
Pauline.   Il vient!
Félix.   Tu le vas voir.

There, in *Polyeucte,* we have a mere fragment of dialogue, but like that in *Horace,* two lines of which were cited above, it is in itself thoroughly dramatized. Every morsel of information is made to count, with climactic force. It does so, however, by virtue of the dramatic and rhetorical method and logic, the structure and arrangement, the preparations and developments, rather than of the plastic touch, the semblance of a human voice and stumbling tongue of passion. Mere passion, indeed, in either of the characters for the moment before us, would, we know, have spoken less sparingly and to the point. And here, as in Corneille and Racine generally, there is more of art and drama, less of the feeling of life itself.

6

But while Shakespeare does not, whether in the scene or the succession of scenes, secure so uniformly and emphatically effects of suspense and oscillation, he does — and far better than they — secure a dramatic effect of tension and release, of ebb and flow.[9]

[9] This subject is finely handled by Mr. Bradley, *op. cit.,* chap. ii.

The passion pulses; the scene itself rises and falls, swells and subsides. And the requirements of this fluctuation are provided for
in the very management of the stage. In the long scene the chief
character retires and reënters, and at the end all the characters
are replaced. Indeed, of this branch of his art, which depends on
his own vitality and tact, a spontaneous sympathy with the subject
and an instinctive comprehension of the capacity and endurance
of the actor and his audience, rather than on analytic skill and
careful psychological preparations — on the action fitting and holding the stage rather than on the design and symmetry of the fable
in print — Shakespeare is, by long odds, a far greater master than
any. This is a matter of accommodations and compromises, of art
not pure and absolute but mingled and amphibious, and of the
passions not steadfast as a star but changing like the planets and
their satellites, the winds and tides, the orchestra and the dance.
The art of the theater is the art of preparations — and of fluctuations, of limitations. And Shakespeare has a range of emotion,
even — despite his violence — to the point of temperance and restraint. His tensest scene, as well as the whole play itself, begins
and ends quietly, as with the Greeks.[10] The last scene in the second
act of *King Lear* is an example. It does not conclude with the old
man rushing out upon the heath into the tempest, but with his
daughters and their followers muttering their misgivings or lifting
up their eyebrows, shrugging their shoulders or making fast their
doors. (Here again we have not only the full and unbridled passion
itself but also the effect of it duly registered upon the stage.) And
like the single scene, the whole tragedy ends on a quieter note
than has hitherto prevailed, one seldom of consolation, but of

[10] The recent favorite opinion is that this is owing to the want of a curtain,
the difficulty in making exits. In addition to what I have already said (*Shakespeare Studies*, pp. 377–378) I should like to point out the fact that Lear makes
his exit here at the pinnacle of his passion, and that one of the beauties of the
quarrel scene in *Julius Caesar* is in its gradual subsidence, though the exits of
the two principal characters are still far distant.

mournful reflection and hopes of restoration for the realm. A wild and tumultuous scene, moreover, is followed by one of lower tone, a passionate one by a pathetic one, or a tragic by a comic, all of which furnishes a contrast or relief, not only for the actor but for the audience, though this is the better when the contrast is only apparent, the relief a little in vain. Then it really heightens the tragedy, as in the scene where Duncan pauses kindly, yet blindly, to contemplate, before entering, the peaceful-looking, martlet-haunted castle; or where the porter, as he comes out to answer the knocking, which (we know) has startled the murderers, jokes about the effects of the liquor, which (we know) he had shared with Duncan's now bloodied grooms, and, grimly, but ignorantly, toys with the notion that the gate he keeps is the gate of hell. Irony lies in such proximity to the truth. And in all these various ways Shakespeare respects the limitations of the character, and of the actor and the spectator, if he does few others. The limitations give his freedom aim and point. Unhampered by rules and a formal structure, by the exigencies of an external tragic dignity or the *style noble*, he has the uttermost range and variety of expression at his command.

7

THE STILL SCENES

Shakespeare's still scenes, whether comic or tragic, are among his greatest achievements. Long ago Sir Joshua Reynolds took notice of the scene before Macbeth's castle, just mentioned, as an example of repose in art. Sheridan Knowles declared it was not repose; and both in a way were right. It is a lull before the storm: the silence tingles, the peace hides a menace. But there is unmistakable and most welcome diversion — a lowering of the pitch, a slackening of the tension, an apparent though not an actual change of theme. And this is such an artistic relaxation as there is little of in classic French tragedy, although, to be sure, it is little needed.

There the action is in continual fluctuation — there we have drama and almost nothing but drama, without diversions or distractions, artistic or inartistic (as in Shakespeare they sometimes are); the tension is high and unrelenting; and though there is variation in the tone, there is little lowering of it and less repose. This is a stricter but a more limited logic, a narrower gamut, a harp with fewer strings. The alexandrines may falter or waver but are never interrupted; the *style noble* does not fail. Indeed, the oscillation of purpose or of fortune becomes a little insistent and mechanical, like that of a pendulum or metronome.

But Shakespeare has still scenes (or portions of them) even more significant, which are not diversions at all. Such are those of the sleep-walking in *Macbeth* and of the willow-song in *Othello*, of Lear's awakening and of his and Ophelia's madness, and those where ghosts appear. They are not to be confused with such as that between the Old Man and Ross in *Macbeth*, and those between Kent and the Gentleman in *King Lear*, which serve mainly to explain what has happened and to focus attention on what is yet to be, and are useful but not indispensable in a drama so thoroughly narrative and popular in method and purpose. They are scenes of substantive and primary importance, although the action subsides; they are such as those touched upon above, where the leading character does not act but suffers, in the presence of sympathetic or wonder-stricken spectators not only in the house but on the stage. The spectators who are also actors — for instance, Kent, Gloster, Edgar, and the Fool, in *King Lear*, Enobarbus and Menenius in the Roman tragedies — are like the Chorus in Greek tragedy, and give the passion scope and range, volume and resonance. Without the awestruck comments of the Doctor and the Waiting-woman, Lady Macbeth's tragic mutterings and murmurings would fall a little dully and feebly upon our ear. Doctor and Waiting-woman together serve as a sounding-board to her taut and quivering heartstrings, as a whispering-gallery to her sighs. And we in our seats are permitted ourselves to catch a glimpse of the deep pit of darkness into which by her ambition she has precipitated herself, as these honest and faithful souls look down into it and recoil. There is also a contrast between the doctor and the woman themselves, between what he would learn and she would by no means reveal, though they are wholly at one in their humanity. And what is more, for the expression of this Shakespeare has the right and fitting words as never had any one before him or since, for humanity both pitiful and aghast.

This device of the passion witnessed, a simple but noble one, is variously employed. On similar spectators upon the stage the supernatural is made by Shakespeare to depend for its whole effect of reality — or rather of unreality. We believe in it because of the ghost-seer's awestruck wonder, but the gulf between it and our mortal flesh our imagination learns to perceive and measure when his doubt gives way to faith, as with Horatio on the platform; or when his faith holds out against the unseeing and incredulous, as with Macbeth defying the Ghost. It is an art of limitations, but they are those of human nature.

There is, as I have intimated, somewhat the same method in comedy. There is wit and humor rather than the unconsciously comic situation; there are humorous or witty characters like Mercutio and Falstaff, Rosalind and Beatrice, rather than comic ones like Alceste and Arnolphe, Harpagon or Dandin. Or if a comic situation there be, there are fun-loving spectators of it like Prince Hal and Poins, Sir Toby and Maria, Gratiano and the hostile courtroom; and laughter crackles on the stage before it resounds in gallery and pit. Here they laugh by sympathy and contagion, at comedy both developed and delighted in on the boards. In Molière (as also in Jonson) the best comedy is often unconscious; but it is so prepared for, so carried through by devices of contrast and surprise, of repetition, variation, or inversion, that, with or without a claque, it cannot fail. This sort of situation also is in a way projected — like a rocket, exploding in the air.[11]

And it is somewhat the method employed in presenting the background of nature. As we have observed above, nature is by Shakespeare scarcely brought to bear upon the audience directly, by effects of sight and sound. The means are almost entirely the words spoken; and even there, as Mr. Granville Barker notices,[12] the dramatist is less concerned with the picture itself than with the emotional effect upon his characters, and so eventually with that upon ourselves. "His actors are the prism through which all light must pass." The storm in *King Lear* is presented by an imitation of wind and thunder, indeed, but otherwise only by the emotional effect, whether upon those who, as we have seen above, recoil from it at the end of Act II, or upon those out on the heath — Edgar and the Fool, Kent and Gloster, and above all the King. In

> How sweet the moonlight sleeps upon this bank,

and even in Casca's account of the storm and portents, there is more nearly direct description or narrative; but Lear describes incidentally, dramatically, like the characters imparting information in a good first scene, as he bids the storm do its worst. As his passion rages and his reason totters, he acclaims the storm, upbraids it, bows before it; while the others shrink from it or bewail it. There is no symbolism [13] as there is commonly supposed to be, the storm is not the picture or outer embodiment of Lear's inner

---

[11] See the chapter on the Comic Method in my *Shakespeare Studies*, especially pp. 147–157.

[12] *Fortnightly Review*, July, 1926, p. 10.

[13] I am indebted to Mr. Barker's fine and just interpretation; but here and there, as in his *Prefaces*, pp. 142–143, he seems to identify Lear with the storm and to turn it into a symbol. If this be so, he would, in my opinion, be turning the play into something like the *Princesse Maleine* or the *Master-Builder*, untrue to Shakespeare's spirit, and thereby be losing much of this effect of the dramatic.

tumult; but there is action and struggle, a contrast between Lear and the others — there is drama. But in the last scene of *Ghosts*, when after the rain and mist of the preceding acts the sun rises over the glacier and the snow-peaks, nature is brought to bear immediately upon the audience. The effect of contrast with the rain before this, and between the happiness expected at sunrise and the tragic despair when it comes, does not reside wholly in the words. The staging here counts and tells in its own right, though of course not independently — no portion of a work of art does that — and the irony is owing to the passions. It is these that "make a goblin of the sun." Yet the sun is there, and because it is, the lurid effect can be more suggested than conveyed. There is economy, there is force. Shakespeare appeals only to the ear; Ibsen also to the eye. Shakespeare makes fuller and finer use of purely dramatic devices; Ibsen also reaches out to those of the stage.

In the same way for the most part Shakespeare deals with gestures and facial expression. There is little or none of this in the stage-directions of the first editions: it is nearly all in the text. "And yet I fear you," cries Desdemona,

> for you're fatal then
> When your eyes roll so.
> .   .   .   .
> Alas! why gnaw you so your nether lip?

And in the same scene the expression on the faces of the other characters is reflected by Othello himself when he acknowledges the slaying:

> Nay, stare not, masters; it is true, indeed.

Again the characters are the prism through which all light must pass, but the limitation is turned more unquestionably to advantage. Such description by effect is not only more dramatic than any stage-direction could be, and more part and parcel of the structure, but it is more certain than the mere facial expression itself of getting noticed. Shakespeare is not so much descriptive as narrative, deals not with looks, but with changes, gestures — Macbeth's face like a book, where men may read strange matters when he utters the dark saying, "as he purposes," or his starting at the witches' words that sound so fair. There is life in this, before us. And the mere stage-direction, which deals with such matters, is, and indeed must be, too frequently only for the reader. How can an audience take account, as if they themselves had scanned the italics, of George Rous with eyes "that have stared at death," in Galsworthy's *Strife*; or of O'Neill's Andrew, back from the Argentine, with "a suggestion of ruthless cunning about his eyes"; or of his Jim Harris entering in a late scene, as not before, with "a queerly baffled face"?

8

But most of Shakespeare's scenes, and the best of them, are, like the Greek, *still* when compared to ours. This is a strange thing to say, when we remember Shakespeare's extraordinary and incomparable energy, not to say violence, of language; but the word does not apply to that. Or when we remember the swift movement of the story in plays like *Othello*, *Macbeth*, and many another; and the word does not apply to that. It applies to the structure, the adequate preparation, the full and telling effect of suspense. For, as we have seen, whether the dramatist proceed according to the method of anticipation or according to that of mystery, an effect of suspense or expectancy should alike be present. And except, as we have noticed, for the sake of the ironies of an artificial situation, produced by overhearing or disguise, by oracle or prophecy, the method of mystery has ordinarily the advantage. The expectancy and anxiety are thus twofold, in part received directly by the audience, not transferred to it. So the surprise also — or shall we rather say disclosure? — is when it comes twofold, is not merely for the character on the boards.

What Oswald means by the "dread" and the "coming to the rescue" in the last act of *Ghosts* is the concern of Mrs. Alving and of us as well, and is therefore doubly dear. And once these fearful and fateful meanings — the menace of idiocy and the purpose of death — transpire, they in turn serve for preparations still more material and important. Heaving up like clouds before us, they will, we know, not easily be scattered; and though to the outward eye the day dawns splendidly, our ears are to be pierced by the still sharper terror of Oswald's utterance, "Mother give me the sun . . . the sun, the sun!" Without explanation or comment, simply under the huge weight and momentum already accumulated, these words strike home. And this whole last act is charged with anxiety, loaded with disclosure. It is, through its structure, its deep and concentrated suspense, dynamic: Shakespeare's best scenes are often more nearly static. (Not static as they are in Webster — or Maeterlinck, who from him learned the art — the chief characters brooding, the dialogue almost stationary, the atmosphere heavy with fate, and the spectators on the stage divining the passions behind the countenances as they change before them. Though Shakespeare taught both dramatists the value, in dealing with the supernatural, of doubts and misgivings, of a vague dread or anticipation, of simplicity and brevity, of repetitions and echoes, and of questions or commonplace perfunctory utterances betraying a thought that is baffled and all astray, he nevertheless retains more of an apparent or superficial movement.) At the climax Shakespeare cannot afford to be so simple and quiet as Ibsen, being not so dependent for his results upon a far-sprung and irresistible current. Lear's madness comes on with more finely graduated effects of anticipation than does Oswald's imbecility, but without its mystery or surprise, without its accentuated force. And in general Shakespeare's scenes are dread or piteous spectacles, the exhibition of an effect of passion, and of the effect of that effect upon other persons on the stage, rather than of a cause. The audience listens and sympathizes, yet sits superior, stands aloof. Its point of view (again) is taken, rather than that of the stage. The footlights are a barrier, a distinction and separation — in Ibsen and modern drama, as far as possible, they are none. On some modern stages, indeed, they have, as it were symbolically, been done away with.

So in a measure with the best scenes in *Macbeth* already discussed — those of the sleep-walking and of the banquet preëminently, those of Duncan's murder and of Macduff's murderous news in less degree. The banquet scene is a picture of Macbeth's passion on the Apparition's repeated appearance, with the effect of it on his lady and the guests. There is striking contrast, there are telling and thrilling sensations on the stage, but there is no suspense, save such as must be (to be sure) in a striking story. All the preparations are mere matters of fact — the murder and the previous invitation to the feast; and the only disclosure is another — Banquo's grim and vindictive acceptance. No secret is kept, for till Banquo's tongue is nerveless there is no secret to tell. There is *hybris* — impious Insolence — in Macbeth's pretence of regret for Banquo's absence and in the drinking of his health, and there is surprise only in his supernatural appearance. And for us it is a greater surprise than for the Elizabethans, not unaccustomed in tragedy to ghosts and their ironical visits, and not unfamiliar in fiction with the situation of one thus coming to a feast, invited, though little enough "expected." [14] Yet even that would be greater if Macbeth had been looking forward more joyfully to his death. Likewise, there is little suspense in the murder scene, as we have noticed, or in that of the news brought to Macduff. The former scene is a picture of the effect of the murder on the murderers — we shudder but simply look on. More than that we should do if in those tense but still moments a spark should flash, the magazine explode, and, with the right previous preparations, the truth

[14] It is the situation of Don Juan inviting the Statue. Cf. my *Shakespeare Studies*, p. 194.

should appear that Lady Macbeth had urged him on, or he had obeyed her, not from ambition but love. (There is affection, on both sides, beautifully, suggestively, expressed, but save once — "such I account thy love" — it is dramatically dormant and there is no surprise at all.) Then there could not but be still greater effect on us, as on the murderer; then one and all we should be startled, and see deeper than we saw. As it is, the scene is awful, tense, but still.

The Macduff scene has rightly been compared by Chateaubriand to that of the news for Curiatius, touched upon above. In itself it is almost as skilfully constructed as Corneille's, and in respect of the character's own utterances it is far more humanly and imaginatively phrased. In itself, but not in its connections. Here again is the great passion at the great moment, but still more of a passion than a situation. Like Lady Macbeth's somnambulism, like the passions after the murder and at the banquet, it would have been greatly heightened in its effect upon the audience by preparations, by previous expectations or anxieties on the part of the hero, and of the audience, and by a surprise which the audience could share. It of itself carries conviction, by its imaginative sweep and its truth of tone and phrasing; but then it would, with a simple heart-felt word or two, have carried conviction merely by virtue of the situation alone, as the climax, the pinnacle, of the dramatic movement. Before the appearance of Ross, Macduff has shown no interest in his wife and children; in the scene before, we remember, his wife reproaches him, though in absence, for his flight; and while we are not apt to take this too seriously, noting that he has kept his wife's and son's affection, we cannot, on the other hand, receive such an impact from the mere news now imparted to him (but not to us) as we do from that imparted to Curiatius. There we share the shock; there the news is news to us, flung straight into the house from off the stage; and we both feel it more deeply and also know better how he must feel it. And not only the news but his conduct is surprising. We have seen his solicitude for his City, on the one hand, but (far more amply displayed) his love for Horatius and his sister, on the other; and (though only for the moment) we wonder that he can so promptly, intrepidly accept the "honor," hearken to the call. Macduff has no choice to make, no inner contention to quell, being now all love, remorse, revenge. In his case we are moved only by the present thought and passion — "He has no children!" — some of the noblest and most vibrant words ever uttered, and by the effect of these and of his demeanor upon his friends; in this other case we remember what is past, still more consider what is to come, and are moved by the sheer accumulated weight of the situation. It is dynamic. It is poised, suspended, projected, both held and holding, by a system of thrusts and counterthrusts, like a stone in an arch. Shakespeare's scene is, as regards construction, comparatively static and inert, like a wall. It is more aloof and unaided.

Not that the scene in itself is anything less than admirable, only it is not charged with the force of those which have gone before. There is preparation within it, if not before it, more than is usual in such scenes in Shakespeare, and much as in those of Curiatius and Pauline cited above. There are Macduff's anxiety (though a little belated) and his troubled questions, on the one hand, and Ross's timorous, evasive answers, on the other. That is, there is suspense of a sort; but it is merely that of anticipation, without surprise or disclosure for us. Since we know Ross's news already, our attention is wholly focussed on the effect of this upon Macduff. We look on and listen sympathetically. In the other case we know, like the heroes themselves, only that a combat impends and the Horatii are designated, and that Curiatius laments his friend as if he were dead already. And now that we learn that he himself, if he make the choice, is to fight him, kill him or be killed by him, and lose both his friend and his love, we are ourselves involved. In one case we know the news but not the hero; in the other, the heroes but not the news. And when it comes, it startles not these worthies merely but us, the spectators, in our chairs. Light is thrown not only upon the present scene but back over what has gone before and onward over what is to follow; and the whole situation rises and looms up bodily before us. By its accumulation and structure it prevails.

Here Corneille and Racine are far nearer to the modern dramatists, not only to Ibsen but to recent cunningly reticent ones like Jean Jacques Bernard, author of *Martine*. "The moment has been so thoroughly well prepared," says Mr. John Palmer, "that everything is already there, and the silence in which we receive it is the sum of all that has so far been uttered and performed." [15] "Un sentiment commenté," says the author himself, "perd de sa force." It needs the comment and ample expression in the Macduff scene, mainly because, in the multiplicity of the material presented, the moment has not been prepared for sufficiently to dispense with that. Not that the drama of Corneille and Racine is less than Shakespeare's a drama of words — of poetry and eloquence — but it oftener approaches the great moment so adroitly and indirectly as to be in a position to be sparing of them. Then there may be less individuality to them, but a greater weight, a sharper point.

9

THE EFFECT OF EXTENSION RATHER THAN OF VOLUME

I have used above the figure of volume for drama, and it applies in some measure to Shakespeare as well. But in this matter of suspense, and somewhat in his art as a whole when compared to the modern, as in the ancient compared to the French, we have rather the impression of spaces and distances, of approaches and retreats, and if of planes and masses, it is more as in painting than in sculpture. It is a story, and a great one, a vast and mighty canvas stretched out upon the stage, with nearer, middle, and farther

[15] *Studies in the Contemporary Theatre* (1927), p. 98.

distances, not one or two, as when the unities are preserved. It is a picture, with a perspective. Hazlitt, praising *Antony and Cleopatra*, for its "fine retrospections, which show us the winding and eventful march of human life," observes acutely, but in the end not wholly without bias and acrimony: "The jealous attention which has been paid to the unities, both of time and place, has taken away the principle of perspective in drama, and all the interest which objects derive from distance, from contrast, from privation, from change of fortune, from long-cherished passion; and contracts our view of life from a strange and romantic dream, long, obscure, and infinite, into a smartly-contested, three-hours' inaugural disputation on its merits by the different candidates for theatrical applause." On the canvas there are points and peaks of excitement, and also nooks of repose. There are several stories, not one, many figures, not few — and yet in groups not involved and entangled but separated by intervals — as not in Racine or Ibsen. The supernatural, as we have noticed, is set, not on a level with ordinary life, as on the Elizabethan stage it is wont to be, but discreetly aloof and apart. Doubt and faith, fear and wonder, make it different and distant. There is an approach to it from the natural and a retreat from it in turn. So there is, though by another path, from and to the realistic and the romantic. In the *Taming of the Shrew*, the realistic inn and the drunken tinker's delusion are the frame or window through which we look, far away, to Padua, and witness, in a poetic isolation, two fantastic intrigues. And Athens, somewhat romantic by daylight, gives place to an enchanted wood at midnight, and this in turn to Athens by daylight again, and to a reminiscence or retrospect which imparts to all the marvels the right and proper semblance of a dream. "The storm is a good storm," says Sir Arthur Quiller-Couch of the first scene in the *Tempest*; the shipwreck is a right English shipwreck, and it serves as the proper approach and indispensable contrast to the enchanted isle. Here, and everywhere, there are gradual approaches, wide prospects, deep alluring distances and vistas, and the effect of remoteness for what is remote.

And just as the story as a whole is approached and retreated from, so are the stages of it, the scenes. As we have remarked, they begin quietly, and slope and taper down to a close. They contrast variously; and there is not one single group of characters in changing relations but several, some excited and some in themselves unmoved, some of these latter, like the Doctor and the Waiting-woman, serving only for interpretation, and (to use a radio figure) amplification, as well as a contrast and a measure of the effect. It is a little wasteful to bring them in for that purpose alone, in the fifth act; but Shakespeare is not the poet of concentration and economy. Everywhere time and space play a part, instead of being (as far as may be) classically eliminated; and there are room and occasion for shadows and reflections, for memories and comments. In *Coriolanus* the figure of the hero is variously reflected in the speech of almost every other person in the play, with a dramatic harmony. Much the same may be said of *Hamlet, King Lear, Macbeth,* and *Othello.*

It is, of course, not really a picture, unless a moving one; time and its changes, action and its effects, passion and its influences take their course. Hazlitt's "fine retrospections" are really to be found in Dryden's *All for Love* [16] as well as in *Antony and Cleopatra*; but here (as not there) "the winding and eventful march of human life" is within the confines of the play. Shakespeare's stories are natural and satisfying. In Webster's *White Devil,* immediately after the murder of Vittoria's husband and the Duke's wife comes the trial, as if it were in the cinema, with no disclosure of the effect of the news upon her and their friends (her enemies) and no allowance (though in the news it would be provided) for the interval of time. In Shakespeare our sense of reality is not thus affronted, our craving for illusion not thus set at naught. Above

[16] See the *Times Literary Supplement,* October 11, 1928, p. 717.

we have shown the varied use of the spectators on the stage, to
demonstrate and measure the influences, to heighten and amplify
the passionate effect. How much more Shakespeare is in general
concerned with this than with analysis and objectivity appears
nowhere more clearly than in the ample presentation of the admiration and pity for the hero and heroine in every heart but the
villain's, in play after play. These beings are not seen in a dry
light, like specimens detached — they breathe the vital air, touch
and move each other; and the way the principal characters do
this to the numerous minor ones, is, as in Greek tragedy, with its
Chorus, half the drama. Even where the passion is not now before
us, the influences and effects, positively or negatively, sympathetically or ironically, assert themselves, as in the narrative scenes between the Old Man and Ross, Lennox and another Lord in *Macbeth*, Kent and a Gentleman in *King Lear*, the Gardener and
servants in *Richard II*, Enobarbus and various others in *Antony
and Cleopatra*, or such comic scenes as those of Peter and the
Musicians and of the Gravediggers, or such pensive ones as that
of the soldiers harkening to the eerie music of the god Hercules
deserting Antony. There are, then, not only mirrors and reflections
in the play but also impacts and reverberations, and the wave of
tragic sound and fury spends itself on distant shores.

And it is the impression of masses and spaces, of light and shade,
that one gets even from the mere arrangement and ordering of
the abundant matter. The very development and transitions are
those of a story, spatial and external. The story is not one of
struggle and continual agitation, we have already noticed, centered within. The struggle is without, against fate or fortune,
against persons or environment. The hero's character, in some
cases, has defects which betray it, but the betrayal is not clearly or
fully revealed. The gradations here are less carefully and finely
traced than in Racine; the gradations best presented are external,
not internal. There are preparations for the turns of the story but

fewer for those in the character. There are skilful and plausible approaches to the coming event at the beginning of *Hamlet, Macbeth, Othello,* and *King Lear,* with effects of excitement in all four and of mystery in the first two —

> Upon the heath [*hathe*],
> There to meet with Macbeth
>
> . . . .
>
> A drum, a drum!
> Macbeth doth come! —

but little is revealed of the heroes' innermost nature and fatal failings. And there is all the preparation one could desire, in the words of the Soothsayer and in Enobarbus' talk with Menas and Maecenas, for the mere fact of Antony's desertion of Octavia and return to Cleopatra; but no presentation of the focal consideration and decision itself. What a story — what a canvas — with Rome and Alexandria, Athens, Actium, and the Mediterranean — with Pompey, Ventidius, Canidius, and the rest of the great but casual company in it, and the central struggle, whether between love and ambition, or domestic and military honor, left out! And it is because the psychological preparation and development have been so meager and intermittent, and the action so expanded and dispersed, that at the great moments the scene of apocalyptic disclosure and interpretation must be employed, as in the sleep-walking scene, or the lime-light emphasis of sheer passion must be applied, as to Lear out on the heath, to Othello after the poison is in his veins, to Cleopatra abandoned and Antony disgraced. Old Horace or Curiace, Racine's Hermione, Phèdre, or Agamemnon, can, with tragic accent and consequence, speak simply and quietly because we have already seen so clearly what they have been thinking and feeling, and how therefore they must at present think and feel. In Shakespeare effects of space and emphasis, and the amplitude and reality of the external characterization, fill in some measure the place of internal organic development and structure, of the bare and high-piled form. The great moments must be dilated upon and prolonged with passionate exultation or lamentation because the internal struggle has not been distinctly traced or indicated. The points of excitement must be marked with patches of light, the canvas not being suffused with it.

The impression given by Shakespeare is, in general, that of bold juxtapositions and plausible transitions, of wide comprehension and well-manipulated mediation, rather than of logical, concentrated structure. The struggle is not, as with the French, between such spectral combatants as love and honor, duty and ambition. It is between Hamlet and Claudius, Othello and Iago, Antony and Octavius, the immortal young lovers and the hatred of their houses, Coriolanus and the hatred of the People, Macbeth and his conscience; [17] and for the most part there is no visible struggle at all, as in the tragedy of the Greeks. Œdipus does not struggle or hesitate, nor does Antigone. There is prolonged and varied tension and opposition, or "interaction," to use Mr. Firkins' phrase, instead. There is a conflict between the duties, but none in the choice. As in *Macbeth* also and *Richard III* there is flying in the face of Fate — there are effects of *hybris* and *ate*, Insolence and Infatuation, which are cases of juxtaposition again. There is contrast between conduct and its consequences, or between the promise of "the expectations raised by the hero's personality and the disappointment caused by his subsequent career." The contrast is not at the center, in a nature divided against itself, whence the career must ensue; and we do not see at all clearly why the hero acts or how he comes to act. The rays of light run parallel, in prismatic contrast, do not converge into a burning-point or focus. It is not even one light, one emotional tone. With the tragic is set side by side the comic, just as in comedy itself there is also the sentimental, the fanciful, the serious. In tragedy, however, the tone is

---

[17] See below, p. 96. And for a fuller discussion of the subject of this paragraph see the third chapter of my *Shakespeare Studies*, where, as here, I am indebted to Sir Robert Bridges and Professor Frye.

prevailingly tragic, as in comedy it is prevailingly comic; at best a transition, an "enormous harmony" is effected, or (shall we say?) an all-reconciling poetical atmosphere, as in a painting, is poured over the whole.

Often the dramatic contrast not only is not fairly seated within the hero's bosom but depends on juxtapositions or oppositions which are somewhat outward and artificial. I mean those devices, already mentioned, of soliloquy and aside, of deception and feigning, of overhearing and disguise, of improbable misunderstanding and the slander too readily believed,[18] and of letters, rings, or handkerchiefs lost and found, miscarried or stolen, some of which are employed, though less abundantly, by classical French tragedy also, but are avoided by the modern. They are like Siegfried's and Tristram's magic potions. An ironic, or at least a well-contrasted, situation is attained which somewhat corresponds to that arising from the use of oracle or prophecy, and of a story already quite familiar to the audience, as on the stage of the ancients. Thus Hamlet playing mad, the fiendish Iago acceptably playing the honest friend, and Othello led to play a jealous and bloody rôle almost despite himself, are well-nigh two persons in one. So is Œdipus the King, who in the effort to avoid them had done all the dreadful things that it had been foretold he would do, and cursing now that man who had done them, rains curses on his own head. Thereby the demands of realism are somewhat disappointed, as they are indeed in the *Œdipus*, but striking situations are expeditiously secured, telling contrasts achieved. The loss in illusion is more than made up by the gain in sympathy; and the loss is less

[18] See my *Shakespeare Studies*, pp. 93–94. Mr. Barker (*Prefaces*, 1927, p. 203), who no doubt had never seen anything I have written, remarks that in the case of Gloster, in *King Lear*, "Shakespeare asks us to allow him the fact of the deception." The opinion of an accomplished dramatist, actor, and producer is what your Shakespearean militant most highly prizes, most sorely needs. In my *Othello* (1916) I undertake to show that the dramatist does all that he can be expected to do — by preparations and gradual approaches makes the improbable probable.

on the stage than in the closet, and less for the unanalytical but imaginative and passionate Elizabethans and the ancients, accustomed to the method. In the circumstances Iago, Edmund, and Iachimo would have no right to speak up as they do, Othello, Gloster, and Posthumus, no inclination to listen; but once you accept the convention, how much more appealing and truly tragic is Othello, without a suspicious and jealous, proud and vindictive nature, than the French and Spanish heroes, with it.[19] Webster makes use of some such convention too; and his Bosola is, on the one hand, a macabre and cynical but noble and poetical meditator on life and destiny, on the other, a mercenary cutthroat who will do anything for gold; and for no other discernible reason he goes roundly to work, torturing and slaughtering like a Sultan's mute. He abhors his employers, admires and pities their victim, yet spares her not the uttermost of the bitter cup; his subsequent remorse does not carry conviction, for his revenge in behalf of the Duchess immediately follows his failure to secure his pay; and, as sometimes in Shakespeare, what holds the character together is mainly his individual tone and accent. Beaumont and Fletcher make use of it as well. The beautiful brute Evadne is as vividly presented in speech as is Sebastiano del Piombo's Salome in paint; and yet in a single scene she is by her brother forcibly converted, like an infidel at the point of the sword, though not to the faith but to virtue. That is another instance in drama of the omnipotence of persuasive arts, like Othello, like the outraged Anne wooed by the

[19] It is, no doubt, a "fallacy," and in a longer discussion than his "Tragic Fallacy" (*Atlantic*, November, 1928) Mr. Krutch would probably have taken some account of this and of the similar one of the Greeks. With Shakespeare the villain, with the Greeks Fate, bears the burden. But now that the villain is no longer credible or acceptable, and the cause of the trouble has been seated in the hero himself, it is not so much our smaller opinion of man that makes our modern tragedy mean and depressing, as our imperious craving that the presentation of his character shall be real and true. We see, indeed, more clearly that a man bears his fate, or at least the seed of the fatal passion, within him; but we demand that we shall see this in the play. The ancients, even Shakespeare, could present ideal heroes, because the struggle was external.

outrageous Richard. But immorally, yet psychologically and artistically, the new life is made like the old. She is Evadne still. She taunts and kills her paramour, and confidently claims her husband's love in return for the blood upon her hands.

Save in the last instance, contrasts here amount to contradictions. In Shakespeare at his best, unless we consider too curiously, they do not. Without hesitation or struggle, without the clear presentation of processes or developments which would show how they arrived at this dire pass, Othello, who lacks a jealous or a gullible nature, and Hamlet, who has no sufficient reason to feign or dissemble, are nevertheless attended by all the authentic effects of tragedy, as, in the brothel scene in the one play and the nunnery scene in the other, they utter a mingled emotion, delight turned to anguish, love putting on the poisoned mask of bitterness or hate. The brutal degrading imaginations of a jealous soul that Othello utters were not really born in his generous and noble one, which at intervals raises its voice:

> Lest, being like one of heaven, the devils themselves
> Should fear to seize thee.

And though in their origin so external or unexplained, these contrasts in Shakespeare are really not much more unplausible than are the less obvious ones in him elsewhere and in the modern drama and novel. Hamlet delays without being a moral or physical weakling, Lear knows not his daughters without being (as Stopford Brooke would have it) self-centered and compact of vanity, Macbeth murders without the native bent. In all three instances we must in a measure grant and allow the fact, as in the case of the slander believed. The psychological test — even the strictly modern dramatic test — which requires the character to be the source of the action and author of his fate, does not quite apply. Shakespeare's heroes are really heroes, as are often even those of the moderns. His contrasts are somewhat contrived and arbitrary, but these are somewhat touched with sophistry. In either case a contrast is desired — a noble character in a plight. Where merely and only the characters' own passions spin the plot, and

We are betrayed by what is false within,

the contrast is weakened, and either the characters are less appealing or the plight less tragic or pathetic. And where the passions are not quite theirs, as when Masefield's Nan and Hardy's Tess shed blood — sweet and patient women, both of them, and engaged neither in their own nor in another's defense — the price paid by these authors for effect is at bottom as great as that by Shakespeare. (And what shall we say of the lesser, more ruthless ones, to whom love in its beginning means adultery and in its consummation, murder?) In the novels not infrequently, as often with Dostoevsky and in the heroines of *Diana of the Crossways* and Romain Rolland's *Âme Enchantée,* the rather incredible, entangling misdeeds are in the last analysis attributed to the subconscious — a second person, again. But this duplicity is one remove away, and is in some sort countenanced by Nature.

More abundantly duplicity is provided in Nature elsewhere — in the complications of sex. By Shakespeare left almost unexploited, they are well-nigh the richest mine or repository of situation. Though worked for another reason — the inherent attractiveness of the material — it lends itself to the purposes of art. Here are contrast and compression to hand, ironies and paradoxes craving expression. Man and woman become one flesh, one spirit, are even united in the birth of another, though still remaining two. In vain — *nequicquam,* groaned the Roman — is all the ardor of their embraces. Or, thwarted, love turns to hatred, though still love underneath. There you have both contrast and irony, a dramatic struggle. And because in love one is two, and two are one, there is paradox — opposition and apparent contradiction, which are of the essence of drama. "His honour rooted in dishonour stood." What in Lancelot's eyes is honor — fidelity to Arthur, abandonment of Guinevere — is dishonor in the eyes of the Queen, and hence in his own. Not easily can so deep a vein of irony and paradox be found in life elsewhere. For it is the peculiar quality of love that the one person should identify himself with the other, and the other in turn with him; that their points of view should for the moment merge and interchange; and nowhere else can be found in Nature so much of the artificial compression of ancient and Shakespearean drama.

On the stage, however, artificiality is more telling; its effects of contrast and compression are more vivid and varied. Action — simple and bold strokes — is what counts on the boards. Hence, amid all their psychological or philosophical subtlety, their interest in the subconscious and in apparent and actual reality, our dramatists have taken again, of late, to soliloquies and asides, as in the *Adding Machine* and the *Strange Interlude*; to disguise and feigning, with frequent changes, or to interplay between actors and audience, as in the *Great God Brown* and some of the plays of Pirandello. It is done with a difference, with a new import, and a dubious success, but essentially the method is old.

10

CHARACTERIZATION

In character, of course, lies Shakespeare's supreme achievement. His people live if they do not struggle — and they act, and above all talk, as if they lived. They start up from the printed page before you; and if in Corneille and Racine they but tread the boards, here it seems as if they had flung away from them, to walk the earth. Again Shakespeare is less strictly dramatic than the French, and thus in another sense is more so. As several critics have recognized,[20] the character is generally bigger than his rôle. That is, he has thoughts and emotions quite beyond the requirements of his part in the action or plot; and indeed few things about him do

[20] Mézières, Sir Robert Bridges, Professor Frye.

more to lend him an air of reality. The figure cuts through the canvas, it strays over the limits of the frame. Contradictions and omissions, casual allusions and unelucidated reminiscences abound. The classical instance is Lady Macbeth. She declares that she has given suck and knows how tender 'tis to love the babe that milks her, though otherwise we know nothing of this. And just before that she speaks of an occasion when Macbeth was ready enough to do the deed, though time nor place did then adhere, in such fashion that some commentators think a scene must have dropped out of the text. Likewise, Othello tells Iago he will not expostulate with Desdemona, lest her body and beauty unprovide his mind again, though no previous occasion has appeared. The whole business of "double time" in Shakespearean drama — whereby one system of references, or "short time," gives the effect of rapidity to the action (necessary for stage interest) and another more covert and unobtrusive one, or "long time," gives the effect of the slow processes of normal human emotion and endeavor (necessary in a play which presents the story from the beginning) — has the same purpose or upshot. In all these ways the dramatist bursts through the confines of his art. In some measure carelessness is the cause, and the result confusion; in greater measure, a surcharged imagination is the cause, and the result (or is it purpose?) something of the full unconfinable quality of life. In perfect art, form and content are one and indissoluble, and the rôle and the character are practically the same. In Shakespeare we have not the impression of perfect art, whole, clear, and harmonious, but of irregular, irresistible genius. It is not the art which conceals itself but that which contradicts and overrides; and his excesses, which are those of life craving life, and creating it, do not so often destroy the illusion as establish and extend it. He has an irresponsible, contagious way of forgetting that his drama is but drama, that his stage is not the world.

11

How, more exactly, does Shakespeare deal with character, how does he present it as compared with his great corrivals? There are perhaps four different ranks or ranges of material available. The first and most external is the thoughts and words which may properly occur in conversation. This almost alone is considered admissible on the stage today, as in the social drama of Ibsen. Second, there is emotion or passion, which, indirectly indeed, may appear in ordinary conversation, and so in modern stage dialogue, but in the older drama, both the Elizabethan and the Greek, crops out upon the surface, in repeated apostrophe or outcry, lamentation or rejoicing. Third, there is the material of motives or the personal mental attitude, likewise in the older drama frankly presented, but which in real life the character himself may be only in part aware of and at least does not freely divulge to others. And fourth, behind it all, there is the subconscious.

Of these elements the first three alone are to be found in Shakespeare. Critics have thought to find the subconscious in Hamlet and Iago; but of that, except by the most explicit indication, there is very little even in the drama that has been written since the notion of it became current, and whether Shakespeare ever drew it also into his web is a question that may be ignored. Only the conversational, as we have seen, directly appears in Ibsen. In Corneille and Racine frank passion and analysis of motives abound, but of mere conversation there is little, even after allowance for verse and rime.

12

What is the essentially and strictly dramatic method, so far as we know it? The modern, as represented in drama since Ibsen, and in the novel since James. Limited to the scope of probable and plausible human speech, it is the most compact and suggestive, as the method of drama should be. It keeps the point of view of the

character or the other characters — of the stage, not the audience —
and presents the elements of passion or analysis only as they
naturally break through to the character's own lips or to those of
others, and are implied in the contrasts or involved in the situation. "Below the surface," says Mr. Lubbock of the modern novel,
"behind the outer aspect of the man's mind we do not penetrate;
this is drama, and in drama the spectator must judge by appearances." The inner man appears through natural talk and action,
and thus gradually but definitely takes shape. Every available
light is shed upon him; in every feasible way his figure is thrown
into relief; but he is not permitted unnaturally to reveal himself.
And even naturally he is not permitted, in the interest of suspense
and suggestiveness, to reveal himself to any degree. There is "no
statement where we look for demonstration,"[21] not even such
statement as the character may plausibly utter.

Now this method works within limits, and limits — except, as
we have seen, those of the actors' and spectators' endurance —
Shakespeare scarcely knows. He has the advantage of liberty, which
is also a disadvantage. Not only does he not give the artistic effect
of a fixed point of view and a delimited field of vision, and of the
vividness and concentration which are the happy consequence,
but at the same time he thus loses a great effect of reality. It is dis-
illusioning, as well as distracting, when the point of view is arbitrarily abandoned by the character himself, and the author speaks
up from behind him; and as we have noticed, even when the point
of view is kept, and the character naturally (but unnecessarily)
discloses his inner nature, there is lost the effect of suspense. By
the modern method the very character is dramatized — the audience kept listening and wondering, probing and exploring. On

[21] Cf. Mr. Percy Lubbock's *Craft of Fiction*, p. 162. To this illuminating discussion, as the reader will have already recognized, I am throughout the article
deeply indebted; but especially in this and the following paragraph. Mr. Lubbock is dealing with the novel; but many of his principles, as he shows how
the novel in its perfection approaches to the character of drama, apply as I
show how the drama in its perfection becomes more dramatic.

the one hand, the veil of everyday personality is left intact — an effect of reality in itself. On the other hand, by the cunning changes of attitude and the shifting light of situation and contrast, the nature behind the veil is gradually, excitingly laid bare. This is drama, and it is life. We come to know the character before the end, as we come to discern a soul imprisoned within the flesh; though in drama, which is life in a nutshell, we do it far more certainly and speedily. What is better, we are kept thinking. Great art in one way or another either tempts or forces us to think, or it is not great; Shakespeare tempts us only, being a popular artist. But, as Mr. Lubbock says, this indirect and roundabout method is for us really the most direct: "In the end we have seen." By the mere delay and difficulty this our spiritual vision or second sight is made more piercing, more momentous. Of this inner life which is not described or narrated but finally through its remotest manifestations enacted before us, we gain a far deeper and more forcible impression of the place it occupies, of the bulk it possesses.[22]

Yet there are restrictions upon this method in drama as there are not in the novel. After all, drama depends on immediate effect. It cannot like the novel choose its public, or bide its time, appealing from the judgment of the present to that of the future. Neither can it count much upon leisure, upon reflection and recollection. The immediate moment may profit by moments long past, but not those — irrecoverable as in life itself — by this. It of itself engrosses our attention. Hence, though the novel at its best tends and approaches to the condition of drama, drama itself, paradoxically, cannot be wholly dramatic. In practice the perfect form is from one point of view too roundabout, from another too condensed. The perfect process is too exacting, is too costly to the immediate emotional effect. And this is a shortcoming which may be observed even in Ibsen and Pirandello. Their characters seem a little cold and intellectualized, at times too much of a study or a

---

[22] *Craft of Fiction*, p. 179.

riddle for the stage. Only passion can awaken passion, and often for the ordinary audience the indirect process of presentation does not suffice or avail.[23]

Moreover, in drama the author himself must be much farther in the background. He cannot, as in the novel, speak out of his omniscience, whether using the first person or the third. He must avoid both soliloquies and asides, but not so much because they are not true to life as because by them (again) we are told. Hence, where suggestion and implication are insufficient, he must fall back upon analysis in so far as it can be dramatically motivated and warranted, whether uttered by the character himself or by others. In Corneille and Racine, it is instilled, not immediately into the ear of the audience, as in soliloquy, but (often not more dramatically) into that of the confidant. In Ibsen there is more not only of plausibility but of restraint. The character discloses to the person concerned what he thought and how he felt at critical junctures in the past, and thus partially reveals what he is today. Or he may reveal himself by defending his conduct, past or present, or by advocating a point of view near and dear to him; and by the fact that he is arguing his disclosure is motivated, as it is in both Ibsen and Browning. Thus it becomes before the end a problem play, like the *Doll's House* or *Little Eyolf*; the characters revealing themselves only in so far as the problem touches them, and fulfilling the needs of the action, meanwhile, by the momentous fluctuations of the discussion and solution.

When, however, it comes to analysis by others the dramatist has a greater resource than a novelist such as James. He is not limited to one point of view alone. James's dialogue is only such as the one character whose point of view is taken engages in, and if the dialogue is to be plausible, he is not likely to hear much that is true about himself. But in the drama the author assumes one point of view this moment, and another the next, as character after char-

[23] See below, p. 138.

acter takes the floor; and out of the character's hearing there may be various disclosures, colored, indeed — prejudiced or prepossessed — but, in spite of differences, illuminating. The spectators within the drama or out of it, not the person speaking, see and judge. Here again the strictly dramatic, indirect method comes into play: the commenting characters themselves are dramatized, are gradually and naturally divulged. Allowances are then made, conclusions drawn.

For drama and novel alike, however, there is, of course, whether in characterization or in plotting, not only no fixed and perfect form, but not even a uniform and certain tendency. The greatest novels were written before James, the greatest dramas before Ibsen. Genius is what counts, and the form must fit the matter and suit the public. If Shakespeare in his day had, against the laws of nature, contrived to write like Ibsen he would not have been a great dramatist, for he would have left his audience (and the audience him) out in the cold. He would have spoken to the deaf, have acted for the blind. Art is not art when without point, purpose, and result. And any form, even though in its own day and for its own public, has its special and peculiar advantages, not others. Shakespeare's form has, we have seen, the advantage of range and liberty, not that of the spectators' point of view. It has the advantage of omniscience, not that of life unfolding before our eyes. It has the advantage of anticipation and expectation, not that of uncertainty and suspense. These advantages which are lacking are demanded by the better public today. This public craves an unimpaired and uninterrupted illusion, and, not supposed to be present, resents tips and hints flung to it, whether as the audience at a play or "the reader" in the novel. It demands the privilege of discovering and judging for itself. It delights in suggestion; it cannot dispense with stimulation. By Shakespeare these tastes and demands are less amply satisfied, but are in part, as we shall see, in other ways.

13

Of the indirect method Shakespeare has, as we have already intimated, little or none. His characters take shape not gradually but at once, springing full-grown from his brain. Their inmost passions break out boldly and even violently to the surface; and if their motives and purposes and general intellectual attitude do not come clearly to the light from out of their own words or those of others, it is simply because the dramatist somewhat neglects them or intentionally slurs them over. The indirect method is little employed: the direct and analytical is employed neither consistently nor with perfect care. Ambition in Macbeth, though in the text it is said to be, and in fact must be, the mainspring and justification of his conduct, is not that of his meditations. His thoughts are not on the crown, whether the glory of it or his superior fitness for it, but on the horror of the crime. He considers not why he should act but why he should not act, and as readers if not as spectators we nowadays cannot but wonder why he acts at all. We must revert, though Macbeth is morally free, to the fascination of fate, and to the influence of his wife, though neither is insisted on in order that he may not be lowered in our esteem. There is contrast, effective juxtaposition or opposition of the man and his conscience, but no quite acceptable logic, no quite intelligible psychology. Patriotism in Brutus, though in the text it appears to be, and in fact must be, the mainspring of his conduct, is not that of his meditations either. He is acting from some solemn sense of duty which he seems himself not to understand.[24] (Not that there is any mysteriousness, in the hazy style of Maeterlinck or the symbolists: it is in nowise intimated that Brutus or Macbeth cannot, or is not intended to, understand.) To show it clearly Shakespeare lacked the technique of analysis and debate as we find it in Corneille and

[24] Coleridge, long ago, wondered, "What character did Shakespeare mean his Brutus to be." Mr. Granville Barker (*Prefaces*, p. 63) fears "that Shakespeare can in the last analysis make nothing of him."

Racine, and the technique of suggestion as we find it in the moderns. Or he lacked the interest which might have developed either. However it be, in Brutus and Macbeth alike, as in Henry IV and Henry V, John and Richard II, Cassius and Coriolanus, the man but not the patriot or statesman, the person but not the thinker, comes to light. In Caesar there is not even the personality, but only a portentous, empty figure. Likewise he fails to explain or hint at an explanation of Cleopatra's trafficking with Octavius and her concealment of the treasure after she has resolved to die. Was it womanish treason, coquetry, and cunning for their own sake, or was it a deep-laid scheme? And three times her imperial lover changes — deserting her, his wife, and his fleet in the midst of battle — and each time, with emotional advantage, no doubt, the dramatist takes refuge in narrative and report. In general his characters are, as we have seen, not adequately analyzed; their motives and mental anatomy are not indirectly or even directly laid bare. Soliloquies abound, but they serve rather to reveal the character's plans and purposes. Comment by the other characters abounds, but it serves rather to guide our sympathies and judgments. By soliloquy and comment together we learn whether the hero is good or bad, or is changing for the better or the worse, and what he intends to do and how he will do it, rather than what he is and what motives are prompting him. Even the succession of the moods wherein, as we have already noticed, his countenance shines so clear, and his voice rings so true, is not always made intelligible. Mr. Clutton Brock has remarked on the common objection of critics to Hamlet's unconcerned talk with the Player directly after his agonized conversation with Ophelia; I myself have elsewhere drawn attention to the lofty and exalted mood of Othello at the beginning of the murder scene, so soon after his fierce and bloody outcries, when already on his way to Desdemona's chamber, in the scene before. The mere touch of the poet is always alive, his stroke

instinctively certain, but his design and composition are not uniformly painstaking or infallibly correct.

And he presents no studies of single passions or vices, with their
origins and developments, in all their diverse and various manifestations, as do Corneille, Racine, and Ibsen, Jonson and Molière.
He presents people powerfully animated by such passions but always by others as well. Yet he does not, as we have seen, in the
narrower sense dramatize them, in a clash or struggle. He proposes
and solves no problems. There is love in play after play; but this
is the normal, healthy emotion, in equilibrium (as in right drama
it is not), and intact and untroubled, not betrayed or thwarted; if
hindered, it is hindered by a person or persons; and even in
Antony and Cleopatra it is not fairly pitted against other emotions
or the restrictions of society, or analyzed and clearly related to
these. It is generally love at first sight, owing to the beauty of the
woman and the noble bearing of the man; and it is an affair of the
affections and the imagination, but little of the intellect, not manifestly springing out of a community of tastes and aspirations, on
the one hand, or leading to a new envisagement of life, the form-
ing of new plans and ideals, on the other. What makes this attractive is the mere charm of it, and the identity of the lovers' tone
in their new ecstatic state; what makes it lively and interesting (but
not always dramatic) is the lovers' wit and fancy — and such external situations as those of misunderstanding or disguise.[25] There
is none of the excitement of the chase or combat; the poet's earlier
lovers engage in sally and repartee; Florizel and Perdita, Ferdinand
and Miranda, only in endearments. And it is attractive and interesting because — it is love, still more than (as we have seen)
the situation of Macbeth and his lady is terrible and sublime because it is murder.

Amplitude of characterization, indeed, involving contrasts and

[25] See Mr. Frank Harris' *Shakespeare the Man* and Professor Herford's "Love
and Marriage in Shakespeare," *Edda*, Vol. VI, to which I am here indebted.

sometimes incongruities real or apparent, often takes the place of the dramatic clash or struggle. Hamlet loves a woman as well as his father, but simply and irrevocably, with no struggle apparent, he puts the less relevant love behind him; Macbeth and Lady Macbeth, Brutus and Hotspur love too, but the fact plays no clearly perceptible part in their fate; and really nothing else plays a part in Romeo's. In Coriolanus and Antony love and manly pride dwell rather strangely and unfamiliarly together, and, without ever fairly coming to grips, succeed one another in command. The barriers between Orlando and Rosalind, the Duke and Viola, Benedick and Beatrice, Othello and Desdemona, Posthumus and Imogen, Leontes and Hermione, are the quite external ones arising out of misunderstanding or disguise, deception or slander. Antony and Cleopatra are at cross purposes and actually play one another false, but though this is externally prepared for it is never explained. This latter, personal inconsistency is not an inconsistency in the artist, as it is where Leontes becomes jealous, Orlando's brother, Oliver, embraces virtue, and Valentine bestows Silvia on Proteus. It is like the real and actual inconsistency more clearly and consistently depicted by the naturalists, Meredith and Hardy, Ibsen and the Russians. In Shakespeare it is a matter more naïve. Either he does not appreciate the need of explaining, or as we have seen, he has not the interest, the adequate faculty or technique.[26] The naturalists, though they have known Corneille and Racine, believe in psychological inconsistency, in illogical, partly but not wholly unaccountable impulse, as a fact. With them, in a way, *abit in mysterium*. No mystery is made of it in Shakespeare. They fairly face the question of motive and consistency, and endeavor to answer it. It is unlikely that Shakespeare did either.

[26] There are repeated instances of Shakespeare's ignoring the motives assigned in his sources, as the cases of Hamlet's undertaking to play mad, Lear's division of his kingdom, Iago's plotting against Othello. He quite rightly prefers no reason to a poor one.

With him, as with his fellows, perception — imagination — by far outran the reason; he has the English mind, which like the Russian and unlike the Latin, has, as Mr. Basil de Selincourt says of it, "a native affinity for unanalyzed adjustments and reactions." He sees more than he can explain, feels more than he understands, and depicts or presents it without hinting at a reason.

Of psychology as distinct from character-drawing there is little in Shakespeare, though there is little for that matter in Racine or Ibsen. One and all they deal in what is clear and recognizable. They are not scientists but artists. When Racine's Pyrrhus and Ibsen's Peer Gynt and Hialmar Ekdal deceive themselves we know it, and the chief difference between them and Hamlet (when really he deceives himself) is that he knows it too.[27] And of the unconscious self-deceptions or fleeings from one's thought or purpose, of subliminal processes, masked movements, defensive reactions, and the like, there is in Shakespeare, as in the Frenchmen and the Norseman, only what we could make shift, whether on the stage or off it, to recognize for ourselves. The later dramatists deal more in subtleties but they make these clear; the critics, strange to say, attribute to the elder and more popular poet subtleties that neither are clear nor even are indicated. An audience of psychologists would have difficulties with the Hamlet of the critics; and Shakespeare's audience, with whom he found favor above every other dramatist of his time, was the same as that of Marlowe and Marston, Dekker and Jonson, Beaumont and Fletcher, to whom the critics attribute no such subtleties at all. But the difference between Shakespeare and these is one of degree not of kind, one of artistic mastery not of artistic exactingness. If anything, a play like *The Alchemist* or *Volpone, Philaster* or *The Maid's Tragedy*, requires more attention from the audience than *Othello* or *Mac-*

---

[27] See my *Shakespeare Studies*, pp. 127–141. And see *Andromaque*, II, v; where Pyrrhus is resolutely abandoning Andromache for Hermione but shows that his thoughts are upon the former, as Phoenix sees.

beth. Unlike some of the dramatists of our day, but like all the greatest dramatists of any, Shakespeare needed no intermediaries or interpreters, and for that matter needs none now — if he hadn't had them.

The sort of psychology we are justified in finding in Shakespeare can be perceived by an intelligent person of himself, or else by the raisonneur it is pointed out to him. Cleopatra is voluble when excited. She is so in the first act, when she quarrels with Antony and would scarcely let him put in a word. And when the monument is scaled and she is taken prisoner by Proculeius, we are justified in recognizing this excitement as holding over in her volubility with Dolabella who replaces him.[28] Antony, again, in defeat and disgrace, when he catches Thyreus, Caesar's emissary, kissing the faithless hand, "his playfellow," wreaks himself upon him, as he would not have done if this were not Caesar's follower, his conqueror's. But this simple point Shakespeare fears we might miss, and lets Enobarbus observe:

> 'Tis better playing with a lion's whelp
> Than with an old one dying.

And when the night before his last battle, Antony, taking each man's hand in his, speaks effusively to his officers, Enobarbus must needs remark:

> 'Tis one of those odd tricks which sorrow shoots
> Out of the mind.

Yet without such assistance we readily perceive the psychology of Menas and Pompey, after refraining from the triumvirs' throats, at the end of the galley scene; Pompey compensating himself for his rectitude by another reference to his father's house, unlawfully held by Antony — "but what? we are friends" — and Menas, as he orders the salute, venting his vexation, "Sound and be hang'd, sound out!" And so with Macbeth:

---

[28] See above, p. 22.

> Your children shall be kings.
> *Banquo.*   You shall be king.
> *Macbeth.* And thane of Cawdor too; went it not so?

In his first speech, obviously, his real thought is of what appears
in Banquo's reply; and in the next it comes impatiently to the
surface. "Goats and monkeys," cries Othello as he makes his exit
after striking his wife. It echoes what Iago has said about the
lovers being hot as goats, as prime as monkeys — animals proverbially lascivious. The inflammatory image has lodged in his mind
and now in his rage it spontaneously breaks forth again. But all
these are such mental phenomena as come well within the scope
of any intelligent person's observation and of any sound dramatist's imagination — what is good about them, as in all character-
drawing, and as in all art, lies in the touch, the proper stroke at the
proper place — and they are not at all the recondite psychological
or pathological ingenuities and profundities continually discovered in these characters and in Iago and Hamlet. The recondite has
no place in drama. Indeed, the comment provided by the dramatist, who is of an age but for the ages, does not so much comfort
the discoverer as disconcert him.

14

THE EFFECT OF EXTENSION ALSO IN THE CHARACTERS

Here, then, in character too, we are given the same impression
of surface and extension rather than of volume. We have seen this
in part already, since character cannot be separated from situation;
and have noted how Shakespeare inclines to the ample, concrete
exhibition of tragic passion and its effects, rather than to the pro-
duction and effectuation of the tragic cause. Though the spectators
on the stage speak naturally, plausibly, still they tell those in the
audience what they might often be led to discover for themselves;
and from the beginning the character is, in so far as it is revealed
at all, spread out like a scroll, which every man may read. Hedda

Gabler, at first, we do not know. But by the end of the first act we have secured a firm and clear though still incomplete conception of her inner nature, as well as of her husband's, wholly by indirect and quite dramatic means. We have learned that she is esthetic and romantic, but bored and disappointed, despises her husband but is a little interested in Lövborg, whom she had once had occasion to threaten with her pistol, and (jealous of Mrs. Elvsted) is eager to reëstablish her ascendancy over him, now that through her he has achieved fame. Claudius and Iago, too, we do not know at the outset. Unlike Richard III they do not then wholly lay bare their hearts. Yet after a moment Iago lets even his victim and tool, Roderigo, understand that he follows the Moor but to serve his turn upon him, and "is not what he is"; and what Claudius is we surmise before the scene is over from Hamlet's opinions and suspicions, and before the night is over, learn it once and for all from the Ghost. What remains is imparted in soliloquy; but we might have arrived at conclusions simply from Iago's demeanor and bearing, and have come to judge between Claudius and Hamlet for ourselves. Or, as in the case of Hamlet, Othello, Macbeth, and above all Antony, Cleopatra, and Coriolanus, we are told, though at a single remove, by the comments of the various characters, dramatic only as they are occasioned and as they differ from each other, as they are emotionally charged and are fitted to the particular character's lips. Of Hedda we are told little or nothing, and fairly win the knowledge of ourselves. *Quae ipse sibi tradit spectator.* And thus we look not upon her but within her, do not merely observe and contemplate but penetrate and detect.

Not that in Shakespeare the characters wholly appear at the outset or do not develop or unfold. Lear and Macbeth, Othello and Hamlet, all change in their various ways, as we have seen in part already. But in their change is not centered our interest, does not reside the drama, and (save by dint of disguise or feigning) there is no prolonged contrast between what they are and what they

seem to be. Except for the moment, as in the cases of Claudius and
Iago, considered above, the change is only the slighter one which
comes about in the character as it is — one of development under
passion or of a presentation completed. In the tragic atmosphere
the character darkens and deepens; or as with Hamlet quarreling
at the funeral of Ophelia, Othello striking Desdemona, or Cleopatra lying, and cheating, and raging, when at the point of ven-
turing into the temple of death, the character does startling and
surprising things. But in a moment we see that they are still the
same, and we recognize the acquaintance.

By Shakespeare's direct method, to be sure, certain effects of
irony are more quickly attained, as well as a keener interest in the
story. The great intrigue is at once under way, full steam ahead.
And there is a sharper stage-contrast presented — between Iago's
duplicity and knavery, on the one hand, and Roderigo's and
Othello's, Desdemona's and Cassio's credulity, honesty, or innocence, on the other; between the noble bearing of the court of
Denmark and its inner rottenness. In both tragedy and comedy,
moreover, in *As You Like It* as in *Othello* and *Macbeth,* there is an
irony which is wholly dependent on the knowledge previously imparted to the audience.[29] Orlando plays at wooing his sweetheart,
who is before him; Macbeth recklessly confronts Macduff, who is
his fate. But such a contrast is more external. It is between the
blindness of Orlando and Macbeth and the light of truth which
has been set, not before their eyes, but ours. In Ibsen's play it is
between the elegant appearances and the bitter, desperate reality
— this less steady and certain but more startling light to which we
have attained, as the character himself or others might have, unaided. This irony is focussed, piercing the surface, not playing upon
it. It is that unclothing of the soul as we find it — still more amply
contrasted and sharply pointed — in the *Doll's House,* where the
frivolous and reckless Nora turns out to be serious and true, and

[29] See above, pp. 57–58.

the sturdy and virtuous Helmer to be craven and feeble. In Ibsen's characterization, then, as in his plots (but seldom even in Corneille's and Racine's characterization, though in their plots more commonly), there is the method of mystery and disclosure. The character, like the very situation, is thrown into relief.

And so with the self-deceptions. Hamlet and Iago when really they deceive themselves do it, we have seen, in the open; as when the one catches himself like a whore unpacking his heart with words, and the other plays for the moment with the notion that he is not a villain,[30] and — "divinity of Hell!" — jeers at himself, or (before that) alleges a reason for hating the Moor, but, admitting that he knows not if it be true, will for mere suspicion in that kind "do as if for surety." But in Ibsen and Becque they deceive themselves indeed. They neither acknowledge the fact nor recognize it: others on the stage may do this, but not within earshot, and they can judge only from appearances, as we do. Again we are not told. There is contrast and irony, therefore, not as between person and person, but within one soul alone. There is the contrast, not between appearances and our cheap positive knowledge, but between the character's professions and his conduct, or between his criticism on the conduct of others and similar conduct of his own. For (as in such case would be necessary) we have been permitted to perceive the reality before the evasion or pretense appears. We have already caught the tune — we instantly detect the false note.

The very dialogue, in so far as it can be separated from character and plot, shows these qualities. It has power of suggestion but little of suspense. It is flat (though in the literal sense of the word alone), not thrown in relief or projected. It is alive and mobile, not mysterious and "intriguing." There is wit and humor in it but not paradox; and if we are led irresistibly on from speech

[30] Here, as in some other passages of this chapter, I am, with the permission of the Macmillan Company, reproducing, though in a different connection and to another purpose, ideas already expressed in my *Shakespeare Studies* (1927).

to speech, and then to another, it is not in order to solve a problem or rede a riddle. The writing is less economical, though vastly richer and more various, than in Ibsen, Corneille, and Racine, and more intimately fitted to the lithe contours and changing colors of the character and to the spirit of the moment. It is a stocking of silk, not a legging of brocade or buckram. It will not stand alone. It has not ordinarily the virtues of mere structure, does not because of the mere mystery lead us on, and in that respect is not so thoroughly dramatized. It is both less so and more so than that of Beaumont and Fletcher, who arrived on the scene as Shakespeare departed. On the one hand Shakespeare has no scenes like the second in *Philaster*, where despite his own misgivings and the warnings of his friends, the hero, in response to her invitation, appears in the boudoir of Arethusa, his enemy's daughter, and step by step learns that she will not yield to him her claim to the kingdoms but will make good the claim — by marrying him; or like that in which disclosure follows upon disclosure, thrill upon thrill, in a fashion that Sardou and Ibsen himself might have envied — the colloquy between Amintor and Evadne, their wedding night. On the other hand, he has none of the defects of the method, as in the scene last mentioned, and here and there in such plays as the *Master-Builder*, a mystery that at times degenerates into mystery-mongering, a suspense secured by juggling with words and paltering with motives. Shakespeare never stoops to throw dust in our eyes.

And his dialogue is dramatic in other ways. If it does not give the effect of volume in itself, it gives that effect to the things described. Browning, as Professors Herford and Bonnell have noted, does that in some measure by the use of touch images, not relying, as some poets do, almost exclusively upon the senses of sight and hearing. Shakespeare, in his imagery, is lord of the senses five. Like Browning, he gives things a body — hollows and recesses, projections and an edge. For him even light *thickens*, and night *strangles* the lamp of day. And if less sculpturesque, less pictorial than Browning, he is more dramatic. He gives more of the effect of movement and life. His touch is a grasp. Macbeth is too full o' the milk of human kindness to *catch* the nearest way; Macduff tells Malcolm that in Scotland daily new sorrows *strike* Heaven on the face; and Banquo after the murder cries out that fears and scruples *shake* us. If a person has news to give, he will, like Lady Macbeth and Iago, *"pour* her spirits" (or "this pestilence") in his ear, and if a woman has news to seek she will like Cleopatra bid the messenger *ram* into the same tender organ "thy fruitful tidings." Of color, as appealing to a less dramatic sense, there is far less use than in Browning; of light and darkness, more. And to a greater and finer degree than in Browning, or any other poet, the inanimate is made animate. To the murderer in his trepidations the earth seems to listen and the stones to prate; to the husband, as he considers his wife's offence, Heaven seems to stop the nose at it and the Moon to wink. For Shakespeare's impassioned souls, things themselves have a soul, have a body — noses, ears, and eyes, and especially lips. They cry or groan, shriek or whisper. "Religion groans at it," in *Timon of Athens*; "Grief whispers the o'er-fraught heart and bids it break," in *Macbeth*.

Indeed, the dialogue is dramatic in a still better way, being wholly created for the character and the occasion, "loaded with life." If there is no process of disclosure, there is an immediate presence. If the situation is not thrown in relief, it is reflected, vividly revealed. Who in the mere words spoken ever quaked and shuddered like Macbeth, in the manifest presence of a ghost?

Thy bones are marrowless, thy blood is cold.

Or like Gloster ever looked down into a precipice?

> There is a cliff whose high and bending head
> Looks fearfully in the confinèd deep;
> Bring me but to the very brim of it . . .

the last line thrilling and reeling with his desperate resolve. Or like Othello smiled serenely in the very teeth of danger

Keep up your bright swords, or the dew will rust them!

Or felt like him the exquisite pangs of despisèd love?

O thou weed,
Who art so lovely fair and smell'st so sweet
That the scene aches at thee, would thou hadst ne'er been
born.

And though on a lower level, the rhythm of Shakespeare's prose is almost as alive, supple, and sympathetic as that of his verse. Who in words ever longed and yearned, though in our hearts we all have done it, like old Gonzalo for firm dry land:

Now would I give a thousand furlongs of sea for an acre of barren ground, lońg heáth, brówn fúrze, ánything.

Everything for anything, where there is nothing at all! And not only situation but character is in the lines — in a sense they have volume enough! Intellectually, both in structure and also in point and suggestiveness, they often leave something to be desired. The wit may be blunt and verbal (and nevertheless be labeled); the thought, as a philosopher would judge it, may be commonplace. But imaginatively they leave nothing. They suggest not ideas but character, and as no other lines do. The form and pressure of a personality is in them — the live limb under the silk. Not one trait but several, not one star but a cluster of that constellation which is Cleopatra, gleams and twinkles out of her saucy, exultant apostrophe —

O couldst thou speak,
That I might hear thee call great Caesar ass
Unpolicied.

And when Pandulf, the Cardinal Legate, condescends to the King of France —

How green you are and fresh in this old world! —

the line, without analysis, or psychology, or any notable intellectual subtlety, seems, nevertheless, in its phrasing and its rhythm,
to embody the spirit of all Browning's haughty and crafty prelates,
yet unborn.

How Irving or Booth would have spoken it, have acted it! And
Shakespeare's lines cry out for the right speech and gesture, as his
songs do for the singing voice and the viol. They are truly of the
stage, for the ear and for the eye. They not only crave but intimate
a definite tone, look, and gesture; as does the line above, and
Hamlet's "Thrift, thrift, Horatio," and Othello's "Here comes the
Lady, let her witness it," and as do for that matter a thousand
more. Often the gesture is indicated rather clearly; as in Lear's
holding of the mirror and Richard's breaking of it; Othello's and
Iago's kneeling to register the vow; Antony's "business" with
Caesar's will and bloody mantle; Hamlet's with his sword, the
portrait, and the recorder; or that on the platform, with the Player,
at the play, in the churchyard, or at the fencing-bout. Oftener it is
not; stage-directions, as we have seen, are few, mostly they are in
the text itself, and when they are not they are little needed. The
personality is in the lines. And here again, more than in French
drama, and (despite the stricter conversational turn of it) more
than in the modern, is produced the illusion of life. Time, place,
circumstances, and even the very physical presence of the persons
themselves! And such dialogue cannot, for all the want of suspense,
seem flat or empty.

And for another reason it cannot. There is little suspense, but a
masterly use of contrast and of the illimitable resources of expression at the poet's command. In painting, complementary colors
(like red and green) "in apposition" may give the effect of volume
without recourse to the gradations of modeling. Such an effect is
frequently got by Shakespeare through the juxtaposition of characters like Lear and the Fool, Mercutio and Benvolio, Macbeth

and Lady Macbeth. But the best parallel I can think of, to his use of contrast and variety of expression both, is in music. Shakespeare has not only verse at his command as the modern dramatist generally has not, but he has also prose, and, in either, a far wider gamut of rhetoric to traverse. He is not meagerly restricted to what is conversational and plausible. He can be lofty or eloquent, lyrical or fantastical, as well as simple or plain. He can take the highest notes as well as the low, the loudest as well as the soft and tender. And as in a masterly orchestral composition, they then seem higher or lower, louder or softer, than they really are. They throw each other into relief — the comic does the tragic; the real, the ideal; the homely or humble, the grand or sublime. As we have seen, Shakespeare depicts passion fully and directly, in outcry or apostrophe, curses or ravings, lamentations or jubilations. But as Mr. Barker has finely shown, he continually descends to simple and lowly talk. After Lear's first sublime outcries on the heath comes the Fool's "shrill pitiful chatter":

O Nuncle, court holy-water in a dry house is better than this rain-water out o'door.

The poet carries "us into strange regions of thought and passion, so he must at the same time hold us by familiar things." And he does it here not only by a contrast with the talk of the other characters, as of the Fool and Edgar, Gloster and Kent, but by "Lear's own recurrent coming down from the heights to such moments as:

No, I will be the pattern of all patience,

or

How dost, my boy? Art cold?
I am cold myself. Where is this straw, my fellow?

or

Make no noise, make no noise; draw the curtains; so, so, so."

". . . And the tragic beauty of his end is made more beautiful by his call for a looking-glass, his catching at the feather to put on Cordelia's lips, the undoing of the button." That is, more beautiful because more real, because given a more tangible shape and form. And something similar to all this might be said of Hamlet and Othello.

Other dramatists, to be sure, have had recourse to simple, pregnant, and poignant expressions at the great moments, notably Corneille and Racine as we have already found. The chief difference between Shakespeare and them is that his count more in respect of character; theirs in respect of situation. The two things cannot be quite separated; but such sayings as "Qu'il mourût" and "Non, mais il me surprend" (as we have seen) and Hermione's "Qui te l'a dit?" (as we have not seen) count not only as *mots de caractère* but as the surprising climax of a gradual development, in a way that Macduff's "He has no children," or Lear's "I gave you all," or Othello's "I do not think but Desdemona's honest," does not. These too have their place in the action, but owe less to it. They count less by virtue of structure and in relation to the play as a whole, but more in relation to the other utterances of the character. They are a flash of vision, they are a throb of pain. They are like such sayings in Browning, who only less than Shakespeare, in the midst of all his own mannerisms and eccentricities, catches for us the very accent of a human voice; as when Caponsacchi groans,

> Sirs,
> Only seventeen!

or, again, at the end of his story, as he composes himself:

> Sirs, I am quiet again. You see, we are
> So very pitiable, she and I,
> Who had conceivably been otherwise.

And we either hear the voice or we don't hear it — but what matters less is what has been said and done before.

15

THE IMAGINATIVE IMPRESSION

In general, however, we are told far more than we see disclosed before us; and the inner nature of the characters is less definitely and intelligibly revealed in Shakespeare than in Corneille and Racine, less forcibly than in Ibsen or Browning. Yet we know them, for all that, if not so exactly or profoundly, more at first hand. They are the creatures not of analysis and construction but, as we have said, of the immediate imagination. They are not dramatized like Ibsen's; they excite little suspense and satisfy little psychological curiosity; but they are more variously shaped, more vividly colored, more instantaneously and irresistibly alive. Why at bottom they act, or what in their heart of hearts they think, we may not clearly see, but we know well enough what they are, and better still, that they are there. They have less structure to them, yet more of the quintessence and attar of art, which is simple, sensuous, and passionate. Indirectly they touch us less; directly, far more. Shakespeare has a greater power of individualization and differentiation, by the more external ideas and sentiments, and by the tone and accent, the vocabulary and rhythm. He is less exact and careful in analyzing, ordering, organizing, but he has a more potent and magical touch. He depicts, not intellectually, but emotionally, sensuously. What each man or woman, lord or lady, king or clown, prelate or layman, so vivaciously utters, belongs unmistakably, though not always quite intelligibly, together, and to him or her alone. Our ear, not our reason, is the judge. As in no other theater of the world, the puppets — Hamlet and Brutus, Rosalind and Beatrice, Mercutio and Falstaff — speak *in propria persona*, with their own particular tongue, not the showman's.

These puppets, they are people. They have voices, if we have ears to hear them; they have faces, too, though so seldom portrayed. Mr. Chesterton says of James's characters, which are endowed with just the qualities lacking in Shakespeare's, that they are figures which have no faces. They have minds — the particular point of view, the inner nature, conscious or unconscious — concerning which in Shakespeare's characters we are frequently left in the dark. But these have the reassuring material traits in which those of James for their part are lacking — bias and idiosyncrasy, prejudice and predilection, tastes and fancies, turns and tricks of speech, and the qualities of youth or age, of sex or profession. If we have not the effect of volume through a process of suspense and disclosure, we get something of that effect another way. Though we are not always given certain or consistent glimpses into the interior we are (as is noticed above and will be again below) permitted to see clearly and vividly the many planes and facets of the surface. Hamlet and even Henry V change with the company, are all things to all men, and have not only countenances but profiles, not only fair and goodly fronts but backs. Though from within not so definitely revealed or forcibly projected, they outwardly take form and shape.

And, in a sense, the characters have souls, though without a psychology. That is, they are enveloped in poetry, both heroes and heroines, both clowns and villains. "And all Meredith's psychological richness and acuteness," says Mr. Priestley, "would be of little avail if he too had not been able to create this atmosphere, to bathe his women in light and make them move to music." Meredith did this even in prose. In poetry, where art and reality are incomparable and incommensurable, as well as in prose, Shakespeare in this respect outstrips both him and everyone else. It is the *sense* of reality that he gives us rather than the bare thing itself; and his characters are less transcripts of it than Ibsen's. But Ibsen's are a hard and meager lot, or it is a bleak and frosty light that he lets fall upon them. Shakespeare's are mellow and abundant natures — of such certainly was his own. Macbeth and his lady are unjustifiable — inexcusable — traitors and murderers, and yet, without prejudice to morals, they elicit our sympathy. They had for their purpose discussed murdering Duncan before this, but not in the play; and they murder him now off stage, not before our eyes. As fact, as mere matter of morality, this makes not the slightest difference; but it makes vast difference in drama. And they suffer, in conscience, by a popular logic only the more because in their crime they are without real or apparent excuse, whereas by the laws of nature it would be the less. Above all, the glory of poetry is shed upon them, as is that of color and chiaroscuro upon the villains of Velazquez. And Iago, in morals what a monster, in manner how engaging and human, in speech what a poet! This, too, is not reality; yet Iago is one of Shakespeare's immortal creations. Antony and Cleopatra are two such. We are not suffered to forget that their relation is illicit and pernicious. But how much is touched lightly or passed over — duties to hearth and home, to their children and the state — and the virtuous, deserted Octavia is kept in the shadows of the background. Poetry is showered upon the pair, if indeed it does not rather well up out of them; their speech is passionate and lofty, not voluptuous or corrupting; and all that Antony has to repent of is his flight from battle, not that into Egypt, and all that Cleopatra has to regret is that she bears not the title of wife. And Caliban is a lustful, murderous brute, but with the imagination and affections, the gratitude and resentments, the delight in discovery and in sharing it, of a boy. He likes to be stroked and to be told stories and the names of things; and he will show his new master the best springs and "a jay's nest," his treasure. Like a boy in a plight — like a dog newly clipped — he cannot bear to be laughed at. "Lo, how he mocks me!" — "Ha, ha, ha," he cries with the schoolboy's *rire de vengeance*, "beat him enough. After a little time, I'll beat him too!" But he likes the tunes the spirits play, he cries to dream again, and he had listened wide-eyed to Miranda's stories about the man in the moon.

In general, our poet's villains are not hideous and hateful, his paramours not licentious, his bores not boresome — as in reality they are! Literature, though (save in reading my pages) we are prone to forget it, is not life. A fact in literature is not a fact, though in history it must be. And what is ugly or painful in life —

> In the affliction of these terrible dreams
> That shake us nightly —

takes on a loveliness in the situation and in verse. The greatest art is a compromise — in any case, a simplification, if need be, a sacrifice, of truth for effect. Even the medieval epic poet knew this, at least in France. Ganelon in his traitorous rage was beautiful, and the paladins could scarce take their eyes off him —

> Tant par fut bels, tuit si per l'en esguardent!

"And this is the particular crown and triumph of the artist — not to be true merely, but to be lovable; not simply to convince but to enchant." And this is the crown and triumph of Shakespeare.

16

The illusion of reality, but the certainty of beauty — that is what we find in Shakespeare, as in art we ought to do. In dramatic figures beauty is necessary not only to make us follow the action with interest but also even to make it hold together. In Ibsen, above all in plays like O'Neill's *Strange Interlude*, we see little reason why the characters on the stage should be so much more concerned for the hero's or heroine's person or fate than we are. Why should Rosmer fall under the spell of Rebecca West, or why in the other play should four men who appear, and some others who do not, crave so desperately the love of a woman no more worthy or alluring than Nina? Concerning Cleopatra or Juliet, Desdemona or Ophelia, or (for that matter) Antony and Romeo, Othello and Hamlet, the disconcerting question does not arise. The characters themselves justify the play. The very certainty of their charm imparts reality to the whole illusion.

Another thing that enchants us into a sense of their reality, strange to say, is the characters' own sense of their spiritual unreality. Shakespeare is not a religious poet like Calderón or Sophocles; nevertheless most of his characters, at moments, look upon themselves as travelers betwixt life and death. They are "crawling between earth and heaven," the earth being a "sterile promontory" and our place on it a "bank and shoal of time," ourselves being such stuff as dreams are made on and our little life rounded with a sleep. The humblest characters have glimpses of the other world, and the rude grave-maker becomes himself fairly spectral and visionary as he solves his own conundrum about the grave-maker — "the houses that he makes lasts till doomsday." Above we have used the figure of Shakespeare's mighty canvas, with distances and vistas. Still deeper ones are depicted upon it. And they are illumined, though seldom hopefully; long and lurid rays, as out of a magic lantern or a supernatural searchlight, flash and flicker through them. At a distance everything becomes a dream.

Nothing else so enchants us and deludes us, unless it be, on the other hand, their humor, which shows them to be at home on the earth. They are like human flesh and blood, are both ghosts and beasts. Humor they all have, or their nature appears in the mere lack of it. And nothing so well as a smile convinces you that a puppet is not a puppet; though that is what Corneille and Racine have (willingly or unwillingly) dispensed with, and what Ibsen can with difficulty attain. "Among his other excellencies," says Johnson of the poet, "it ought to be remarked that his heroes are men." Not the heroic and public, the religious or philosophical, but the human and private, concerns him. His soldiers and statesmen love their country, but almost as his young men do their mistresses, without principle or reason; he has no just conception of republicanism or imperialism, of Cassius or Brutus, of Julius or Augustus; and he is interested in them less in relation to the state than to wife or friend, sister or servant. With these they unbend —

and thereby, as not in Corneille and Racine, their public character is thrown into relief — having, like their creator, not too much philosophy to do that.

Not that he has a psychology instead — in one sense he has something deeper and in another something not so deep, the plastic, differentiating principle in art. It is the *poet's* gift, not that of a *seer* but of a *maker*. It appears in the fairies and Caliban, for which there was no model, as clearly and happily as in the "human mortals" — as in Falstaff and Iago, for instance, and that does not make it the more likely, of course, that the one was done from the life or that the other is wholly within the limits of nature. They have the semblance of truth but are the birth of the poet's brain, and (as with those born of the flesh) what makes them so unmistakably real or so inimitably different as this humor of theirs? Laughter — it is the epitome of character, the soul disporting herself naked, her life-story all in a word. Titania's at the big-bellied sails has all the delicacy of a sprite's, Caliban's at the deed which he would he had done, all the grossness and earthiness of a satyr's. The humor of Rosalind is not that of Beatrice or Viola, Perdita or Cleopatra; nor Hamlet's that of Jaques; nor Falstaff's that of Autolycus; even as no earthly body's laugh or smile is that of anybody else. And Iago, monster of humanity, he has his proper devilish humor too, which more than anything else brings him within the pale:

These fellows have some soul.

By the Mass, 'tis morning;
Pleasure and action make the hours seem short.

Ay, too gentle!

Edmund, less inhuman, is, in the same way, made still less so, by his witty imagery and reckless cynicism:

Fut, I should have been that I am, had the maidenliest star in the firmament twinkled on my bastardizing.

And, as in all Shakespeare's characterization, and to more felicitous effect than in any other, it is a matter of identity in the tone. This is, in the last analysis, a matter of the wording. Of ideas, to be sure — of skepticism and cynicism, in this case, cunning and revenge — but mainly of the external ones, the "surface of the mind," which all may scan and know. It is a matter of the unique external shape and form — of vocabulary and imagery, of emphasis and rhythm, even of the very vowels and consonants. Why shouldn't it be, when painting is a matter of lines and colors, sculpture a matter of lines and masses? The motives of Iago and Edmund will never be adequately reconciled and cleared up; but for Shakespeare's purposes they need not be. The man's accents of themselves convince us — Iago's in his very first speeches, Edmund's in his first soliloquy. Here the mere sounds and rhythms, quite dependent on the sense, to be sure, but lifting it into poetry, give the effect of a sneer or a jeer, in the midst of the descriptive power:

> Why brand they us
> With base? with baseness? bastardy? base, base?
> Who in the lusty stealth of nature take
> More composition and fierce quality
> Than doth, within a dull, stale, tired bed
> Go to the creating a whole tribe of fops
> Got 'tween asleep and wake.

It is the selfsame spirit that follows him into the valley of the shadow of death, as he thinks of the two women who pursued him, but are gone before:

> I was contracted to them both: all three
> Now marry in an instant.

And likewise the hard, sly soul of Iago lurks and coils not so much behind the lines as within them.

> . . . 'tis not long after
> But I will wear my heart upon my sleeve
> For daws to peck at. I am not what I am.

Ere I would say I would drown myself for a guinea-hen, I would change my humanity with a baboon.

Do it not with poison; strangle her in her bed, even the bed which she hath contaminated.

There he is, not only in the thought but in the imagery, not only in the mood but in the very syllables and intonation! Who does not quail under his metallic accents, or (as it were) seek to evade the quick glitter of his eyes? The poet *felt* the character, the actor now feels it, and what more or better can we do? He made it by the touch, by the touch we know it now; and the best criticism of Shakespeare is the only sort he ever expected, a sympathetic reading of his lines.

17

THE IMPRESSION OF REALITY RATHER THAN THE IMAGE OF THE AGE

The very accents of Shakespeare's people convince us, but not quite as of those whom he really knew. Their speech is Elizabethan — that and nothing else is the raw material in which (when they were not indulging themselves in traditional stage rhetoric) Shakespeare and his fellows worked. But there is (again) none of the hard and dogged truthfulness or dreary and hideous literalism which nowadays prevails. "A likeness of truth" (to use Dryden's phrase) contents him. Scholars delight in Elizabethan drama as a social document — otherwise some of them would hardly know how to delight in it — but finding, to be sure, far more comfort in Dekker and Jonson than in Shakespeare, though even then one rather precarious. Mercutio is an Elizabethan buck and gallant, but only at a perceptible remove. His speech is literary and poetical, colloquial, indeed, but little touched with the current slang and cant. J. M. Synge was averse from contemporary drama because of its "sterility of speech." What he did himself to remedy this we see in the *Play-Boy*, the *Well of the Saints*, and the *Riders to the Sea.* He did, even in prose, to the contemporary vulgar speech in Ireland what the Chicago School have unsuccessfully endeavored or ignorantly neglected to do, whether in prose or in verse, to the vulgar speech in America. He adopted but adapted it, and turned it into a thing of beauty. And this was lost on many of his worthy and zealous countrymen, who, as really the Shakespeare critics would have done had they known his original, resented the speech, like the morals and manners, as a misrepresentation or libel. What they resented was his art. On the one hand, he did not distort and debase the literary tongue but enlarged and enriched it. On the other hand, he did not employ an artificial and narrowly intelligible jargon, the concoction of blackguards and hoboes, drummers and comic journalists, but, though much refined and modified, the hereditary Irish English, colored by the Celtic idiom, smacking of the Hibernian soil. Yet the words are all familiar or intelligible — it is the rhythm and turn of phrase, the spirit and not the letter of the Irish speech — that he has seized. Shakespeare made no such new creation, or innovation, for his medium; but much as he may have enriched the literary tongue with colloquialism, he remained at a still greater distance, it would seem, from the crude, raw speech of everyday.

For it is in the style — it is as a writer — that Shakespeare works his wonders. He is a great plotter, too; but of structure, as we have seen, he does not always make so much as he might, whether in fable or in dialogue. He is a poet — not the most faultless but the most opulent and magical — from first to last. As the characters are creations, so is their speech, wherein they have their being. The elements of it, as we have seen, are old, and the familiarity and concreteness of it in comparison with the speech in other great tragedy make us think of life at once. The heroes and heroines in Greek and French tragedy keep their state. But by their nearest and dearest among the survivors Romeo is called "churl," Desdemona "girl," Cordelia "my poor fool," and Cleopatra "lass un-

paralleled," after death. And in life Cleopatra is called "girl" by
Antony, Lady Macbeth, "dearest chuck" by the King of Scotland,
and the Princess Katharine of France, simply "Kate" by the conqueror of Agincourt. In general, however, these and Shakespeare's
other heroes are stately and lofty enough. They are heroes or po-
tentates, every inch of them. Like the classical tragic poets Shakespeare too keeps *decorum*, though at the great moments often only
to break it.[31] It is the prerogative not of their rank but of their
passion — it is his own as a poet. And this contrast and apparent
contradiction is in life, indeed, though, like humor, it was to the
classical tragic poets, amid their restrictions, inaccessible; but it is
in the life of any time.

So it is especially, both in speech and in thought, with those
whom Shakespeare could not have known, the foreigners. There
is the same distance — no race psychology, no *Culturgeschichte* —
but the same all-prevailing poetic power. As we have seen above[32]
a little genuine first-hand observation went into the making of the
Scotch, Irish, and Welsh, and of the Princess Katharine, both in
their English speech and in their ways of thinking and feeling.
But for the most part these ways are according to the traditional
report among the English — the Scotch being canny and intrepid;
the Irish, boastful and bellicose; the Welsh, fanciful, sentimental,
and superstitious; the French *jeune fille*, artful and sophisticated,
coy and demure. But when it comes to races more remote, the
Jews, the Moors, and the ancient Romans, Shakespeare must needs
draw still more upon his imagination. In the Jews' case, indeed,
he had something to go on, not only the European tradition concerning them but the reflection of them in the Bible. These definitely appear. Shylock has the avarice and miserliness, the keenness
in argument and at a bargain, the Pharisaic literalness and casu-
istry, the racial pride and scorn, and the cringing and fawning to

[31] See above, "Cleopatra," pp. 13, 23.
[32] See above, "Henry V," pp. 47–51.

cover his revenge. But he is (though a fine one) a caricature. He is not a profound or wholly sympathetic study of a Jew's point of view; and what makes him a great artistic success is above all the tone and manner, the hard and grating, cunning but picturesquely exalted style of talk that he is given throughout:

> An oath, an oath, I have an oath in heaven!
> Shall I lay perjury upon my soul?

His speech befits his gaberdine.

With the Moors, however, Shakespeare had presumably nothing to go on at all — no more than had the eighteenth-century dramatists and novelists in depicting the noble savage — and yet one of these is his greatest achievement. In Aaron he depicted a brutal barbarian, in Othello a noble one. Aaron is a crude melodramatic figure, but in his racial resentment and paternal pride as he champions his offspring he is a character as much as any, a raw, blatant, grossly and bestially jocular creature, though, save in looks, without the special qualities of the Moor or Negro or of quite any primitive being as we know him. He is atheistical as the primitive are not, and not superstitious as the primitive are. And Othello, save in looks again, has nothing of the Moor or Negro about him either, whether in religion or superstition, in attitude to woman or to the ruling race. There is superstition, perhaps, in his tales to Desdemona of the men whose heads do grow beneath their shoulders (though Raleigh had given a report of them), and of the two-hundred-year-old Sybil who sew'd the handkerchief, but there is nothing barbarous about him until he falls into Iago's toils. And tragic passion is often barbarous in Shakespeare. He is simply such a conception of the noble African or Oriental as the supreme English imagination might conceive by itself — rich in emotions, generous and unsuspicious, poetical and yet not naïve or unsophisticated, delighting in war and adventure, in friendship and (though belatedly) in love. He is simply the noble African, long in the service of the state, whom old Brabantio would have loved, often invited, and questioned concerning the story of his life, and to whom, despite his color, a Desdemona would certainly have yielded up her heart. And the unmistakably individual and richly colored utterance does the rest.

And the Romans — like the other foreigners, they are more human and English than truly foreign. Brutus and Cassius, Coriolanus and Volumnia, have something of the dignity and gravity, the rigor and stoical virtue of the great days. Yet for the most part Shakespeare merely avoids anachronism (and comic effects, which in an English historical play involve it), as Heywood does not, and inappropriately soft and romantic emotions, as do not Beaumont and Fletcher, or even Corneille and Racine. But he gives us little of a positive, historically Roman characterization like Corneille's, or of an accurate study of Roman manners like Jonson's. Here is no paternal power or civic duty overriding personal affection — no Horace or Curiace. As so often in Shakespeare, it is a matter of tact and touch, of illusion rather than of reality. The page is not burdened with historical fact or local color, which would be lost on an ordinary audience; but much is made of a few expected, familiar matters like the Capitol, the Tiber, and the Tarpeian Rock, the Senate and the Tribunes, Jupiter and Juno. And above all the Romans talk like Romans, if they do not think like them, or at least talk like heroes, in stern, resounding terms. A simple but effective device is that the words *Rome* and *Roman* should be so continually upon their lips.

18

THE VARIETY OF CHARACTER AND THE POET'S ATTITUDE TO LIFE

And so many these real, unreal people are, so various! Corneille's and Racine's, Browning's and Ibsen's creatures are not the poet over again, but at least are pretty much of the poet's own breed. Shakespeare's sometimes resemble each other, but from their creator differ almost as widely as we creatures of a day do from ours. With him, we are out of the study, out of the house, where the sun shines and the wind is blowing. Indeed, it is not as a dramatist that (however unreasonably) we think of him, but as one who made a world. In a single play like *King Lear* the characters, one after the other, are clearly and forcibly distinguished by sentiment and accent, tone and manner — Lear and Gloster are, Kent and Albany, Edgar and Edmund, Goneril and Regan; and the same is as true of *Othello*, *Hamlet*, and, to a less degree, of many another. The first and sanest critic of Shakespeare said a thing which should be longest remembered. "He was the man who of all modern, and perhaps ancient poets, had the largest and most comprehensive soul." It comprehended the *good* and the *bad*, the *big* and the *little*, the *clever* and the *stupid* in its understanding and sympathy, both far wider than these epithets. It is not that of a critic or satirist, of a thinker or analyst; and there are some nooks and crannies of comedy and tragedy known to Molière and Ibsen, who are such, but unknown to Shakespeare. Yet he is not indifferent or undiscriminating, a mere prey to his creative bent. His world is not a chaos. He has the common sense and the respect for fitness and order which the higher vision cannot overwhelm. His creative imagination it not only the most comprehensive but also the best balanced. He is a lover, not a hater, and yet a judge. His imagination is normal, like that of Sophocles, Molière, and Tolstoy, not Jonson, Ibsen, and Dostoevsky. The wicked and criminal, the base and ignoble, he makes human and humorous, healthy and strong. He knows little of perversion or degeneration, nothing of our pathology. He avoids (if he knows them) the byways and the subterranean channels. He neither dissects nor burrows, neither engages in research nor studies disease. What a gallery of lovers he has portrayed for us, and yet only one love of importance — Antony and Cleopatra's — is illicit, and none is morbid or abnormal, though every great drama or novel today exhibits some new variety of one or the other. It is partly owing, no doubt, to the fact that in his art he depended, like his fellows, on external situations, not like the French, on love contending with pride or honor, generosity or duty. But the fact remains.

He is neither of the study nor even of the stage. Ibsen is a little of the first, Corneille and Racine a little of the second; but it is no small part of Shakespeare's glory to be free from the limitations of both. Here and there we have seen that Shakespeare is less consistently and essentially dramatic than these later dramatists; and this is a shortcoming, but also an advantage. He has no designs upon us. He has no program to follow, no rules to observe, no experiments for their own sakes to work out or carry through. His eye is on the object, the thing itself, or rather on the vision that he has of it. Of his technique he is scarcely more conscious than of his native tongue. He has learned the one as he had learned the other, growing up like Molière in the theater, as the rest of us do (and Shakespeare also had done) in house or street. And he developed it as he practiced it, and observed the effect of it, without recognizing it as a thing in itself and apart. His hand followed his eye, his tongue his thought, with no purpose either of keeping within the boundaries of his art or of enlarging them. He could not but enlarge them, or override them, as he unfolded, as he obeyed his impetuous and irresistible impulse to express life as he continually saw it and felt it anew. His style changed from period to period, even from play to play, but his thoughts were not of style, of change. Out of the depth of his nature and the abundance of his resources, rather than from deliberate effort, he was original.

He was no theorist, no virtuoso. The subject was to him not a matter of indifference but in itself a delight. His stories were really stories, often old ones, but turning in his hands to something new and strange. His persons were great persons, fair women and brave men, whose faults and whose fall touch us more deeply, though not more nearly, than those of ordinary people. And not only what they say and do, and see and hear, but what they eat and drink, wear and wield, enjoy and desire, and the places they inhabit, the horses they ride, the dogs they follow, the music they hear, as well as the very skies above them and the birds and flowers about them, are not forgotten, and are likely either in themselves or in his treatment of them to be marvelous. In matter and manner he can be simple but can never be humdrum. His lines leap or ripple, his phrases flash or glow. He is like the great painters of the Renaissance, who eagerly chose fine subjects — illustrious people and exhilarating landscapes — not, as nowadays, mean folk and dumpheaps. But unlike Corneille and Racine, Molière and Regnard, he does not renounce the large and solid substance of reality, seeking only the elusive tragic or comic essence; and yet, unlike Ibsen, in keeping his grasp on life he does not strip it bare. He does it no violence, though not always faithful to it. No one in imagination ever so embraced it without a philosophy to prompt or support him. He loved it like Homer and Virgil, Odysseus and Æneas, who would not drink it, as we would, to the lees.

> Vivite felices, quibus est fortuna peracta
> iam sua; nos alia ex aliis in fata vocamur.
>
> Quae lucis miseris tam dira cupido?

His voice is clear, his countenance serene, but his philosophy of life is melancholy. He had nothing of the mystical adoration for it, not uncommon in our Victorian and twentieth-century poets as they saw the other life sink under the horizon. He loved it still though he knew not why — as how else indeed could he do, having been so mightily favored.

IV

The Old Drama and the New

Two of Mr. Archer's main purposes in writing his recent valuable book, *The Old Drama and the New*, he has achieved. He has brought our contemporary English playwrights as men of letters more completely into their own; and (with one more blast before the Drama League the other night[1] to make an end of it) he has dispelled the Elizabethan superstition, which for a century, if not for centuries, has hung over our stage like a cloud, blighting original work and darkening the counsels of criticism. In the eighteenth century it was the classical superstition that stood in the dramatist's way if he would be literary; in the later eighteenth and the nineteenth, with the Romantic critics erecting it into a dogma, it was the Elizabethan almost alone. Vulgar and ephemeral writers, to be sure, cheerfully ignored it; but men of letters, until they made out light ahead reflected from the French or from Ibsen, saw no way clear to write for the stage, while the literary critics and historians have bowed under the shadow of the dogma to this day. According to it the little finger of a Jonson, a Beaumont, or a Webster, was as big as the thigh-bone of any of our puny tribe.

On Mr. Archer's achievement in demonstrating the error in this

[1] November 5, 1924, at the Century Theater, on *Elizabethan Worship*.

way of thinking I need not dwell. A few scholars had recognized the error, but mere scholars get no hearing, and the actual slaying of the dragon had been left for the true-filed and well-directed shafts of Mr. Archer. In all error, however, there is some truth; in things literary, at least, most error is overstatement, likely, therefore, when thrust out of the way, to be supplanted only by further overstatement, further error. (In the arguments of others we see this, like the gods!) If the Elizabethans really are not so much bigger or better than our moderns, surely our moderns are not, as Mr. Archer thinks, so much bigger or better than the Elizabethans. And as surely Shakespeare should not be spirited away out of the company of these and set up as an isolated exception. Though a world-poet he was an Elizabethan, through and through and first of all.

1

No one knows better than, I think, Mr. Archer, when not arguing or advocating, that such an exception Shakespeare simply could not be. All art is a function of society, a matter of communication on the part of the artist but of understanding on the part of the public, and by means of a language — that is, conventions, devices, various accepted simplifications — slowly developed and established but immediately intelligible when used. And dramatic art, above all popular dramatic art, dependent for effect as it is on the very moment of presentation, is a community affair in a special and particular sense. Sculptor or painter, poet or prose-writer, may be individual and aloof as a dramatist cannot. He must write for the same audience as his fellows or rivals; he must use the same language or medium; and, as with them, his very thoughts must in a sense be the thoughts of the audience, his ways their ways. He cannot go "voyaging through strange seas of thought" — or he will *be* alone, and that, of all things, is the last your dramatist desires. Failure has for him no consolations. As with a business man, a general, or the very actor in his play, nothing succeeds but success. To be *great* is to be misunderstood, say the philosophers and reformers, but never the dramatists or actors — save when in that plight. To those of the craft they would scarcely say it at all.

Now it is to this language, these conventions or devices — disguise, soliloquy and aside, vagueness of time and place, superfluity of horror, blank verse, high-flying rhetoric on the one hand and grossness of speech on the other, the expression of passion rather than the sober and discreet imitation of reality, and romanticism rather than realism — that Mr. Archer particularly objects. He admits that some of the Elizabethans besides Shakespeare were men of genius, not lacking in matter or in poetry; but he cannot abide or endure the form of art they cultivated or the medium in which they wrought. It was too soft and easy — was water-color, so to speak, not oil; was sandstone, not marble. But he seems to forget that it was exactly the same medium wherein Shakespeare wrought, by the early Elizabethans mixed or rough-hewn for him, as it were. And never since the days of Sophocles was there a great dramatic community — authors and audience together — so much at one, all employing or comprehending one medium or idiom, engrossed with the capabilities of it and with the import of what was communicated, untroubled by the thoughts or idiom of other authors, audiences, or times. Of Shakespeare himself this is truest, who apparently took no interest in dramatic theory or technique as such, and did not print his plays. And so well does Mr. Archer know all this that at unguarded moments he himself shows how from his form and medium Shakespeare suffers, though ordinarily of that subject he keeps well clear. As a strategist, Mr. Archer, one cannot help suspecting, attacks the weakest places, well aware that against the fortress of Shakespeare's reputation he should for long be tilting in vain.

By our standards, to be sure, most of the great Elizabethans are poets rather than dramatists. But Shakespeare, then, is too. By

our standards many of the conventions and licenses in the Elizabethans are crude and objectionable. But they are too in Shakespeare. In three centuries, however, drama in general has become
enormously more dramatic and less poetic; just as in the same
period prose has become more like prose, and lyric verse, on the
other hand, has become less like a song. Are we, then, to take no
pleasure in any prose, lyric, or drama other than such as ours? If,
as he reads or witnesses the greatest Elizabethans save Shakespeare,
Mr. Archer gets so little pleasure as he says he does, Shakespeare himself, one thinks, he must read or witness with only a
much mingled and sadly qualified delight. And the same in a
measure must be said of Mr. Archer when confronted with the
drama of other periods, as indeed he more than once betrays.
Many of the above licenses and conventions are to be found in late
seventeenth-century comedy, from Etherege to Farquhar, and of
that comedy Mr. Archer disapproves; and some of these and others
besides, such as rime in the verse and elaborate etiquette or a high
fantastical style in the dialogue, are to be found in seventeenth-
century French and Spanish drama, and that drama Mr. Archer
but faintly praises. Some are to be found even in that comedy for
which Mr. Archer has a kindness, Goldsmith's and Sheridan's; and
one wonders with what countenance and cheer Mr. Archer contrives to swallow the choruses and the lyric measures, the disguises,
mistaken identities, and recognitions, the indeterminateness of
time and place, and all the hugely improbable assumptions of the
plot, in ancient comedy and tragedy. "Of his comfort we should
despair," did we not remember that sound sense or an exquisite
taste cannot by argument be quite impaired or by a partisan spirit
stifled.

2

What apart from the above-mentioned licenses most offends Mr.
Archer is the careless, slipshod, unplausible methods of the Eliza-

bethans in general; and yet of that Elizabethan who in his best work gives in all these respects least cause for offence, and is most exacting with both himself and his material, he will have none. Ben Jonson is the one man in the period — for that Shakespeare is not — blest (and curst too) with the artistic conscience; but Mr. Archer, who reverences it only after the still small voice within, will do it no honor in Jonson. He recognizes that Jonson is a poet and has a powerful mind, but does not allow him to be a very considerable dramatist, and ignores — indeed denies him — his particular faculty or quality. I do not wonder at Mr. Archer when he complains of the shapelessness of Webster's *White Devil* and *Duchess of Malfy*, but wonder (without admiring) when he says of *Every Man in His Humour* that "a worse-constructed play could not easily be discovered, outside of Jonson's works." Bad plays are so numerous, even as are the sands on the seashore; and Jonson was acknowledged to be the great and cunning craftsman of the Elizabethan Age, both in his own time and after. His plays were *works*, as indeed he called them, but that according to Mr. Archer's own principles should be far from a reproach. In respect of poetry, and the spiritual or imponderable qualities of drama, the verdict of time is not necessarily binding; but in respect of dramatic structure and workmanship it may be, and when in such a matter critics and dramatists so gifted and yet dissimilar as Dryden and Coleridge can agree, we may take it for granted that they are nearly or wholly right. *Securus judicat orbis terrarum* — for if these agree it amounts to that. Certainly Jonson knew and practiced the art of plotting, of preparing and motiving, and of making the dramatic current ebb and flow, in a day when it was too little practiced and less known; and of that art the plots of *Volpone, The Alchemist,* and *The Silent Woman,* and in less measure *Every Man in His Humour* too, are enduring monuments. Little of this cunning construction would it be possible in brief space adequately to lay bare. But to take one or two details out of many,

what an effect of ebb and flow and truly dramatic rhythm, everything prepared for and yet everything a surprise, and all presented
in the simple, sensuous, if not altogether passionate, language of
the stage — in that of sights and sounds and natural human intercourse and action — is to be found at the end of the fourth act of
The Alchemist! The explosion, which is the impostors' triumph,
is, once it has been dramatically emphasized and realized, followed
by the arrival of Surly; that defeat, by the angry entrance of the
gulls, one after the other, who fatuously, though naturally, side
not with him but with the impostors, and blindly drive their de-
liverer away; and that triumph, in turn, by the still more disconcerting but wholly to have been expected arrival of the master!
And what a series of comic changes and true stage sensations, where
rogue meets rogue, not exactly as Greek meets Greek, but as two
well-anointed wrestlers grapple and still continually elude each
other's clutches, is to be found in the last trial scene in *Volpone!*
And yet such cunning and careful work, the absence of which in
Webster or Middleton Mr. Archer deplores, he in Jonson fails to
appreciate, says nothing of the construction at all save to pick
flaws, but has a deal to say of Jonson's extravagance in conception,
disregard of probability, and propensity to caricature. Must a
dramatist, however, like no other artist, constantly exhibit every
quality and virtue known to his art? Being a satirist, Jonson does,
by that very fact, give an imperfect image of life. But he gives all
that should be expected — a vivid and artistically consistent one.
And for satire there is a place upon the stage — for Jonson's as,
two generations after them, for Molière's.

What are these flaws, viewed more narrowly? In all the close-
wrought fabric of causality in *Volpone* Mr. Archer can pick out
one — in the motiving of Mosca's bringing Corbaccio's son to his
master's house. Is there a play even among the greatest of Shakespeare's in which you cannot pick flaw after flaw as serious? Why
does Hamlet feign madness? Why does he give himself away at

the play within the play, the court taking no notice of that or of Claudius' self-betrayal? Why is Banquo, in regard to Duncan's death, so suspicious and yet so warily silent; and yet again, in regard to his own doings at the end, so confidential and incautious? And why does the shrewd but loyal Emilia never once speak up amid all the great to-do about the handkerchief? Though in far nobler plays, these improbabilities are more vital and also more noticeable than that found in *Volpone*.

As for the "presuppositions" and implications of Jonson's fable, they too are paralleled in Shakespeare at his best or in Molière. Unplausible imposture on the part of the rogue, preternatural credulity on the part of his victims — surely one cannot complain of that in Jonson when we have it in the warp and woof of Shakespearean comedy and tragedy alike, in *Much Ado, Twelfth Night, The Merry Wives, Othello, King Lear,* and *Cymbeline*. And in comedy, particularly in satiric comedy, where the characters are dominated each by his "humour," and where in the good cause of laughter they have always been allowed a larger license, it is justifiable as in sober tragedy it cannot be. The Moor is a noble and balanced character, with no right reason to be gullible; but these legacy-hunters in *Volpone* are gullible from the outset, in virtue of their greed. Jonson's comedy is in this respect to be judged by the standards of comedy and satire, by those to be applied to *Le Tartuffe* and *L'Avare*. And the same is to be said to Mr. Archer's complaint against Corbaccio's and the others' incredible readiness not only to believe the flattering and enticing things they are told but to risk so much in gifts. Cupidity, he says rightly, goes with parsimony; but that is neither here nor there. Mr. Archer will remember Sir Walter Raleigh's answer to the complaints against Lear's and Cordelia's conduct (and the critics' ingenious explanations of it) at the beginning of Shakespeare's play — that this unplausible conduct is the "postulate" upon which the play depends. "The falsity of the initial assumptions," growls Mr. Archer, as he weighs the probabilities of Volpone's getting rich in such a fashion; but the author of *Play-making* need not be reminded that the beginning is the place for false or improbable assumptions, as it is not only in *King Lear* but (witness the casket story and the pound-of-flesh story) in the *Merchant of Venice* and in *Le Tartuffe*, and that there they do not much matter if what follows them be logical and consequent. And (here again) in comedy and satire there is, and should be, more latitude; for Lear and Cordelia are not warped and unbalanced, but those who, like the legacy-hunters, are obsessed by a passion, will, with not a mathematical but a human logic, be even spendthrifts and squanderers that they may give it scope. Blind avarice is the postulate, even now not unknown. Did Mr. Archer never look on (at least) at a gaming-table? Did he never read of the stock-market, where the most avaricious men on earth will eagerly, frantically fling away their all? Or of those who buy far-away gold mines, oil wells, or orange groves, or millions and then milliards of German marks, thereby merely giving the sellers gifts? It costs them a wrench, no doubt, not to say a paroxysm, nor of that does Jonson fail to make comic capital when the legacy-hunters actually hand their presents over — but to hand them over is human. "Nothing venture" — the proverb is world-wide.

Moreover, being not a tragedy but a comedy, and a sublime satire besides, *Volpone* is mainly the materialization of one passion, which must be cut and shaped, as it were, in planes or with facets, and quickly turned about in the light. Swift-succeeding aspects — flashes, contrasts and surprises — comic effects in short, must be had, even at some considerable cost to truth and soberness. One might as well complain that a monster of a miser like Harpagon keeps a coach and horses, a cook and a troop of servants, and cry, No way is this to paint a miser, as living on such a scale. Cupidity goes with parsimony without a doubt; but in the comedy, as Sarcey observed, he keeps the servants to stint them, and the

horses to get up at night and steal away their oats. And so it is that
old Corbaccio gives Volpone his bag of bright chequins, though
with a pang. He is but lending them, he trusts, for a little space;
is but adding unto his heritage. "Who ever heard," says Mr.
Archer, "of avarice staking large sums on a problematical post-
obit?" But Volpone is passing away, he is made to think, and
Volpone cannot take them with him. Nor can he, to be sure, and
he is on his last legs himself — another improbability, from a point
of view more logical than human or comic. "Sure, I shall outlast
him," he croaks and chuckles, noting the symptoms one by one.
Memento mori — every man knows of his end but no man remembers it. And Avarice, like Ambition, would stake her all to hold
the prize in hand for one moment, or, like Envy, to keep it from
out of the hand of another.

3

What in view of Mr. Archer's formula of realism and "imitation" is most remarkable is his blindness to Jonson's regard for
time, place, and "decorum," and approximation to the

> deeds and language such as men do use,
> And persons such as comedy would choose
> When she would show an image of the times.

Now and then, no doubt, Jonson's learning and his bent for caricature run away with him — or weigh him down, had we not better
say — but in *Every Man in His Humour, The Silent Woman,* and
The Alchemist, is scene after scene in which he fully lives up to
the program unfolded in these verses. Rightly his comedy is called
the comedy of manners; and, with due allowances for satiric dis-
tortion, we get from him a more real and vivid picture of London
life than from anyone in his time. He imitated reality, studiously
and rigorously, as Shakespeare did not nor needed to do. There
is in him no high-flying rhetoric except by way of burlesque or
satire; and the incidents, though often farcical, are strictly within

the bounds of the comic — not romantic, fantastic, or tragic, as in Elizabethan comedy they often are. There is a perfect, if somewhat external, unity of tone, as well as of form, to *The Alchemist, Volpone,* and *The Silent Woman,* hardly to be paralleled in Shakespeare. Bitter as they are, his comedies are comic, through and through.

And almost alone among Englishmen Jonson has an excellent gift to which a critic like Mr. Archer should not be indifferent, the faculty (in which he anticipates Molière) for working out a single comic theme fully and delightfully, with variations, as in music. There are no scenes in Shakespeare such as that where the jealous Kitely desires to leave the house, but fears to do so, undertakes to confide his secret to Cash, his man, but fears even to do that, and yet in a panic or paroxysm confides it to him after all, anxiously pretending and protesting the while that this is not the secret he had meant; or such as that in *Volpone* where Mosca, absorbed and abstracted, makes up, item by item, with malicious delight, the inventory of his supposedly defunct master's valuables, whilst in swoop the legacy-hunters one after the other, each in turn gloating over the precious items, as mentioned, in the thought that they are already, not the others', but his own. In such scenes, and in many in *The Silent Woman,* you have repetition and variation of *motif,* inversion and transposition, and the comic art approaching that state considered by Pater to be the perfection of art — that of music — as elsewhere you shall find it only in the supreme *maestro* of comedy himself. Such fine economy of means and nice calculation of effects is not after the Elizabethan style, which Mr. Archer despises, but after the classical and Gallic, which both he and we admire.

4

On his own showing, then, Mr. Archer should take some pleasure in Jonson; and the same is to be said of Beaumont and

Fletcher. The scenes just considered are examples, though Mr. Archer does not say so, of what he declares is rarely to be found in Elizabethan art — a nice gradation in the unfolding of a story, a "good, competent theatrical workmanship," and evidence that the artist is making the best use of his medium, to the limit of its possibilities, such as Mr. Archer finds in scenes in Houghton's *Hindle Wakes* and Pinero's *Letty*, though the scenes are of a sort not quite the same. But of the same sort as those last named, in which by gradual approaches and proper preparations a surprise is sprung — as Neville, for instance, discovering that his rival knows (what we ourselves had not known) that he is married — are several artful scenes to be found in the great twin poets. Again Shakespeare is not the exception that Mr. Archer would make of him, and the like of this in him is hardly to be found save in the first act of *Hamlet* and the *finale* of *Othello*. But there is the scene in *Philaster* (a play which Mr. Archer considers) where, despite his own misgivings and the warnings of friends, the hero, in response to her invitation, appears in the boudoir of Arethusa, his enemy's daughter, and learns that she will not yield to him her claim to the kingdoms, but will make good the claim — by marrying him. And there is another scene, in *The Maid's Tragedy*, also a play which Mr. Archer considers, in which disclosure follows upon disclosure, and thrill upon thrill, in a fashion that Ibsen, however he might have shaken his head at the "presuppositions" and "assumptions," might well have envied — the scene between Amintor and Evadne, their wedding night. One here detects something even of Ibsen's retrospective-prospective method as, save in Continental drama, one shall not again down to Ibsen's own day. The psychology of Evadne is indeed obscure, as Mr. Archer notices, and as others have noticed before him; but there can be no question of the stage-effectiveness, for all the staginess, of the scene. And whatever else may be said of scenes such as these, and of Jonson's mentioned above, it cannot be said justifiably that in them

the authors are, as Mr. Archer says the Elizabethans continually
are, "blurting things out just as they came." Here, certainly, there
is art enough, if not of art too much.

5

Much else might be said, which, however, must be left unsaid,
concerning Mr. Archer's book. It is a question, for instance, if the
modern medium, in which, with its difficulties and restrictions,
he glories, as if it were marble and the Elizabethan were sandstone,
be not really flint or granite. It is too difficult, too refractory, to
be worked. Soliloquy, aside, disguise, and mistaken identity are
indeed licenses; but the imitation of reality, which Mr. Archer
prizes, is painfully and anxiously pursued at the expense of the
painting of the passions, which he deplores. Expressionism is a
revolt against it. Only passions on the stage — not virtue's own
feature or scorn's own image — may arouse passions, which in the
audience nevertheless must be aroused. Four boards and two actors
were all that he needed, said Dumas the Elder — these, and a passion. Here, as in the matters already considered, the defect of Mr.
Archer's book lies in his spirit of partisanship and antagonism —
not in his praise and appreciation which are just and right, but
in his censure, which often in part is wrong. He slays the dragon
— but another springs up behind him, out of its blood. He knocks
the Elizabethan superstition soundly on the head; but in lifting
up his hand also against Elizabethan art as distinguished from
the art of its greatest master, he is, like most other iconoclasts past
or present, bowing down to a superstition or idolatry even whilst
he breaks one, *la superstition Shakespearienne.*

V

The Stage and the House

T HE other day, for the first time in a double decade, I went to a football game; and there I was visited, not by passions, whether felicitous or infelicitous, but (of all things) by an idea. As I sat in the million-dollar stadium, along with 50,000 other mortals, but looked, not so much down into the arena or bull-ring as at the roaring audience roundabout it, I thought to myself, This is the American theater, or (in some measure) this is what that theater should be. Here stage and house are in sympathy, have a perfect understanding, are, for a couple of hours that are but as moments, at one. Here at last the spectators know and appreciate the art, instantly perceive the fine points of it, confidently applaud a success and bewail or execrate a failure. And the result is that the players play better, the spectators enjoy the play more. Few there sit ignorant and aloof like me. Knowing the game, they enter into it, join in it, play it in imagination themselves and so help the actors to play it. They "assist at the spectacle," to express the thought in French. For in the theater the French and the Italian audiences are not troubled, puzzled, or indifferent as ours are. They know this defter game, appreciate the fine points of the dramatic or histrionic art, and as spectators participate. Few there sit thinking of football, or of anything else afar. They do not indeed keep up a running fire of outcry and expletive like us in the bleachers, for that would interfere with the performance; but they cry *bravo, bravissimo,* after a speech or a fine bit of acting, weep or laugh when they should, and do not when they shouldn't, and at the end of a scene burst into a frank and wholehearted demonstration. For they hiss as our audiences — save when the sentiments do not suit them — never do; and despite movies and radio, drama with them is still alive.

Football or baseball, of course, is not an art; our national arts — are sports. The right purpose of these is to satisfy the cravings of the players, not the public, but they have been turned into shows and spectacles. The public must have its satisfactions too. Every university or college, whatever else it has, has its million-dollar or hundred-thousand-dollar stadium, and most of them have no theaters at all. They have a hall, perhaps, not for twenty-five thousand, but for five hundred. And not one healthy American in a thousand, whether in college or out of it, but would choose to pay twenty or thirty dollars to see the Yale and Harvard game rather than pay five to see (if it still were possible) Salvini play Othello or Ellen Terry Lady Macbeth. But what does that matter? Is not the theater for those who think otherwise, "fit audience though few"? That was said by a haughty epic poet, not your complaisant dramatist, and applies only to what is perpetuated in print. For the oral arts an audience, and a big and participating one at that, is indispensable. Does any actor, manager, or playwright imagine that if the national theater, which we are continually discussing and proposing, were sufficiently endowed to ignore the box office, it could ignore an empty or indifferent house? If playwright and players learned in some way to forget the spectators, these in turn would certainly forget them, and with the audience would vanish the play. Dramatic art, like all the oral and literary arts, and the

pictorial and plastic too, is a means of expression, demanding a
response; and for drama, oratory, and music the response must be
immediate and passionate. The art resides not in the page, nor
even on the stage, but on both this and the other side of the footlights, up and down the theater. Ideally, stage and house conspire,
and the audience is half the play.[1] Though no longer directly
addressed, it is no fiction, and it counts for more than so many
hundred pairs of empty ears and eyes. The artists play upon the
public and are played upon, get their effects or fall short of them,
and by applause or censure are spurred on to greater efforts. The
drama's laws the drama's patrons give. And all players and playwrights, singers and orators, have learned their art and mastered
it, not in school or study but in theater or forum.

Not that they merely cater and pander and give the public what
it wants. It is a striking fact that all the greatest art, whether oral
on the one hand or plastic and pictorial on the other, has been
popular. Shakespeare was popular, beyond a doubt the chief but
also on the whole the favorite playwright of his age. Æschylus,
Sophocles, and Euripides were popular, holding audiences of ten
or fifteen thousand people; and any one who has witnessed the
Agamemnon or *Œdipus the King*, even without the right effects
of song and dance for accompaniment, can well believe it. At the
Comédie Française, three years ago, the *Œdipus* took the audience
by storm. Never in my life before had I seen such a play, whether
on the stage or in the house. Molière was popular, too, and all
over the Continent he is so still. And the greatest sculpture ever
carved, the greatest pictures ever painted, at Athens or Memphis,
at Florence or Venice, were for temple and shrine, not drawing-

----

[1] Here is one of the many shortcomings of the cinema. "Theatrical Ger
many," writes Mr. Ashley Dukes from Salzburg, "no longer thinks of motion
photography as the art of the future. On the contrary actors are returning in
large numbers from the studios to the stage, conscious above all of that necessity for personal artistic creation in the presence of the spectator which is the
life-blood of acting." *Theatre Arts Magazine,* November, 1928.

room or gallery, were for street and forum, hilltop and square. The greatest epics also, the *Iliad* and the *Odyssey*, the *Chanson de Roland* and the *Niebelungen Lied*, were for the people and their gatherings. Not that these masterpieces were fully appreciated by everybody in their day, like a football match, which is not above the reach or beyond the compass of the meanest intelligence. No doubt there was much in *Hamlet* and *Macbeth*, in the art of Phidias and Polycleitus, of Giotto and Raphael, which eluded the eye and ear of the stupid or vulgar Londoner, Athenian, or Florentine. But their art did not mystify or repel him, did not rouse him to indignation or ridicule. Still less was it meant to do so — to *épater le bourgeois* — and it was not the worse but the better for that. The art of these geniuses, to be sure, was not so stained with the sentimental or the vulgar as the most widely popular (but ephemeral) art must in a measure be; but out of that art it had sprung, to that art it was not opposed. And it profited by the deep-rooted and widespread tradition. It employed the same technique, though a finer, and it was understood. It touched the same simple human nature, though more delicately, and it was acclaimed.

It is cherished still, and more than ever, now that the divorce of our higher art from the popular is fairly complete — now that we have dramas and music that can scarcely be played, pictures and statues that can scarcely be looked at, lyrics that cannot be sung or even read, still less be read aloud. One and all, they must be studied. What is more, they must be expounded — in the preface by the author, in lecture or essay by critic or propagandist. As Mr. Chesterton has well shown,[2] the interpreter has now a necessary place, not as in former times, for the art of an age still earlier, but for this. He is indispensable when first the work of art appears, and must stand between it and the people. He ministers and mediates between the congregation and the mystery, passing behind

[2] See his "True Case against Cliques" (*London Mercury*, February, 1928) to which I am considerably indebted in this and the preceding paragraph.

the veil. But every work of art, says Poe, contains within itself all that is necessary for its comprehension. No right poem (and still less a play) needs preface or prolegomena, as no right statue or picture needs letter-press, no music a "programme." That is not quite true of the art of a time gone by; but it is far truer even of Homer and Æschylus, of Myron and Giotto, than of our high art today.

This cries out for the interpreter, like the stranger within our gates. In the spacious, joyous days art was native and at home. The Parthenon, with all its sculptures, arose as properly and almost as naturally as the olive-tree on the Acropolis, and so did the *Agamemnon* and the *Œdipus* in the Theater of Dionysus. There were no books or lectures upon them, no public or private classes in the subject. Nowadays, instead of being a means of expression, art must itself be expressed. It needs one to come and tell us, and (if so be) to satisfy us, why the landscape does not look like the dear familiar earth or water or the portrait like a human being, nay, why the poem is not a poem, the song not a song. Or if it be not so bad as that, why the poem or song, the picture or drama isn't such save from one particular point of view. And this there-upon we must be instructed to take. A landscape of Rousseau's or Dupré's is solid and indisputable; but as Mr. Chesterton says, a nocturne by Whistler of mist on the Thames is either a master-piece or it is nothing; it is a nocturne or a nightmare. "The moment it ceases to be a splendid picture it ceases to be a picture at all. Or, again, if *Hamlet* is not a great tragedy it is an uncommon-ly good tale. . . . But if we take a play like *Pélléas et Mélisande*, we shall find that unless we grasp the particular fairy thread of thought the poet rather hazily flings to us, we cannot grasp any-thing whatever. Except from one extreme poetic point of view, the thing is not a play; it is not a bad play, it is a mass of clotted nonsense." [3] But as for Whistler, what is he now to Matisse and

[3] See Mr. Chesterton's *Victorian Literature*, p. 219.

Gauguin, and as for Maeterlinck what is he to Chekhov and Strindberg? They are *vieux jeux*, both of them.

This aloofness and mysteriousness may do — though it does not very well, I think — in pictorial and plastic art, which may be studied. It does not do at all at the theater, where there is no opportunity for that. Drama depends on immediate effect; and to the cry there must be a response, to the impact a reaction. Drama cannot rightly depend on criticism, or even on lecture or press-agency, to prepare the way before it. The theater is neither a school nor a temple, or if it endeavors to be it fails. In a western city, of late I have repeatedly noticed tragic moments in Ibsen and O'Neill received with laughter. The audience, unlike that in the stadium, did not understand, could not react or respond appropriately. Much of our high-brow art is so received, openly or covertly, by the uninstructed public. But in the theater, if tears be expected and anything like a snicker detected, the result is fatal.

Does this then mean that in the theater subtlety is unattainable, and that the drama cannot accompany and cheer the human mind upon its march? By no means. It is a recognized principle, though nowadays too little observed, that in poetry words, figures, ideas, even, cannot advantageously be employed unless they be fairly familiar. The poet does not instruct and enlighten, but arouses and stimulates. He makes use of ideas and associations already established in the reader's mind, does not instill them. He turns into figures of speech only those objects or notions that mean something to his public already. And the words and phrases, whether literary or of a dialect, must be of the spoken tongue. He can, I suppose, deal with ideas in the grotesque and fantastic jargon of the Chicago School, as one can in Esperanto, but not excite emotions, awake associations, summon up remembrance of things past. In such guise — without form — a poem is no poem. And still more is this the case at the theater. There his thoughts must be the thoughts of the audience, his ways their ways, his words their words. There he must strike fire instantly — and if he has at command the steel and flint, in the mind of the audience must be the tinder. He cannot (to use the different figure of a previous chapter) go "voyaging through strange seas of thought" or he will be alone, and that, of all things, is the last your dramatist desires. A dramatist he would be, not a prophet in a weary land. He cannot deal with psychological or scientific material which has not as yet been grasped and accepted by the common sort. If he would present the supernatural, he must turn to account their superstitions, and respect their prejudices, as does Shakespeare with his ghosts, not scorn and neglect them like Voltaire. And he must have much the same notion of what is tragic, and what is comic, as they have, and of the way it may be brought about. He cannot suddenly employ a technique unfamiliar to the playgoer.

Such a technique must be approached discreetly, by degrees. All the great popular art of which we have been speaking, not only the dramatic but the lyric, the pictorial, and the plastic, has been the fruit of a gradual development, and the artists have gone forward faster indeed than the public, but not so as to leave the public far behind. Where was this and when? At Athens, at Thebes and Memphis, Florence and Venice, Paris and London, in their golden age. In cities, big enough to yield a variety of mind and material, small enough to be homogeneous in blood and temperament, morals and manners, notions and ideals, in their sense of beauty and propriety, their taste for the tragic and the comic. Great artists seem indeed to be the result of inbreeding, like fine animals; and as the good breeds of cattle and other creatures have arisen on islands or in provinces which then were as islands — Jersey, Guernsey, and Alderney, Malta, Minorca, and the Canaries, Devon, Hereford, and Ayr — so in these fenced towns of ancient days, where everybody was related to everybody else, and migration was exceedingly uncommon, artists arose in a multitude. Only where there were many were there the greatest, who entered into the others' labors — Phidias and Praxiteles at Athens, Haydn, Mozart, and Beethoven at Vienna, Leonardo and Michelangelo at Florence, Marlowe, Shakespeare, and Jonson in London. Or if the genius was not actually born there he came there, and found not the artists only but their art. It was local but public, and interested and embraced fairly the whole city, a living thing. It was of the time as well as of the place. In Pericles' day or the great Lorenzo's there was no coterie or school which deliberately built, carved, or painted, wrote or acted, as they often do nowadays, in the manner of centuries gone by or of lands remote. There was no Assyrian or Egyptian art at Athens, as there is Greek and Russian, Chinese and Hindu art in New York. There was a prevailing style — there was, with personal variations, only one style, indeed, as in clothes, and speech, and manners. And there being many artists, not few, just as today in a family where there is one good musician there is a general appreciation of musical technique, so there would be an artistic spirit pervading the town. But the main thing is that this highly developed and mobile social organism, with an open-air life, with no newspapers and few books, but constantly in converse, and daily in contact with the art in question, steeped in its atmosphere and imbued from childhood with its traditions, would in reacting to it be fairly spontaneous and at one. People had seen so many a fair statue finished or in the making, had listened to so many a good speech in the agora or at the theater, and had heard so often intelligent approval or disapproval of these, that they responded to beauty in art almost as promptly and instinctively as they did to it in life and conduct. Those not related in blood were so in thought and customs; and in agora or theater they laughed, wept, or hissed as they should do, together. And the result was that seldom the artists in their innovations went so far as to offend. They too responded. They knew the public as well as the public knew them, and were exquisitely aware what they could really do, how far they might go. And that is the secret of all art, particularly in drama and oratory, though in the modern world well-nigh forgotten.

Indeed, so far was the art in these cities a means of expression, without need of interpreter, that we may fairly consider it as a language, between artist and public. It uttered his and their notions and emotions, and they understood it and delighted in it. In all cases — not only drama and lyric but sculpture and architecture in Athens, sculpture and painting in Florence, the drama in London — it was an art that had developed through generations. In all cases it had begun very simply and humbly; but if in York or London, for instance, any dramatist knew better, and scorned to write so simple a thing as a mystery, morality, or interlude, he wrote nothing at all. Nowadays these beginnings, whether in painting or sculpture, whether in character, situation, or style, often seem to us fairly childish. In our theater the tragedy of *Cambyses* would bring laughter, the comedy of *Thersites*, if anything, tears. "This is the silliest stuff," whispers Queen Hippolyta at such a performance, "that ever I heard." Yet, allowing for the burlesque, Bottom's and Peter Quince's was the style that had prevailed twenty years before. Then it was as good as the dramatist could give and the audience could take; now it was no longer a gift for either. Comic or tragic, the art steadily progressed. The story on the stage became more compact and unified, casting out of itself bit by bit the merely descriptive and narrative elements, the static or successive elements, and employing more of action and compression, of suggestion and contrast. Yet at any one time in the development, the drama, like the audience, was pretty much the same. Good or poor, it had one technique, spoke the same tongue. Lyly, Peele, and Greene, who were contemporaneous, use pretty much the same conventions, devices, or accepted simplifications; and none of them makes much more of a demand upon the intelligence or attention of the audience than the others. Marlowe, in his first play, *Tamburlaine,* does not either. But presently, in *Edward II,* he does, and the pace is accelerated. The interesting thing, thereupon, is how in the last decade of the sixteenth century and the first of the seventeenth the old plays had to be rewritten.

Company and audience together demanded it. The medium — the technique — was already antiquated. Shakespeare rewrote old play after old play: the *Merchant of Venice, Hamlet,* the *Taming of the Shrew,* and most of the English histories are examples which are certain. Nothing so clearly shows that playwright, players, and public had moved forward together, hand in hand, soul with soul. The story of Kyd's *Hamlet,* like that of his *Spanish Tragedy,* was a good story, which company and audience would not willingly lose. But the style was bombastic, the verse was crude; the serious situations were too violent and improbable, the comic too flat and feeble; and the characters were often ferocious or silly, lacking in subtlety and grace. Neither play was more than a dozen years old, both had been prodigiously popular, but they must now be recast. They were then more antiquated than are *Volpone* and Shakespeare's *Hamlet,* after four centuries, today. Some of the histories the poet rewrote were more recent still. In the last century the English drama, under the touch of Messrs. Jones and Pinero, arose from its ashes, and yet *The Second Mrs. Tanqueray* and *Mrs. Dane's Defence* are not nowadays rewritten before a revival. For the English drama did not begin then all over, at the bottom of the ladder, as in such plays as *Cambyses* and *Thersites* it had done, though Plautus and Seneca were at hand. It began pretty much where the drama stood in Paris at that moment. It was the heir of the ages. But the audience itself was not. The English-speaking dramatic public, long aloof from the theater, was not standing on that level, and therefore it has not followed the drama as it developed since. It has hung helplessly behind at the music-hall or pantomime, vaudeville or movie, at football and baseball. It has been fain, if not to feed its imagination, at least to assuage and purge its passions, in the stadium. The worst of it is that drama, beginning aloof from the public, has suffered all along for lack of encouragement and sympathy, not from the purse only but from the spirit.

That is what both dramatist and company now require, not criticism or propaganda. They need to see and to feel the emotional effect, happy or unhappy, on the spot. They need — an audience. Instruction in the arts of acting and playmaking at school may do something: fortunately, the pupils in the end do not all act or write. But much that is accomplished by that means is neutralized by the movies. And a drama that must be made to suit the dregs of the population, ten million of them at a stroke, can never develop far. The camera knows not its audience. Drama — it is but the playwright speaking and the audience responding, and it can develop only as the intercourse happily proceeds. Today even the legitimate drama is, like the movies, all eyes and no ears, and, in this bad one-sided sense, universal, fashioned for any theater in London or New York and then for the road, for any audience whatever, and therefore, in the good sense, for none. In failure it is divorced and barren, in success it is base and promiscuous, but in either event the felicitous and fertile relation is lacking. Yet of late history has repeated itself. In Dublin a few playwrights writing for one company and one theater, and in immediate contact with it, have revived something of the Elizabethan conditions. Both company and audience they have humbly and patiently trained and led. Something the same has since then been done in Manchester and other English towns, and at the Old Vic in London; and there have been some scattered, sporadic efforts in America.

If, then, history teaches us anything, drama, like the other arts, is not a matter of individual and arbitrary invention, on the one hand, or of mass-production and mechanism, on the other. It is not individual but communal, and yet not national or cosmopolitan (in the movie or any other style) but particular and local. Not that it deals with local interests or in dialect, but only as drama learns deeply to touch and delight one set of people will it do something the same to any. Football has the audience. Like the movies, it is national and international. Like the movies, it is mechanized, with its manipulated emotions, its orchestrated outcries and syncopated cheering. But football is a social function, not an art. The movie is a sort of art but not a social function. Drama must be, as it has always been, both the one thing and the other.

That is, drama worthy of the name. When it isn't both the one thing and the other — and it very frequently isn't — drama falls into intellectual and moral degradation, on the one hand, or into preciosity, on the other. When it was delighted in by the people as a whole, as by the Athenians in the great age, and by the Parisians in the time of Corneille and Molière, and by the Londoners in the time of Marlowe and Shakespeare, there was no danger of either evil. But when the respectable or the common people turned away, because of indecency or because of too great ingenuity, the indecency or ingenuity naturally increased. The gap between the theater and the people widened, as greater effort was exerted to attract the special clientèle.

Such is the condition of affairs today, as in the reign of the first Stuarts and at the Restoration. Novelty and sensation, whether in morals or in method, take the place of a balanced interest. Low-class plays depend on violent and prurient situations and settings, on gross, profane, or grotesquely exaggerated speech. High-class plays depend on ingeniously novel situations, style, and settings — cubistic, futuristic, expressionistic, what not? — or present the text and the stage methods, now of Russia or Japan, now of the present, the Renaissance, or the Middle Age. The high-class plays are to their clientèle often interesting, but they leave it emotionally cold. They do not last. The low-class plays are to their clientèle interesting, too, but they leave it emotionally or sensuously jaded. And they last but only too long. In either case it is for both producer and spectator expensive, speculative; and for both, the low-class theater is by long odds the safest bet. Removed from the hearts and thoughts of the people, as all the drama is, this is nearer at least to their bodies. And when not a social function, drama justifies all that the Puritans can say of it, and becomes a social disorder.

Though this may be truth, it is not the whole truth. Culture counts; the difference between the most cultivated and the least cultivated is greater now than in the day of Shakespeare and Sophocles; the public itself is far larger; and it is more difficult now than then to gather it together, all with one accord. Nowadays there must perhaps be theaters for high-brows and for low-brows, for the esthetic and for the average man. There must perhaps be even a theater cosmopolitan in range, which embraces all styles, all techniques; and one where the extremest frenzy of originality is given rein and scope. Even so our observations seem to hold good. Such more specialized forms of drama will flourish only so long as they speak a language understood by the particular public or coterie. They each must have their own public, indeed, upon which they can depend, at a particular theater or theaters. This is the case in London, Paris, and Berlin, as less commonly in New York. Company and audience know better then what they can expect. The foreign and exotic, the ingenious and exquisite, is offered to the appropriately enlightened public alone. But if it is to hold and keep that public it must really strike home, be human, fairly popular. That is true of all art, but particularly of the drama. At best an audience at a play can never be counted on as at a concert or opera; to theaters of every sort will always come the average man, ignorant of technique, expecting entertainment.

And he must be provided. Drama cannot be for the actors and dramatists, as painting can be for the painters, music for the musicians. And though never again it will return to the stadium and the solidarity of the Greek spirit, its course, for its health, must needs be more than at present is the case in that direction.

VI

Spenser

Spenser is the high priest of English romanticism. Not only was he the leader of the romantic spirit in the Elizabethan Age, but he afterwards presided over what we call the Romantic Revival. Shakespeare and Milton were the names then held most in reverence, but the spirit abroad was Spenser's. Without him, of course, there would have been a revival, but one wonders if it would have been quite the same. All the leaders and chief personalities felt in some way his impress, came at some time under his spell — Thomson and Shenstone, the Wartons and Chatterton, Gray and Collins, Wordsworth and Coleridge, Byron and Shelley; and towards the end of the period his presence towered still higher, and benignly overshadowed Leigh Hunt and Keats. The poets' poet Lamb called him, Hazlitt said he was of all poets the most poetical, and perhaps no English singer has taught so many. The chief critics, also, of the romantic age analyzed his qualities and celebrated his merits — not only Lamb, Hazlitt, and Hunt, but the Wartons and Coleridge.

NOTE. In part this essay was delivered as a public lecture at Vassar in January, 1927. I have not undertaken to remove certain direct and intimate touches, and *argumenta ad feminam*, which were suggested by the occasion.

What is romanticism, what do we mean by this over-used, ill-used word? Primarily we mean what has to do with chivalry, a life devoted to love and glory, with adventures and tourneys, and the showy fairy-tale life of knights and ladies. That we find in Spenser. Sometimes we mean what has to do with romance (a kindred word, with a kindred meaning), a life high-uplifted above the practical and humdrum, and devoted to a dreamy or rapturous love, even though no knights and ladies may be there. And that we find in Spenser. Sometimes we mean the subtle and mysterious aspects of the poetic imagination, whereby more is meant than meets the ear, as in Wordsworth's or Shelley's poetry of nature, or in the supernatural or legendary as touched to new life by Coleridge in the *Ancient Mariner* and *Christabel*, or by Keats in *La Belle Dame Sans Merci*. And that we find in Spenser too, though it is, of course, not quite like theirs — how like and how different I hope before the end to show.

Now behind all these meanings — the more literal, the more spiritual, and that which is rather esthetic — there lurks a background of the medieval. The Romantic Revival was a medieval revival; and the spirit of romance was born not in the Middle Ages, indeed, but under their influence. Yet Spenser is not medieval but of the Renaissance; and the Renaissance, as we ordinarily think of it, turned its back on the Middle Ages and faced the world, directly or in the mirror of ancient art.

2

What then is the Renaissance? You may sometime have seen Leonardo da Vinci's St. John the Baptist. He is a beautiful young man, bowing before the little Saviour with a bewitching smile, with a cross in his hand and some raiment of camel's hair about him, but looking as if he had fed not on locusts at all but only on the wild honey. Or, on the other hand, you may have seen Botticelli's Venus, newly arisen out of the sea, the goddess of love and laughter, but here with the wistful look in her face of Botticelli's Madonnas, a goddess (the ancients had none) of sorrow and tears. Here, and there, is the Renaissance — the Middle Ages discovering and entering into the classical world, Christianity and paganism, holiness and happiness, meeting and mingled, and the spirit reluctantly or unreluctantly reunited with the flesh.

To be more explicit, the Renaissance also (as the word of course signifies) is a revival — of learning, of the arts, above all of interest and delight in the world as a whole. The Middle Ages lay under the shadow of the Church, and though men there often contrived to take their pleasure it was not with the best of consciences. And they were ignorant, hardly knowing how to take it; the treasures of antiquity were as yet closed to them, and the arts they practiced were traditional and simple. Some of the fine art was very noble — for instance, the poetry of Dante and Chaucer, the architecture of France, the painting of Italy. But medieval literature, even the best of it in some measure, and the less good in greater measure, suffered for the lack of certain qualities now to be introduced through an acquaintance with the classics. The ancients were distinguished by an appreciation of the principle of beauty and harmony. In ethics and conduct they looked to the ideal of balance, of the golden mean; in art they did the same. In the best period they did not despise the senses; neither did they worship them. They loved life but they loved their ideals too. They were neither ascetics on the one hand nor debauchees on the other. In the Middle Ages men were. But now it was a new and freer life that men were entering, the old having gone stale; it was a new and freer art that men were beginning to practice, the old having become almost meaningless.

In their delight in the new, the whole-hearted children of the Renaissance, like Ariosto, Spenser's master, even turned, as Spenser did not, ironically and cynically against the old. In the *Or-*

lando Furioso Ariosto was a poet of chivalry before him, but half in sport. The high-flown sentiments and extravagant adventures are there, and all is very gay and gallant, but his knights and ladies are at heart almost satyrs and nymphs, courtiers and courtesans; and their romance is but skin-deep. His knights are to Spenser's somewhat as are the gallants of Charles II's time to Sidney and Raleigh. And in part, though, as we shall see, not wholly, the difference between the two poets is owing to the English temper as compared with the Italian, to Spenser's character as compared with Ariosto's, and to the fact that though the latter comes more than two generations earlier than the former he belongs to the late Renaissance, Spenser to the early. For in that movement England was more than a century behind.

3

Spenser looks back reverently to the Middle Ages but is certainly of the Renaissance. Still young in heart, with the bloom on his soul, and his pure romantic dream untroubled, he entered into the new world and the spirit of classical poetry. And he did it with a sprightly and delicate delight. He knew the classics as no English poet had known them before him; and in his verse he was closer than any had ever been to their spirit. He had a finer taste than his predecessors and many of his successors. He knew the Greeks, whereas even many of his contemporary Elizabethans knew them only in Latin; and he knew some of the Greek tragic poets, who to Shakespeare and his fellows seem in any form to have been strangers. He seems to have preferred Virgil to Ovid, as few Elizabethans, including Shakespeare, had learned to do; and Plato and the Platonic doctrines were his particular joy and enthusiasm. Indeed, Spenser is the one great poet of the early Elizabethan Age to drink deep of the cup of classical literature and also feel the new life tingling in his veins.

The two then went well together, though they do not today. For

us the reading of classical literature does not any longer mean the
discovery of life itself. It meant that to Italian painters like Botticelli and Leonardo, as well as to the poets of Europe. It opened
men's eyes, freed them from their medieval fears and superstitions,
revealed reality and its beauty. For instance, men now began to
draw, paint, sculpture, or poetically describe the nude — a thing
which men had not done for a thousand years. The fact may be
taken as typical. Men were discovering the very world, the world
about them — the thrill of that discovery is the Renaissance — and
what is the discovery of the moons of Jupiter, or of the American
Continent, to that?

But Spenser was not a classicist, any more than he was a realist,
though he came in contact with reality. Few in the Renaissance
were. Few then were so classical as Milton was to be. And the
special and peculiar charm of the early Renaissance is the medieval
spirit in a classical garb. Or without a garb, perhaps we should say.
Botticelli's Venus with the soul and face of a Madonna, stands
there like the Greek goddess that she is, unclad. Just so Spenser
blends elements strangely incongruous — Christian and pagan history, Christian and pagan mythology, saints and satyrs. In the
Fairy Queen, the lady Una, who represents the Church, lives for
a time with the satyrs, at her ease. Even at school you read Browning's *The Bishop Orders his Tomb in St. Praxed's*. There is the
Renaissance, though the late Renaissance, materialistic and cor-
rupt as Spenser was not, but not yet cynical or mocking. It is thus
the dying Bishop's tomb is to be sculptured, if his sons will heed
him in his pleading: Give me, he says,

> Those Pans and Nymphs ye wot of, and perchance
> Some tripod, thyrsus, with a vase or so,
> The Saviour at his sermon on the mount,
> St. Praxed in a glory, and one Pan
> Ready to twitch the Nymph's last garment off, —
> And Moses with the tables —

There's a mixture for you, from a bishop's deathbed at that! So the tomb in which Luini, Leonardo's contemporary, in the picture now at the Brera, has the angels place the corpse of Saint Catherine, is sculptured over with Tritons and Nereids.

And much in Spenser is, whether consciously or unconsciously, deliberately or inadvertently, old-fashioned and medieval enough. There is almost no allegory in the classics, and Spenser abounds in allegory. And, besides, the *Fairy Queen* is a tale of chivalry, and the vocabulary is intentionally archaic. Chivalry and feudalism are dead and gone, and quite properly Spenser puts a medieval flavor into his language as he treats of them. Really, he is like Sir Walter Scott in his poems and novels, Coleridge in the *Ancient Mariner,* or the Preraphaelite Morris and Rossetti, as he turns from the present to the past. He takes to the poetic beauty of a period now gone by. But though he returns to it, like them he is not of it; there's the blue haze of distance upon it, or the ivy and the mellow patina of time. It is romantic not much more because it is of chivalry than because it is unreal and remote. Like the Romantic poets and the Preraphaelites, he relishes old words like *eftsoones* and *whilom, wight* for *man* or *person, eke* for *also,* and *paynim* for *pagan.* Like Scott, from afar, he delights in battle and all the paraphernalia and bravery of battle. "Fair shields, gay steeds, bright arms be my delight," cries his Sir Guyon. And like Keats he dreams of the loves of knights and ladies, their courtesy and gallantry. To him these things were still more picturesque and precious than to Chaucer simply because he had read of them rather than seen them — read of them in Chaucer himself, in romances like *Sir Gawain and the Green Knight,* or in Malory. He does not invoke the muse, it is worth noting, in the regular style of Homer, Virgil, and Milton, and beseech her to sing, but prays her to vouchsafe to him the yellow rolls of manuscript. "Lay forth out of thine everlasting scryne, The antique rolles which there lye hidden still, Of Faerie knights and fairest Tanaquill." Chatterton, Scott, or Keats might have said the same.

Indeed, despite superficial appearances, and the difference between him and Ariosto, Spenser's deepest debt, perhaps, was to the classics and the Italians and to the new spirit in the world about him. What made him romantic was not the medieval life which he knew of but his attitude toward it, the glamour of the past, the esthetic delight of the poet himself. There is, as Professor Mackail has noticed, a romantic spirit in Theocritus and also in Virgil, though with no age of knighthood behind them; they too look to the past with a tender regret; and while this attitude of theirs as such may never have affected Spenser at all, the exquisiteness of the ancients and the Italians did. And exquisiteness, a delight in beauty and in emotions somewhat for their own sake, and a regard for detail, are, as later we shall see more clearly, at the bottom of the romantic spirit. Before, then, we attempt to define Spenser's romanticism and to distinguish it from Milton's and our own, it is well to consider Spenser's indebtedness further, and not only the nature of his art in general but those qualities of it which are not specifically or necessarily romantic at all.

4

To the ancients and the Italians Spenser and others like him in the Renaissance must have owed something of their extraordinary exquisiteness and refinement, their delight in emotions and the expression of them for their own sake, since these were little known in England before that day. Such things are slow in developing of themselves, and come, like Theocritus and Virgil, towards the end of a poetic movement. The Italianate English poets ripened quickly, profiting by these high examples. And there is something precocious and premature, mellow and overripe about Sidney and Spenser, as not about Shakespeare, who was comparatively untouched. In them the love of beauty and splendor, like that of fame, characteristic of the Renaissance, is a more all-engrossing passion. Spenser feels them both, and both were either inspired or fostered in him by classical literature. He was profoundly affected, as I have said, by the doctrine of love and beauty in Plato; but he delighted in physical beauty as well as the ideal, inspired by classical and Italian literature again. Love of beauty (with hatred of ugliness, its counterpart) is the motive which animates his poem. Love of beauty, of course, needs no instilling or fostering, but taste and exquisiteness do. The *Fairy Queen* is an allegorical moral poem, but it is a Palace of Pleasure, a Paradise of Dainty Devices. It is a treasure-house of lovely descriptions of lovely things — processions and pageants, garments and trappings, landscapes and gardens, trees and flowers, birds and animals, but, above all, women and girls. Spenser is like Benozzo Gozzoli in the Campo Santo at Pisa and the Riccardi Palace at Florence, delighting in palaces and processions, birds and beasts; and like the Venetians, reveling in the glory of the nude. And that the delight in the beauty of these things may be perfect and complete, they are all spirited away into the past, to a land of dreams.

5

His delight in the physical beauty of women is exquisite but eager, sensuous but sane. Classical and Italian influence had opened his eyes to the beauty of the body, and had given him the courage, and shown him the way, to express it. Few things in the *Fairy Queen* are so delightful as the figures of ladies, maidens, and nymphs that go glancing through its changing vistas. Nowhere is the play of his fancy happier, or the cadence of his verse tenderer, than here. I well remember as a boy my delight at coming upon this description of Belphœbe:

> Upon her eyelids many graces sate,
> Under the shadow of her even browes.

Such a gracious shadow there is under the brows of the Praxitelean
Aphrodites, which Spenser never saw; both he and Praxiteles saw
it where we all may see it today for ourselves. "The beauty of
women," as Mr. de Selincourt observes, "again and again suggests
to him imaginative effects of light and shade." The damsels who
dance before the knight in Acrasia's Bower —

> every of them strove, with most delights,
> Him to aggrate, and greatest pleasures shew;
> Some framd faire lookes, glancing like evening lights,
> Others sweet words, dropping like honny dew.

They "used their eyes," as women will. And the eyes, lips, and
hair of women play a great part in Spenser, as in Dante, but more
richly and sensuously, as in our Preraphaelites or in the fancy and
memory of any lover. Britomart, again, the disguised maiden
warrior, when she unlaces her helmet, and lets her golden hair fall
down to her heels, springing a surprise upon the natives, a *coup
de théâtre*, reminds him of the northern lights:

> Like as the shining skie in summers night,
> What time the dayes with scorching heat abound,
> Is creasted all with lines of firie light,
> That it prodigious seemes in common peoples sight.

And even of Acrasia, the queen of voluptuous pleasure, he says,
that

> her faire eyes, sweet smyling in delight,
> Moystened their firie beames, with which she thrild
> Fraile hearts, yet quenched not; like starry light
> Which, sparkling on the silent waves, does seeme more bright.

With which she thrild fraile hearts yet quenched not — the sentiment and style (before the time) of *Epipsychidion*; and that figure
to picture the eye of a woman in love George Meredith does not
disdain to use in the great farewell scene of *Richard Feverel*. And
all three figures — this one, that of the evening lights, and that of
the Aurora — show how sensitively his imagination responded to

the most intangible and ethereal beauty, natural or human, that there is in the world.

Such exquisiteness and audacity of expression seem classical or Italian; the tenderness and deep spirit of chivalry seem rather English, though the racial line cannot be clearly drawn. It is all of the Renaissance, and is as romantic as heart could desire. The spirit of chivalry, indeed, is medieval, for he follows the example of the old romances, and presents every knight as the servant of a lady, and the chief source of virtue in the poem as woman's love; but the Renaissance had refined upon the idea, Spenser joining with it. If the love of money is the root of all evil, the love of woman, Spenser and Sidney together would have said, is the root of all bliss; and the *Fairy Queen*, though a code of conduct, is a book of gallantry throughout. For the poet the path of virtue is the service of the fair; and even the pursuit of wisdom is not more arduous. His hero is taught by some allegorical character, and this is oftenest a fair woman, who takes him aside, with his hand in hers. Instruction in Spenser, and in medieval allegory generally, is as it used to be (and probably still is) in the Sunday School — males are not taught by males. Spenser himself must have been as fine a gentleman as ever lived. Greater geniuses like Chaucer and Shakespeare are sometimes coarse and low, but Spenser, though for the purposes of allegory sometimes coarse, is never low. No one is sweeter or more tender. He was the friend of the first gentlemen of the day, Sidney and Raleigh, and the purpose of his poem as he described it in his letter to Raleigh was to fashion a gentleman or noble person in virtuous and gentle discipline. And according to Spenser as well as the courtesy-books of the time the source of virtue was love — love for friend or woman. Gentlemen then frequented the court, and as Spenser himself says of the court of Elizabeth,

love most aboundeth there,
For all the walls and windows there are writ

> All full of love, and love, and love, my deare,
> And all their talk and studee is of it.

That is, the windows were inscribed with love-sonnets, cut with the lover's own diamond, as is the glass, I notice, in the windows of some college fraternities. Is that all of the old-time court life that lives on in college? At court the study of love and the study of virtue were one — no wonder we call those the good old times.

Even at college, however, the court of Elizabeth would seem today to be a little absurd. As at that of Urbino, where dwelt Castiglione, author of the great book of courtesy, every courtier was not only a lover but must needs be in love with the lady on the throne. Thus love of woman becomes love of country; and in the *Fairy Queen* it is well-nigh life itself. Not only is almost every man and woman, good or bad, a lover; but he lives to love or to fight, and fights even for love. How romantic — all love and sport, all play and no work, as at college again! But for that matter it is almost so in Shakespeare, and Shakespeare is not tiresome or silly. As in Shakespeare, all high-born women in the *Fairy Queen* are beautiful, just as all high-born men can ride,[1] fight, and make love — it is a romantic world. And as in Shakespeare, though more than in him, but not more than in Dante, love conquers all, and even when in error, lovers are liberally indulged. Dante is almost swept away from his moral moorings by his own tale of Francesca; and Spenser, while Sir Guyon is destroying Acrasia's Bower, makes her and her maidens touch him so nearly that the reader wonders how he can bring himself to do it.

> And in amours the passing hours to spend!

The sweetness of the verse betrays him — Spenser would have liked so to spend them himself. Chastity is represented by Britomart, a lady, armed like Athena, but cherishing a passion.

---

[1] As feates of armes, and love to entertaine,
But chiefly skill to ride, seemes a science
Proper to gentle bloud. II, iv, I.

> A harder lesson, to learne Continence
> In joyous pleasure than in grievous paine,

says the poet, contradicting Aristotle, in the true spirit of romance. And the one lesson in the House of Holiness that the Red-Cross Knight finds "too too hard for living clay" is to abandon his romantic career:

> But deeds of arms must I at last be faine,
> And ladies love to leave, so dearly bought?

But it is not required of him.

Yet Spenser was not infatuated or obsessed. Like most romantic persons, he was conservative; and like most romantic men, he wanted a woman to be ladylike rather than womanly — Una and Britomart when they are not quite ladylike are only the *more* romantic — even as romantic women want a man to be gentlemanly rather than manly. He believed in what in America is no longer believed in and what perhaps you, in these latter days, have never even heard of — women keeping to their sphere. Those who don't keep to it he puts in hell, to recompense them for the hell they have made of heaven:

> Amongst these mighty men were wemen mixed,
> Proud wemen, vaine, forgetfull of their yoke:
> The bold Semiramis . . .

but the catalogue I spare you. And some of his heroes are shrewdly aware of women's wiles —

> And all the wyles of wemen's wits know
> passing well, —

though one has a rather naïve way of warding them off:

> But he was wise and wary of her will,
> And ever held his hand upon his hart.

Concealing, he reveals. He is simpler than a farmer at a fair, with his hand clutched in his pocket. But against their wiles what but simplicity ever availed? He is not a farmer.

6

It is as a descriptive, picturesque, and (in the good sense of the word) sentimental poet that Spenser is chiefly remembered, as a romantic poet might well be. He is too descriptive, and diffuse, and tangled, to tell a story so well as Ariosto; and though we know that he wrote nine comedies, now lost, we wonder whether they were very comic or dramatic. Yet even in his epic he is at times dramatic, and in two respects — the creation of character and the full and round realization of great moments. Romantically enough, his women are his best-drawn characters, for in them allegory less interferes, and emotion and sentiment prevail.

To one who consumes only the luscious and highly-seasoned nutriment of the modern novel, Spenser's good women may seem thin and ghostly. And indeed there is some moonshine about them. What at times interests us most in Una is Spenser's exquisite tenderness and enthusiasm for her, rather than the lady herself. It is the worshipper as much as the idol that wins our hearts. How the verse quivers in the first three stanzas of the third canto, about her desertion! Yet even here there is characterization; the worshipper reflects the image of the worshipped. But once in Una's own words there is more of a heart-throb — the word tastes ill today! — than anywhere else in Spenser. When the Lion spares her and follows at her heels like a Newfoundland dog, she thinks of her knight who has left her.

> But he, my Lyon, and my noble Lord,
> How does he find in cruell hart to hate
> Her that him lov'd, and ever most ador'd,
> As the God of my life? why hath he me abhord?

The last is one of Spenser's most admired lines; but it is not only exquisite meter but drama as well. We hear the very cry of a sweet but thwarted affection, of love wondering that it can fail of love — in a world like this!

Her knight had left her, with medieval or (perhaps) American abruptness, at daybreak; but she instinctively feels that only a misunderstanding can be the cause, and with a romantic unmaidenliness follows on her palfrey in pursuit. She afterwards tells Prince Arthur, her champion, of her heart's mischance —

> How I him loved, and love with all my might,
> So thought I eke of him, and think I thought aright.

Exquisitely doubtful faith — a faith in her own faith, a hope against hope, though with fear and trembling! And when Arthur delivers her knight from thraldom, she thanks him and prays heaven to repay him, like one who herself belongs there. Yet even in that moment she remembers Duessa, who had led her knight astray. "Don't let her escape," she cries, like a woman; she must be unmasked or there will be trouble again! But for her knight, when she sees him, she has, as one critic has noticed, no reproaches save for wronging himself. Arthur then tells them his own story — the secret of his devotion to the Fairy Queen. And when he has ended Una bursts out in sympathetic exultation, though as she recalls her own experience she sinks into a sigh:

> O happy Queene of faeries,[2] that hast found,
> Mongst many, one that with his prowesse may
> Defend thine honour, and thy foes confound:
> True loves are often sown, but seldom grow on
>   ground.

As one who knows the mingled sweetness and bitterness of love, with almost no stain of experience, Una is dear to the poets — her profile is so delicately drawn that only a painter can praise it. Two, says Wordsworth in a sonnet —

> Two shall be named pre-eminently dear, —
> The gentle lady married to the Moor;
> And heavenly Una with her milk-white lamb.

---

[2] Spenser is writing before the *Midsummer Night's Dream*, under the influence of the older tradition; and the word means nothing dainty or diminutive.

7

A bolder and more substantial character is Britomart, the maiden disguised as a knight, who unhorses doughty young warriors with her spear, and then takes their breath away yet a second time by letting her hair down; and who, like Shakespeare's Rosalind and Viola, finds a natural satisfaction in the feminine interest excited by her fair face and manly form. Yet, like both these ladies, she has a tender secret, and thinks ever of a fair visage written in her heart.

Una's tenderness is no secret at all; and between Spenser's heroines there is a contrast, though since they are in different books, it is not made dramatically effective. Una is a palpitating, disembodied spirit, floating over the earth; Britomart treads it like a queen. Una is love forlorn; Britomart is love questant, triumphant. Both are romantically conceived: they disobey the dictates of propriety, in beautiful obedience to the dictates of their hearts. But Una has no pride or reserve, being so pellucidly innocent and gentle that she has need of none. Britomart, sufficiently infringing upon the requirements of decorum in playing the part of a man while she is a man-hunter, keeps her secret with all virginal diligence. She has seen Sir Arthegall only in a magic glass, through a telescope, so to speak, and, ten to one, is never to see him otherwise. Only after a struggle has she yielded her secret to her nurse. And now, on her quest, she finds relief in drawing her companion out — pretending to have a grievance against Sir Arthegall, though she regrets her words even as she speaks them. The answer, so contrary, makes her inly wondrous glad; but still she feigns, and leads him on to say more and more, letting it all sink into her heart. And as she proceeds in solitude, she turns over in her mind what she has heard, forlornly fancying what her beloved is like, whom she has scarcely seen. She communes with Nature; sympathizes with melancholy folk, so melancholy herself; and roams, and seeks, and fights, and at last, in the midst of a combat, finds. Their beavers fall, their faces are revealed. "He of his wonder makes religion." And she, once she has heard the name of Arthegall,

> Her hart did leape and all her hart-strings tremble,

as in the verse it does. But still she holds her love at bay. Her nurse, letting the secret out, calls them lovers —

> Thereat full inly blushèd Britomart.

Nevertheless she keeps him in awe of her until he duly woos her, for she must needs make to her pride and to decorum considerable amends.

8

Spenser is preëminently the poet of what in the eighteenth century was called "the tender," as well as of what we mean by the word today. It appears in his characterization — it appears above all in his own personal comments. When Britomart's nurse finally gets the secret from her, she soothes and comforts her and puts her to sleep:

> And the old woman carefully displayd
> The clothes about her round with busie ayd;
> So that at last a little creeping sleepe
> Surpris'd her sense: she therewith well apayd
> The drunken lampe downe in the oyle did steepe,
> And set her by to watch, and set her by to weepe.

As Mr. de Selincourt remarks, "the stanza that closes the midnight scene between them would be hard to surpass in its homeliness, its dramatic truth of detail, and its climax of tenderness." And in all poetry there is no tenderness for a woman's deepest feelings more intimate and delicate than Spenser's. When Britomart, in her travels, hears her knight praised by another and learns that he is "worthy of her secret devotion,"

> The loving mother, that nine monethes did beare,
> In the deare closet of her painefull side,

> Her tender babe, it seeing safe appeare,
> Doth not so much rejoyce as she rejoyced theare.

The childless Matilda, when she receives the baby which Sir
Calepine has rescued from a bear —

> She gladly did of that same babe accept,
> As of her owne by liverey and seisin,
> And having over it a little wept,
> She bore it thence, and ever as her owne it kept.

And these are not the only places where Spenser speaks tenderly
and reverently of childbirth, and the woman's relation to her
child. Such matters to him are sacred, and his touch is as soft and
light as the mother's hand. "And having over it a little wept" —
because it has no mother, because she has no child.

9

This has to do with character, but by way of description. The
poet speaks also for himself, and generally he has no notion, as we
have seen already with regard to Una, of keeping in the background. He is not aloof, objective, like a modern, as the poets of
the Revival are not. He is like the medieval romancers, like
Chaucer and the balladists, and praises the hero or heroine and
curses the villain.

> An ill death may he dee,

is the standing phrase in the ballads. So Spenser curses out Archi-
mago, as he speaks of the evil spirits,

> Fluttering about his ever-damnèd head.

And that too has a distant charm today. But he is a poet of tenderness and wonder rather than of vituperation, and these are his
native gift, his particular vein. They are romantic emotions —
the modern romantic poets abound in them — but in Spenser they
are more spontaneous and instinctive. He is wide-eyed as a child,
soft-hearted as a girl. Questions, exclamations, apostrophes are his

natural and congenial utterance, and half of his wonder and tenderness is in the movement of his verse. He exclaims — and the
lines "with tears" are steeped — as he considers the plight of
Una:

> To think how she, through guilefull handeling,
> Though true as touch, though daughter of a king,
> Though faire as ever living wight was faire,
> Though nor in word nor deede ill meriting,
> Is from her knight divorced in despaire
> And her due loves derived to that vile witches share.

When he considers the case of his hero, Sir Guyon, who has been
rescued, he is moved to question — but in grateful admiration —
God's care for men;

> And is there care in heaven? and is there love
> In heavenly spirits to these creatures bace,
> That may compassion of their evils move?

There is, through the ministering angels:

> How oft do they their silver bowers leave
> To come to succour us that succour want!
> How oft do they with golden pinions cleave
> The flitting skyes, like flying Pursuivant
>
> .   .   .   .
>
> O Why should heavenly God to men have such regard?

Or as he puts it in another line, not an exclamation nor a question
either, but as buoyant and uplifted with wonder as if it were:

> Providence heavenly passeth living thought.

There is something angelical about Spenser; he, if any one, had
drunk the milk of Paradise. Likewise, his characters beautifully
wear their hearts upon their sleeves, or, as in a sacred picture,
beating visibly through their bosoms — Una, as we have seen, telling her story to Prince Arthur, or he returning the confidence with
his own:

> Ah Love, lay downe thy bow, the whiles I may respire!

In Spenser the golden years return, ere love must needs sigh in secret, and, for speech, but murmur.

10

So sweet and dreamy, descriptive and lyrical a poet might well be quite lacking in humor or dramatic power; but he is too great for that. He has situations, contrasts dramatic and even comic, in his fairyland. One is when the Red-Cross Knight, in combat with the Paynim for the shield as a prize, reels for a moment, and Duessa, his companion, betting on the wrong horse, precipitately throws off the mask and casts in her lot with his foe:

> and lowd to him gan call
> The false Duessa, Thine the shield, and I, and all.

But her knight, not having heard her, in the end prevails, and then is brought home to bed and medical attentions. And there, beside him,

> . . . all the while Duessa wept full bitterly;

like Becky Sharp on a notable occasion — with reason enough, though not that reason which does appear.

This situation, however, is not made so much of, the contrast is not so clear-cut, as in the following case. Her nurse, Glauce, brings Britomart to Merlin for counsel what to do for her, in love with a man whom she does not know, and worse, knows not how to find, and worst, has never seen. Merlin at once prophesies her union with him, though, lost in his prophetic rapture, he dwells on their glorious progeny, which is to ascend the English throne. He expatiates, thinking of the nation. Like a man he talks politics — like a philosopher, or dame Nature herself, he is careful only of the type, not the single life. But Glauce breaks out — breaks in upon him — in her affectionate distress:

> But read (said Glauce), thou Magitian,
> What meanes shall she out seeke, or what wayes take?
> How shall she know, how shall she find the man?

That's the question — the question of almost any girl's life and her guardian's; and after that I wonder whether the nine comedies were not an irremediable loss. It is such a contrast as in Sir Arthur Quiller-Couch's story of the clergyman who had been apprised of his designation to be a bishop. His daughter is writing about it to her school friend. "Even now," she says, "he is in the library seeking guidance." "Dear mama," she adds, "is upstairs packing." *She* is not waiting for the word of the Lord, lost in the future; nor is her daughter. That's the difference, says Sir Arthur, between Macbeth and Lady Macbeth after the murder, the man lost in his emotions and imagination, the woman, compact and practical, thinking only of business, the affair in hand. It is a difference that reappears in the relation of Milton's Adam and Eve.[3]

Another dramatic moment in Spenser is an utterance of Sir Satyrane's, and it is also one of the most truly romantic, I think, in the world. This noble son of nature, born in the woodland, of a satyr and a Christian mother, has rescued Una from one of her numerous diurnal perils and is now escorting her. Already he is devoted to her, as he could not help but be. Meeting an old pilgrim, they inquire of him concerning the Red-Cross Knight. He was slain, says the pilgrim, with Paynim knife. Una cannot believe it, of one so invincible; but the deceiver reasserts it. Then Satyrane bursts out —

> Where is (said Satyrane) that Paynims sonne
> That him of life, and us of joy hath reft?

Not "us both" — that would have been a touch less rare — and through love they have one loss together, even the death of his rival. Was ever anything so simply and beautifully generous? But it is not realism — it is too beautiful to be true, though not too untrue to be beautiful. He is no milksop. Where is this Paynim's son? — he does not speak out freely, but we well know what he has it in mind to do.

[3] See pp. 240–243.

This tune goes manly, and in Spenser it often does — he is not
all tenderness and tears. There was a good stroke in him too, no
doubt, as Carlyle would have put it; and there is in all his knights,
once the time for that has come. How the verse resounds, as to the
trumpets' or bugles' call, the morning of the combat, canto v of
Book I.

> The noble hart, that harbors vertuous thought,
> And is with child of glorious great intent,
> Can never rest, until it forth have brought
> Th' eternall brood of glorie excellent;
> Such restlesse passion did all night torment
> The flaming corage of that Faery knight,
> Devizing how that doughtie turnament
> With greatest honour he atchieven might;
> Still did he wake, and still did watch for
> dawning light.

And what a *joie de vivre*, vying with delight of battle, and inspir-
ing and informing Nature itself, there is in the next stanza after,
with its stout and strutting alexandrine:

> At last the golden Orientall gate
> Of greatest heaven gan to open faire,
> And Phoebus fresh, as bridegrome to his mate,
> Came dauncing forth, shaking his deawie haire:
> And hurld his glistring beames through gloomy aire.
> Which when the wakeful Elfe perceiv'd, streightway
> He started up, and did himselfe prepaire,
> In sun-bright armes and battailous array:
> For with that Pagan proud he combat will that day.

Like Shakespeare's, Spenser's heroes are all paladins, who smell
the battle afar off, and cry, aha! None of them are poets or philosophers, Alastors or Werthers, or Hamlets such as our Romantic
critics have conceived. They are tall men of their hands. The
greatest grief that the young squire Timias feels when he has been
treacherously wounded is that he cannot get even.

> Exceeding griefe that wound in him empight
> But more that with his foes he could not come to fight.

And this Spenser has in common with Milton, and not with Shelley or Wordsworth.

But for the most part the common impression is the true one — Spenser is a descriptive and picturesque, tender and lyrical poet, rather than one truly narrative and dramatic. For the highest narrative and dramatic success he is too much concerned with detail and engrossed in his own feelings, too indifferent to reality and deep in his dreams.

12

What, now, is the nature of his romanticism as compared with that of Milton and of a later day? Spenser has, first of all, the right external setting, which has since become a romantic tradition. The scene is in a forest or in the mountains, or both at once and together, or is by, on, or even under the sea. And the spot where the action centers is a glade or a dale, a fountain or waterfall, a grotto or a garden, a bower or a hermitage, a castle by the sea — *Das Schloss am Meer!* — or a ship upon it, an island in a river or a lake. These reappear in Scott and Coleridge, Keats, Shelley, and Tennyson; but Spenser has the less modern ones as well — the chariot for land or water or an enchanted boat, and monsters such as dragons and hippogriffs, dolphins or unicorns. He has also the romantic or fabulous human figures — knights and ladies, squires and foresters, dwarfs and giants, hermits and wizards, nymphs and satyrs. And these are placed in the traditional situations — a combat, a voyage, a triumphal procession, a scene within or without a house or castle.

Though much of all this reappears at the Revival, it is with a difference. The monsters and marvels are introduced warily, for the associations or the symbolism, in lyric verse. They are seldom introduced as in Spenser for their own sakes and with a frank delight. And in Milton the romantic paraphernalia scarcely appear at all except by way of allusion: in *Comus* there are only the forest, the enchanter, and the river-nymph. But Milton is not penning tales of chivalry, and has only distant reminiscences

> Of fairy damsels met in forest wide
> By knights of Logres, or of Lyones,
> Lancelot, or Pelleas, or Pellenore.

The amorous and chivalrous, the adventurous and marvelous, the stagy, spectacular, and glittering aspects of romance are not for him. He is interested in its dark and legendary, supernatural and superstitious ones, as in the *Hymn on the Nativity*.[4] And here Milton is nearer to Coleridge and Keats than to Spenser, who is hardly concerned with these at all.

Milton also has a more modern romantic attitude to nature. Spenser treats it with delight but somewhat conventionally. His forests and mountains, grottoes and fountains, brooks and rivers, now often seem like stage-settings. They are exquisitely touched, but the poet and his characters avow or betray little love for them in themselves. Milton avows little but betrays much, not only in his unconventional treatment of nature, but in the beauty and mystery with which he invests it. This is not merely in the verse, but in the feeling for the light and shade, and for space. When Milton hears

> the far-off curfew sound
> Over some wide-watered shore

or sees the Spirit flying

> Quickly to the green earth's end,
> Where the bow'd welkin slow doth bend,

he is far nearer both to nature as it is and to the romantic heart as we know it. He has broken with Spenser's prim perfection and orderliness, and swept away his enclosures. With the Elizabethan

---

[4] See pp. 267–268.

the scene is often in a garden or a park, where are bowers, trellises, and arbors, and fountains in marble basins, and not only the daintiest flowers but all the fairest trees in the world are gathered together, and

> No braunch whereon a fine bird did not sit,
> No bird but did her shrill notes sweetly sing.

The flowers in Spenser's Garden of Adonis seem to Professor Elton to be under glass; these trees seem to be in tubs, and the birds to be attached with wires.

Like most paradises (as indeed the word itself indicates) Spenser's are duly fenced or walled about. It is so even when Spenser comes nearer to beauty, romantic or real. The garden of Acrasia and her Bower of Bliss are, of course, highly artificial, though exquisite. What of his is more truly in the romantic vein is where the hand of man and that of Nature have happily wrought together. It is where there is a glade, a dale, or an isle, with a cottage, a hermitage, or a castle within it, skirted or girdled by brook or river, trees, hills, or waves. Even now many of the old cottages and manor-houses in England stand by a stream; Henry James's father, advertising for a house where he could fish from his bedroom window, received at once a score of offers. With the immemorial elms also about them, they would each make a picture, as they do on Spenser's page; though for him they are fairly symbolical — set there "like a little nest," or "as a sweet inn from paine and wearisome turmoile." But in Milton there is little of the artificiality; and of enclosure —

> Towers and battlements it sees
> Bosom'd high in tufted trees.

> Hard by a cottage chimney smokes,
> From betwixt two aged oaks.

> Betwixt these rocky pillars Gabriel sat,
> Chief of the angelic guards, awaiting night; —

of that there is only so much as provides points of repose in a wide-ranging scene. Spenser like a cinquecento painter traces delightful boundaries, but Milton is scarce content with less than the unattainable skyline:

> Where the labouring clouds do rest —
>
> Over some wide-watered shore —
>
> Where the bow'd welkin slow doth bend.

Even there the "return to Nature" has begun, the human figures being much subdued. Or if they be not, Milton, still like the later poets, does not forget the sky, the clouds and the daylight, hanging and brooding over all:

> To many a youth, and many a maid,
> Dancing in the chequer'd shade;
> And young and old come forth to play
> On a sunshine holiday
> Till the live-long daylight fail.

The last line, with its retarded movement, suspended couplet, and liquid lapse of melody, dies away as with a sigh.

Like a true romantic, Milton extends the scene, dims and blurs the formal outlines, and sheds mystery over the whole. This is an esthetic development, and that, as we have seen, is characteristic of Spenser, too, particularly in his love of love, and his delight in the past rather than in the present, in pleasurable emotions and exquisite details for their own sake. But with Milton come complications, subtleties. Being a matter of retrospect and reverie, romance accumulates associations as it proceeds, and as one generation inherits from another. It dreams, but enters into all the dreams that there have been before. Certain words gradually widen or deepen in meaning — words like *drear* and *dread*, *wild* and *weird*, *waste* and *desolate*, *lorn* and *forlorn*, *magic* and *enchantment*, *charm* and *spell*, *melancholy* and *gloom*, *dark*, *dim*, *dusky*, *shadowy*; and particularly the words which have to do with passion — *pang*, *throe*, and *thrill*, *sob* and *sigh*, *anguish* and *languor*, *moan* and *groan*. In their original intention, and as for the most part they were still used in Spenser's day, they conveyed little that was pleasant. In the hands of Coleridge, Keats, and Rossetti they convey much. They are enriched and encrusted with memories, have taken on nuances or overtones. A pleasure has grown out of pain, a beauty out of ugliness; and the poet delights, for their own sake, not only in the pleasurable emotions but the unpleasurable. The beginnings of this tendency are discernible in Milton. Though less relentless and insatiable than Spenser in his search for beauty, he more seldom fails of it. He finds it even in Satan and Comus, who are not ugly like Dante's devils and Spenser's villains. There is nothing really hideous or revolting in him as in Spenser and Dante there often is. There is no stench as there is, repeatedly noticed, in Dante's Hell and in Spenser's forest; this not being one of the romantic senses, in bonds to beauty. And the greater directness and simplicity of Spenser appears particularly in the matter of melancholy and darkness. Milton's *Il Penseroso* is very different from Keats's *Ode to Melancholy*; the poet does not indulge and pamper the mood or luxuriate in the passion; and yet he finds "pleasure" in it. Spenser scarcely does. Twice in his great poem he provides music

> To drive away the dull melancholy,

repeating the line, as if such were the proper effect of music, though not only Shelley but also Shakespeare are against him. And night, dearer to the romantics (though not quite so to Milton) than day, is to him "cheerless," while dawn and morning ever laugh for glee.

13

Nevertheless Milton and Spenser have much in common, and in some respects are nearer to each other than to the moderns. It may have been Spenser who taught Milton to take pleasure in effects of light and shade and of distance, and thus to throw a mantle of mystery over the scene. The motley show that Pride makes as she issues forth to the tourney, in a chariot drawn by six very different beasts, bestridden by the six other deadly sins, reminds us, as has been said, of a circus parade. But over the gay fantastic procession hangs a mist, and though the people shout for joy, there are bones and skulls upon the road. Pride's team is driven by Satan, who lashes it, and

> Huge routs of people did about them band,
> Showting for joy, and still before their way
> A foggy mist had covered all the land;
> And underneath their feet, all scattered, lay
> Dead skulls and bones of men, whose life had gone astray.

It is no circus, really. We often hear that Spenser is light and pretty, but Milton called him sage and moral; and he had not only much of Milton's high seriousness but some of his special gift for external mystery — for things vast, vague, and dim, floating many a rood. The tail of the dragon, him of the Apocalypse, whom Duessa rides,

> was stretchèd out in wondrous length,
> That to the house of heavenly gods it raught,
> And with extorted powre, and borrow'd strength,
> The ever-burning lamps from thence it brought,
> And prowdly threw to ground, as things of nought.

What a cosmical sweep, like Milton's own! And though the sense of space, the feeling for the infinite, was in Spenser far less developed, he had something that is as truly romantic, and in Milton seems lacking, the spirit of adventure and of peering into the unknown:

> The wondred Argo, which in venturous peece [*vessel*],
> First through the Euxine seas bore all the flour of Greece.

The last line, in the exhilaration of its melody and rhythm, though these are very different, reminds us of

> We were the first that ever burst
> Into that silent sea.

And Spenser has the sense of space while wandering, as he speaks
of the North Star, which

> firme is fixt, and sendeth light from farre
> To all that in the wide deepe wandering arre.

How the movement of the line — the three long syllables together
— and the harmony of the open vowels realize for us the awe and
loneliness on a wide, wide sea! And this spirit of adventure the
friend of Raleigh shared neither with Milton nor with Shakespeare himself.

He has even Milton's "darkness visible." In the Cave of Error
the Red-Cross Knight's glistering armor sheds

> A little glooming light, much like a shade;

while the Cave of Mammon is almost as rich and mysterious, dusky
and ancient, as Coleridge, Keats, or Rossetti would have painted
it:

> Both roofe and floore and wals were all of gold,
> But overgrowne with dust and old decay,
> And hid in darknesse, that none could behold
> The hew thereof; for vew of chearefull day
> Did never in that house itselfe display,
> But a faint shadow of uncertain light,
> Such as a lamp whose life does fade away;
> Or as the Moone, cloathed with clowdy night,
> Does shew to him that walkes in feare and sad affright.

A faint shadow of uncertain light — and the poet delicately dulls
the glitter. It is old gold, pictorially dusty and dim:

> Car nous voulons la Nuance encor,
> Pas la Couleur, rien que la nuance.

But here, Spenser and Milton are alike,[5] and differ from the
moderns. The esthetic bent is restrained by the moral, the allegorical, purpose. The Cave of Mammon is meant to be wicked and unpleasant, like Mammon himself, for all his picturesqueness:

[5] As I show below, p. 266.

His yron coate, all overgrowne with rust,
Was underneath enveloped with gold,
Whose glistring glosse, darkened with filthy dust,
Well yet appeared to have beene of old
A worke of riche entayle and curious mould,
Woven with antickes and wild imagery.

To Spenser the last two lines are not what they would have been to Keats. Both the elder poets have a meaning or a purpose which keeps them from following their own esthetic devices, and enjoying their emotions and sensations, to the full. They do not "ever let the fancy roam," as Keats and Shelley do. These do not follow whim, to be sure; else they would not make good verse; but often the fancy, the esthetic spirit itself, is the controlling principle. Beauty is enthroned. In neither Spenser nor Milton is it, but in Spenser now and then it plays the usurper. He has the love of the past, of splendor, and even of love itself, and has the lust of the eye and the pride of life, all of which Milton disdains. He is more precious in style, and turns aside, to the detriment of his structure, as Milton never does, for the delights of description, the play of fancy or of phrase. He is less aloof than Milton, and — though more naïvely and simply, and still somewhat like the romantics — wears his heart upon his sleeve. And yet Milton, as we have seen, has the larger, more modern taste, the greater pleasure in melancholy, mystery, and darkness. But both alike are more robust and stalwart than the romantics. Their eyes are on the object, even though in retrospect, not sidelong on themselves. In Milton, of course, restraint and continence of feeling are conspicuous. How any modern romantic would have let himself go, after penning the line

Till the live-long daylight fail!

What one would have filled out the couplet, even though after a full pause, with

Then to the spicy nut-brown ale,

and have immediately returned to mirth? But Spenser is almost his peer when he follows the line

> To all that in the wide deep wandering are,

with this:

> And chearfull Chaunticlere with his note shrill.

Only, in Spenser it is no self-restraint, the darker mood is transitory — often appears mainly in the mere melody and rhythm and but passes like a cloud over a sunny landscape, throwing its cheerfulness into relief.

14

Whether that of adventure or of sentiment, of prospect or of retrospect, romanticism is alike a movement of escape. All romanticism is. But that of Wordsworth preëminently, and of Coleridge, Shelley, and Keats in less degree, is an escape, not clear out of the world, but to the bosom of Nature. It does not flee away and create anew but changes what is already created and accepts it. And of this sort is Milton's, taking a pleasure in melancholy, in Nature somber, wild, and boundless, and the mysteries of heathen worship and legend. It finds a pleasure in what is or was; it flies somewhat nearer to earth. Spenser's is an escape even for the man himself. The Nature he loves is only his vision of it, a garden, an isle, an oasis. His real refuge is a Palace of Art, a castle in the air. He was a sound man of business, but he fled away from it to his poetry, above all to the *Fairy Queen*. This vast but unfinished poem is as it were a long day-dream, continued not only from day to day but from year to year, and stanza by stanza, canto by canto, book by book. What day passed without his retreating from his cares and the Irish roundabout him, to this, a sweet inn from pain and wearisome turmoil, both for him and for us? As Hazlitt, who himself needed such a retreat, well says:

In Spenser, we wander in another world, among ideal beings. The poet takes and lays us in the lap of a lovelier nature, by the sound of softer streams, among greener hills and fairer valleys. He paints nature, not as we find it, but as we expected to find it; and fulfils the delightful promise of our youth.

15

And the painting, the mere expression is exquisite — that is more than half the charm — or the spell, one would more happily call it, which catches us up and wafts us away. Spenser is one of the great virtuosos both in language and in verse, delighting in them, and working wonders by them, almost of themselves, as if for the moment they had been almost reduced to magic and music. More than any of the greatest poets he does this, somewhat like the romantic Poe, Swinburne, and Rossetti. Shakespeare and Milton are even greater masters of style and meter, but in them these things count for relatively less. Like the emotions, they are not so much sought for their own sake — both style and meter are less romantic. Spenser is pictorial, a little like Rossetti and Tennyson, but far more vaguely and indistinctly; his figures are in the clouds, and are gone in a moment. They are visions and move to music, as with Poe and Swinburne. I mean not only that he is melodious but that he has the musical structure and technique in his very rhetoric and style. Themes and motifs, assonance and alliteration, are repeated or inverted, varied or interwoven, in "linked sweetness long drawn out."

These last words, of course, are Milton's, and about music, not verse; but musician that he was, Milton seldom permits himself much of this art in words. *Lycidas* is an exquisite but austere exception. Spenser's rhetoric is like his meter and rime: it intertwines, interlaces. The rimes of the stanza that he invented run *ababbcbcc*, a close, firm pattern, and even the words unrimed often make a pattern too. Mr. de Selincourt likens one case of this rhetorical art to that of the deft juggler who weaves in the air intricate patterns with balls of divers colors and yet never allows them to fall out of his control:

> Amongst those knights there were three brethren bold,
> Three bolder brethren never were yborne,
> Borne of one mother in one happie mold,
> Borne at one burden in one happie morne,
> Thrise happie mother, and thrise happie morne,
> That bore three such, three such not to be fond;
> Her name was Agape, whose children werne
> All three as one, the first hight Priamond,
> The second Dyamond, the youngest Triamond.

This instance is an extreme one, yet not only here but elsewhere the flow of Spenser's rhetoric is as continuous as that of water, and as devious. It ripples and eddies. And rhetoric and meter exquisitely conspire. His nine-line stanzas are neither hard and separate like those in the eighteenth century nor merged and blurred like those of Shelley and Keats. Spenser does not permit himself much enjambement from line to line, and none at all from stanza to stanza. His lines and stanzas keep their contours clear-cut, but are continually varied within these limits, are always alike but are never the same. There is a full pause after the swell of the final alexandrine; and the effect is relieved ordinarily by the repetition of a word or by devices of close coherence like "and," "who," "which," or "whose," that is, not so much by carrying the sentence over into the next stanza as by picking there the thought up anew or echoing it. He would keep the outlines of the meter clear and firm, though veiled.

> And made full goodly joyaunce to her newfound mate.

> Her mate he was a iollie youthful knight.

This use, not of the overflow of a thought but of its refluence, like the eddying of it within the stanza itself, is something that Spenser learned of Ariosto and Tasso, although he developed it farther. And all this, as well as the elaborate rime-scheme itself, is a lyrical method in a narrative poem; for it is the lyric that winds or undulates, repeats or echoes. The vine and the ivy play a great rôle in Spenser, both in the pictures presented and in the images employed; the vine and the ivy, with their wreaths, loops, and festoons, are typical of his art.

But not everything is winding and flowing, undulating and redundant. The thread of the story is never lost. The innumerable stanzas, following one upon another, are, amid all the intricate rhetoric which involves them, like a colonnade, symmetrical and harmonious, distinct and clear. They keep the way straight through the tangle, and in their regular, monotonous succession lead the thought of the reader serenely down the endless enchanted vista, aloof from the world. Or to use the figure of M. Legouis, the stanza "keeps time in this fairyland. It measures the hours in this region of nowhere, this kingdom of illusion." They establish the fact that this is another world, and as by a veil or screen of monotonous music keep the old afar. Or as Hazlitt put it better long ago, "The changing fairy visions are summoned up to the accompaniment of aërial melodies, which lull the senses into a deep oblivion of the jarring noises of the world, from which we have no wish to be recalled."

For within this screen and cloud of verbal music everything is simple and serene. The intricacy in the rhetoric is no hindrance to the movement. What winds and turns soon recurs, what is tangled is soon untied. And there is no bombast or rant as there is in most of the Elizabethan poets, especially the dramatists, and scarcely any of their ingenious quibbling and verbal ingenuity, punning and conceits. Nor is there epigram or striking phrase. Spenser does not, like many Elizabethans or the later romantics, "load every rift with ore." He has the right words in the right places but not such as attract attention to themselves — in style, though not in plot and structure, he is often more truly (though less consciously) classical than Milton himself. Witness the perfect, unadorned simplicity of the passages I have quoted above, especially the line

And set her by to watch and set her by to weepe!

Or of the stanza admired by Leigh Hunt, where without peril

not a word could be changed, not a pause be altered, but there is
no salient beauty:

> A little lowly Hermitage it was,
>> Downe in a dale, hard by a forests side,
>> Far from resort of people, that did pas
>> In travell to and froe: a little wyde
>> There was an holy Chappell edifyde,
>> Wherein the Hermite dewly wont to say
>> His holy things each morne and eventyde:
>> Thereby a Christall streame did gently play,
> Which from a sacred fountaine welled forth alway.

Instead, beauty environs and envelops the whole, and that is
enough. The sinuous, lyrical movement, the aërial melody, would
be broken by the thrilling style of Shakespeare, clogged by the
austere condensation of Milton or the lusciousness of Keats.
Spenser's great poem is a song, in thousands of stanzas; and the
wording of a song must be simple. So he has put simplicity within
his complexity. The other poets have contrived a single compact
structure. Spenser, so far as style is concerned, has, with an exquisite sense of restraint and of relief, placed a Greek temple
within his tangled enchanted forest. The others have built gor-
geous Gothic ones, on the hill.

VII

Was Paradise Well Lost?

THERE are few things in literature so beautiful as the endings of Milton's three long poems. *Paradise Lost, Paradise Regained,* and *Samson Agonistes,* the great Puritan poems of sin and righteousness, end, each in its own way, on a quiet note of reconciliation with life. In all three the story tapers off and there is no final climax. In all three the grand style sinks into the simple, the music dies away on the slow chords of a cadence, the mighty pinions on which the poet was lifted in his flight float him gently down to earth again. And in all three, though he does not cry "back into life, back into life" with Goethe, he drops back into it instinctively. Like the skylark, he is true to the kindred points of heaven and home.

In *Paradise Lost* is the finest of these closes, and concerning the meaning of this one there has, of late, arisen some question.

> They looking back, all th' eastern side beheld
> Of Paradise, so late their happy seat,
> Wav'd over by that flaming brand; the gate
> With dreadful faces throng'd and fiery arms:
> Some natural tears they dropp'd, but wip'd them soon;
> The world was all before them, where to choose
> Their place of rest, and Providence their guide:

> They hand in hand with wand'ring steps and slow,
> Through Eden took their solitary way.

The stern Puritan might have been expected to dictate an ending full of anger and fierce denunciation of the sin which has brought Death into the world and all our woe, or to give place only to the wailing of the sinners themselves. But he does neither. He presents to us, instead, a simple picture of the man and woman leaving home and going out into the world, in tears but not despairing. This is meant, it would seem, to be a picture — a symbol — of the life they were entering upon, the life their children were to lead; and is it not a remarkable thing that the blind old Puritan, amid his quarreling daughters and the renegades of the Restoration, on evil days though fallen and evil tongues, could, after singing of the wrath of God, the rage of devils, and the fatal folly of men, now change his note, stay his hand, and give that life its due?

Does he then simply check himself, virtuously rein himself in? On the contrary he has fully prepared for this benign and magnanimous ending. His thought unfolds as in a drama rather than as in an epic; and from the moment of the temptation of Eve there is perceptible a gradual humanizing of his tone and adjustment in his point of view. Adam really becomes a man, Eve, a woman. She is impelled at first not to share the fruit with her mate, but by her new-found wisdom get the upper hand. And she changes her mind through an impulse still more feminine:

> But what if God have seen
> And death ensue? Then I shall be no more,
> And Adam, wedded to another Eve,
> Shall live with her!

That thought she keeps to herself (and there she is like a woman too), but she pleads with him to share her lot, whatever it be; and he, speaking for the first time the language of sin — the accents of our common nature — yields to her, crying with the first throb his voice has ever felt,

How can I live without thee?

The tie between them now is far closer than before, and their speech is simpler and franker. They give up epic formality, as has been observed. No longer do they address each other as "Daughter of God and Man," or "My author and disposer," or "Thou for whom and from whom I was formed," but as plain "Adam" and "Eve." Their dignity and formality disappear as nature asserts itself within them — as they know what it is to tremble and weep, to reproach or forgive one another, and cling to one another because either has no other in the world.

In keeping with this awakening of the humanity in the hero and heroine is the development in the conception presented of sin and death. In Book xii, ll. 473 ff., Adam, after the vision of the future, is uplifted in soul:

> Full of doubt I stand
> Whether I should repent me now of sin
> By me done and occasioned, or rejoice
> Much more, that much more good shall spring;
> To God more glory, more good will to men
> From God, and over wrath grace shall abound.

And though in Book iii, ll. 207 ff., God had pronounced death to be the penalty on man for the sin that he will commit, in Book xi, ll. 59 ff., he declares that, happiness having been lost to man, death now "becomes his final remedy." So he bids the archangel send them forth, "though sorrowing, yet in peace."

These developments or adjustments in the conception of sin and death are only in keeping, I think, with the general drift of the poem, and with the poet's consistent purpose to make the superhuman life in Eden slope down to the level of the life that men lead and have always led. I consider them as contrived deliberately, in sympathy with the humanizing of Adam and Eve through their sin and with that spirit of natural resignation in which they accept their exile. The purity of Paradise might bear up under the vertical rays of eternal truth, but human nature would wither and shrivel. Professor John Erskine,[1] on the other hand, considers all these developments and adjustments, whether in doctrine or characterization, to be changes and contradictions, of which the poet was hardly aware, and which were owing to more enlightened views that took possession of him as he "finished the last books" of the poem. What I consider a particular and intentional beauty, the foreseen and necessary conclusion, he considers an afterthought. "Indeed, they go out in excellent spirits," says Professor Erskine, "except for the inconvenience, as Eve laments, of leaving the home one is accustomed to. But for the world before them they had nothing but zest. At last they were to travel and see life — in short, to have a Renaissance career." Eden, that is to say, has been something of a bore, and now Adam and Eve, being, so to speak, "on their own," are about to have the time of their lives. But by this interpretation the delicate gradations of Milton's art are obliterated, and Milton, one of the most conscious, deliberate, and unerring craftsmen that ever lived, becomes naïve, inconsistent, not classical but medieval or Elizabethan. Such poets as he have afterthoughts no doubt, but in their poems there are none.

The changes (mentioned above) in the doctrine concerning sin and death are, I must think, no exception. The latest opinion concerning sin is Adam's own humble surmise, not the deliverance of the Lord. That he, at any rate, shall be given no afterthoughts, the poet takes care. For the Lord does not contradict himself in that, having pronounced death as the penalty, he later declares it to be a relief. Death is both, we know. *We* can see that without incurring a charge of contradiction if the immortal poet couldn't. It is what has since been called a paradox. Moreover these modifications or developments in doctrine are not only necessary in the poem as we now descend to the human level, but the truths

[1] *Publications of the Modern Language Association of America*, XXXII, 580.

involved are in keeping with the general principle accepted in the poem elsewhere, nay, are exemplifications of it. That, in a word, is that God brings good out of evil. In Book vii, which presumably is not to be accounted one of "the last books," twice over[2] the heavenly choir sings his praises for doing this very thing with the sins of the angels; and how much more might God do it with the sin of man! In thus representing God as bending both sin and death to his exalted purpose the poet would, in a higher sense, be consistent enough. And therefore it seems unnecessary here to take up the question of the more enlightened opinions which Milton may have begun to entertain near the end. When he "was finishing the last books" we do not know; but the opinions in the *Areopagitica* concerning the flimsiness of "a fugitive and cloistered virtue," which Mr. Erskine finds now prevailing, were, of course, expressed before he had even begun the first. No change in his opinions, therefore, need be involved.

The main objection, however, to Mr. Erskine's interpretation is that it does violence to the text. There is nothing "lively" that I can see about Adam and Eve at their departure. The point is not that they want to go but that they are willing; they weep, as they go hand in hand; the world is all before them, but they do not run to meet it; and it is with wandering steps and slow that they take their solitary way. They are not dejected, but neither are they cheerful: their mood is as pensive as the movement of the verse. Mood and meter both breathe the spirit of the words of the Lord — "sorrowing, yet in peace." In short, this is human life as we know it, and as Milton knew it, of a mingled web, good and ill together, dim, sad, but very dear. And to a poet (and reader too) who conceives it so, all the previous developments and adjustments are necessary as in this poem of superhuman life we approach the human, and as what we call human nature takes, in a measure, the place of sin. What Mr. Erskine considers an after-

[2] Ll. 188–193, 615–616.

thought is but the outcome of that accommodation of religion to life to which every healthy spirit, however illogically, strives to attain, and without which life would rest under a monkish curse. Milton had attained to it, being more of a man and poet than a Puritan. "Nor love thy life nor hate," Adam had just been bidden by the archangel. "But what thou livst live well," he adds — but by that, we may be sure, he does not mean "with zest."

It is a twilight mood, as I conceive it, in which the poem ends, as typifying the twilight in which men dwell. And so, unlike Mr. Erskine's cheerful and lively ending, it readily blends, by gradations, with what has gone before. Twilight and dim horizons at the end — after the darkness visible and lurid splendors of Hell, after the glories of Heaven, after the sweet but unreal light of Paradise. At the beginning the towering passions of the devils and the ecstasies of the saints; the nude and spotless purity of Paradise in between; and now the shame and sorrow, and love and hope, of frail humanity. There is sweetness in the close; but there is also the melancholy that Mr. Erskine denies to it; and were this not the case, the close would be little in harmony with the high and serious spirit of the poem as a whole. The beauty of it Mr. Erskine turns into what seems to me an esthetic incongruity. "Excellent spirits," anything approaching "zest," at the close of the epic of the fall of man, of *Paradise Lost?* If so, pray why *regain* it? Aye, aye, some of us, no doubt, would answer. But Milton was one of those who, accepting this life, heroically cling to their dream of a better, however little they can make of it, when it comes to the point, or really conceive it. And even if he were not such, even if he were so much of a skeptic as to think Paradise well lost, he was too much of an artist, and too little of a humorist, to say so. He was hardly the one to mock at his own poem and at the poem (almost as fine) still to come. Still less was he the one to spoil his music, and end his solemn song of man's exile from immortal bliss on a piping note of cheer.

VIII

Certain Fallacies and
Irrelevancies in the Literary Scholarship of the Day

Importance is one thing, and learning's another; but a debate's a
debate.   (Congreve.)

Censeur un peu fâcheux, mais souvent nécessaire,
Plus enclin à blâmer que savant à bien faire.
                            (Boileau, *L'Art poétique*, IV, 235–236.)

Je disais à mon ami [1] que de savants hommes courent bien plus de
risques que les autres, puisqu'ils font des paris et que nous restons
hors du jeu; et qu'ils ont deux manières de se tromper: la nôtre, qui
est aisée, et la leur, laborieuse. Que s'ils ont le bonheur de nous rendre
quelques événements, le nombre même des vérités matérielles rétablies
met en danger la réalité que nous cherchons. Le vrai à l'état brut est plus
faux que le faux.
                            (Paul Valéry, *Variété*, p. 174.)

W_{HY DO} we find the reading of the scholarly journals a burden? Why do some of us read only those articles which touch upon
what we ourselves are writing about, and to see if they attack us

NOTE. Read, in part, before the Modern Language Association, at Harvard,
December, 1926; reprinted, by permission, from *Studies in Philology and Literature*. Some additions and omissions have been made, in order to bring out more
clearly and adequately the central thought.
    [1] Marcel Schwob.

or if we can attack them? The writers are — Ph.D's. It is their fortune and our misfortune. They came in with a dissertation, and dissertations they are still penning. (I have the right to say this; it has been said of me.) And sometimes the chief difference — sweet to the writer but less so to the reader — lies in the fact that the maiden effort was printed at the writer's expense, the present one, in a little measure, at the reader's own.

What do dissertations in literature undertake to do, of what do they treat? In the graduate school or out of it they undertake above all to prove something; and there lies the root of the difficulty. Even in the graduate school we learned that it is the special distinction and proud prerogative of scientific literary work, not to develop and illustrate what was known but to discover what was unknown, not to expound but to demonstrate, and to defend or assail a thesis. Hence the forced and distorted conclusions so frequently drawn. The burden of proof weighs heavily upon the writer's pen, upon the reader's spirit. The writer is on his mettle to make a point, to score, even though he make the worse seem the better reason (which he dreams not of doing) like the sophists of old.

And what do they prove? Dates and sources, above all, influences (if the subject be more ambitious and the candidate more aspiring), or perhaps a question of different or identical authorship; and the means or medium of proof is commonly the allusion or parallel passage. In the case of influence it may be parallelism or similarity in style, structure, or thought, instead of wording; but a like process is involved. Such subjects are favorites in the graduate school because of their definiteness and tangibleness; they yield results. They yield them, though not easily, abundantly in the end. Most that is necessary is the simple process of comparison — of matching materials — and a good memory and plenty of industry to carry it out. There is always *some* similarity; if not very much, one cuts the garment according to the cloth and makes much of what there is. For the moment one forgets that the two authors in question were gifted beings, who independently inhabited the same planet, had somewhat the same passions, thoughts, and experiences, knew the same sort of people, perhaps lived in the same age, had of their own accord (though possibly quite by chance) chosen a similar subject, and were now writing in the same tongue. And in that moment Q. E. D. crowns the labor.

1

Some of us, as we gratefully remember, were warned against this pitfall in our student days; but we still see others step into it, when not doing it ourselves, and even the greatest among us as well as the least. Shakespeare is a favorite subject, but that ample demesne has been so thoroughly explored, and the sources so diligently traced, that people are tempted to stretch a point in order to disclose another. No one can have more respect than I for the scholarship and literary perception of Professor Gayley. His book on Beaumont is a credit to American scholarship and American letters. But his book on *Shakespeare and the Founders of Liberty in America* is of another sort. It appeared during the war; it was no doubt prompted by the spirit of propaganda; and as often with propaganda (I penitently remember) the end justified the means. Not that Mr. Gayley falsifies the facts, but — the professional failing! — he strains them. He surely does not here see, or (as the critic should) try to make us see, the thing quite as it is. He would fain make us think that in that fateful hour Shakespeare was for us — that even now like Milton, Burns, and Shelley, he watches from his grave. But the argument, being honestly managed, fails of itself He takes great pains to endeavor to prove acquaintance on Shakespeare's part with the promoters of colonizing in Virginia, and sympathy with their motives and aspirations — only, Shakespeare himself says not a word to that effect. Spenser, Daniel, Drayton, and the rest sing of the New World and Virginia, but not Shakespeare. So the argument recoils, and proves, if anything, the contrary.

Mr. Gayley and his followers, to be sure, do not see this. They find in the *Tempest* signs of keen interest in the high emprise. They maintain — and in the November issue of the *Publications of the Modern Language Association* is a clever article to demonstrate it — that he made use of William Strachey's letter, which later appeared in Purchas's *Pilgrimes*. This would indicate not only Shakespeare's keen interest in the undertaking but also intimate acquaintance with its inner counsels — Shakespeare with his prophetic eye upon us!

This proof rests upon a few slight verbal parallels, most precariously. There is not a word in the *Tempest* about America or Virginia, colonies or colonizing, Indians or tomahawks, maize, mocking-birds, or tobacco. Nothing but the Bermudas, once barely mentioned as a faraway place, like Tokio or Mandalay. His interest and sympathy Shakespeare keeps to himself. There are some few isolated similarities in subject-matter, such as a storm, a shipwreck, St. Elmo's fire, a Master, a Boatswain, a harbor, an island, the north wind; but who could tell a sea story without them, even Herodotus or Heliodorus? Had Strachey never been to Virginia or even seen the light of day, or had America never been discovered, these things might have been in the *Tempest* just the same. And the use of identical words — some few dozen such as *cries* or *split*, even in connection with a shipwreck, or as *amazement*, even in connection with St. Elmo's fire, or of identical phrases such as *sharp wind* or *stand upon our guard* — all this but shows that Shakespeare could tell a lively story that wouldn't be far off from the other story, which was one of fact. And he was using the same language, in the very same years. These phrases, were they not his as well as Strachey's? The writer in the *Publications of the Modern Language Association* even seizes upon the word *tempest*, not in Strachey but in another report already in print, as what "may have suggested his very title." But thought, then as now, was free; the language, like air and water, was denied to no one. And old Gonzalo's pipe-dream in Act II, of an ideal but idle commonwealth, which is taken from Montaigne, the writer conceives to be also Shakespeare's defence of colonization as a policy, then much criticized, and an indirect presentation of the right way to go about it. Shakespeare himself, it appears, would have the colonists not idle at all; but how an audience, proverbially so stupid, was to perceive this, or that he was talking of practical colonization of any sort, I cannot make out. Undoubtedly there is some very slight but definite evidence in the *Tempest* and another play that Shakespeare had read some of the Elizabethan voyages or heard the substance of them repeated. Monsters such as the anthropophagi, spoken of in *Othello* and told of before that by Raleigh, are an example. But as regards his interest in America, the result, here again, is negative. He knew something (exceedingly little) of America but said nothing of it as American; and as for opinions on a proper policy there, if he had none on matters nearer home, like the Parliamentary question, or the Irish question, or the question of prelacy, he may be supposed to have had none concerning America, which he mentions but once in all his works and then as a joke.

Indeed, as honest and clever men, Professor Gayley and his followers acknowledge that the evidence bit by bit is not considerable, and may be questionable, but — the ever-ready argument — they consider the effect of it to be cumulative. No one passage of itself indicates that the poet had read Strachey, or any other of the accounts of the Virginia colony, for that matter; but a dozen or so of isolated words or phrases taken together do. A saying of old Professor Child's recurs to me, which I heard, though unconcernedly, in my tender esthetic youth. "As if forty nothings made something," he muttered, to himself or to the deities below. In point of fact, to be sure, these scholars may be right, and Shakespeare may have read and remembered Strachey. But I do not see that they have proved it — and if they have, the poet's interest in America seems less than before.

This supposed cumulative effect is what scholars not uncommonly have recourse to in order not only to prove sources and influences but to identify characters in the flesh or incidents in history. Obviously, it can have force only when the details have individual value; as we learned in our nonage, the whole is *not* greater than its parts. And also only when there is already established an antecedent probability. Verbal borrowings immediately become more likely when the story or subject-matter is virtually the same, or when the text has manifestly been accessible to the dramatist or been used by him elsewhere. Shakespeare had a vivid memory, and when he was dramatizing *Macbeth* or *Henry V* he sometimes followed Holinshed's wording as the line of least resistance. At times, indeed, he followed the text with care, reproducing the veritable words of the famous; but for that there is no occasion in case of a high fantastic tale like the *Tempest*. And could not William Shakespeare make Stephano escape on a butt of sack, without the warrant or countenance of William Strachey, who throws overboard a butt of beer? and make Prospero break his staff and bury it certain fathoms in the earth, without Strachey's Boatswain, who, at sea, "sounding at first, found it thirteen fathoms"? *Fathoms* is a word for anybody, in a sea story well-nigh unavoidable. As many resemblances, I surmise, might be found between the *Tempest* and, say, *Treasure Island*. But who knows? The *Tempest* may yet be demonstrated to be its source, and the ubiquitous Hawkins the incarnation of Ariel.

Not that sources or influences are matters at all trivial or meaningless. Only, the obvious *sine qua non* is proof; and except in the case of close verbal or structural similarity, such as is uncommon, proof chiefly depends on external evidence. The actual knowledge that the poet has read the book in question, as we have it, for in-

stance, from Coleridge's diary, puts a totally different face upon
the situation, though the discoverable indebtedness be slight indeed.[2] Single words and images reproduced and changed, which
as evidence are utterly negligible, assume, now that other evidence
is provided, importance in the study of psychology and the work-
ings of the imagination. Here sources or influences throw light
upon the poet. They throw light also upon the poem when, having
been demonstrated, they involve such close resemblance in wording or phrasing that the poem must in some measure seem to have
been predetermined at the making.

2

Antecedent probability of another sort is ignored in another
article in the same number of the *Publications of the Modern
Language Association,* one on Hamlet's delay. I refer to it only
in passing, for I wish to avoid here anything like personal controversy. In Timothy Bright's *Treatise of Melancholy* (1586) the
author finds indisposition to action to be a symptom of certain
extreme forms of the disease. Discovering, then, a few very slight
similarities in phrasing, she concludes that Shakespeare had read
the book and meant Hamlet's delay so to be understood. But then
would not some comment have been necessary, and the point, so
central and pivotal, have been made clear and emphatic? Even if
Shakespeare had read the book, the audience hadn't; or even if
they had, how were they, without a clue, to know that this particular extreme form of the disease was intended? How strange
a dramatic method, for Hamlet to wonder whether the mere sight
of the ghost was not owing to his melancholy, but when it comes
to the cause of his procrastination to say he does not know; and

[2] See Professor Lowes' *Road to Xanadu.* The external evidence adduced in
this fine book is generally well-nigh irrefragable; only at the internal can one
cavil. Despite the prodigious tenacity of Coleridge's memory, I can now and
then scarcely believe a great poetic faculty to be so dependent for a mere word
or a color, so natural in the situation, upon remote, irrelevant reading.

for others — Horatio, at least, who is in the secret of his grief and his project — not only not to speak up and thus explain it but fail to take notice of the indisposition to action at all!

This would be an historical fallacy; more commonly in connection with Shakespeare it is the unhistorical with which one must contend — the modern Hamlet, the modern Shylock or Falstaff, which is the original overlaid with our predilections and prepossessions. But it is quite as fallacious to connect the drama, or poem even, with its own time in a way that contradicts the spirit of the drama or poem. The prime and the final arbiter is (read Pope, read the Stagirite himself) the discernible intention of the author. Sometimes history and environment can help us to determine that; but the main means are the play or poem itself and other plays or poems of the same author or his contemporaries. Literature, not history, sheds most light upon literature — drama upon drama; and often literature (and drama as well) is somewhat in opposition to the time. The means are esthetic as much as historical, are above all those of fairmindedness and common sense. The anachronistic fallacy is that of looking upon the dramatist like Shakespeare, the poet like Dante, as a philosopher or seer who anticipated our ways of thought and sentiment, and of cheerfully attributing these to him; the historical fallacy is that of treating him as a mere puppet of the *Zeitgeist*, without artistic and poetic autonomy, and the age itself as so entirely disclosed to us that we can positively say, here he got this, here that. A blind and dogged literalism pervades much of our scholarly work, different only in degree (by the bye) from that of the esthetic critic, who treats characters, which in principle he acknowledges to be imaginary, in practice as if they were alive.

It takes various forms. One critic finds Shakespeare following closely, for a tale of adventure, a story from which he borrows only words like *amazement* and *conspiracy* or phrases like *stand on his guard*; others undertake positively to identify the characters or

incidents of an author in the life about him. So Hamlet and Prospero have been identified as Shakespeare himself; but by others
James the Sixth of Scotland and the First of England has been
thought to be the man, though by still others he is (as plausibly)
thought to be Bottom, in *A Midsummer Night's Dream*. To me
personally such identifications seem among the most misguided
and wasted of terrestrial excursions and exertions. They are, so
far as I have noticed, generally disavowed by the authors themselves, even when they concern people long dead, like Arnold of
Brescia, supposed to be the original of Browning's Patriot. Like
much of our research, they entertain no one but the writer and
profit no one at all. How futile to peer into chronicles and archives
for traces of the creatures of a poet's brain, to follow the footprints
on earth of beings all air and fire! Save in the satirical writers, the
resemblance to any particular mortal is generally so slight as to
be meaningless, even though on external evidence the connection
can be demonstrated. And think of the antecedent probability of
Shakespeare, the gentle, silent, and unobtrusive, undertaking to
present, on the stage, the great Virgin Queen fondly caressing in
public her Cousin of Scotland, and with an ass's head on his
shoulders; or to present him afterwards, the author of the De-
monology, now by divine right and favor King also of England
and Ireland, as a princely wizard deprived of crown and throne![3]
Even earls and dukes had to smart for lesser offences than that.
This point, no doubt, scholars see. But they only make capital of
it. For not only is the cumulative argument called in but another
quite as dubious. It is that the resemblance between the character
and the reality is so slender only because the dramatist must needs

---

[3] It might, however, be maintained that, if not poetry and drama, the poet's
psychology has been thus illuminated, as Coleridge's (see above) has been by
the researches of Mr. Lowes. Without meaning to refer to James VI (or to the
Elvetham Entertainment, in connection with the mermaid on a dolphin's back)
the poet had here found the raw material and the first suggestion for his fantasy. But in that case, as not in Coleridge's, the one indispensable thing is
lacking — external evidence.

play safe. By such sleight of hand almost any resemblance can be proved. Evidence is made of the sheer want of evidence. But again and again this argument is made to save the day in the case of identifications in Shakespeare and Molière. What would Shakespeare scholars do without the Earls of Southampton, Pembroke, and Essex, and Mary Fitton, of whose relations (one and all) to Shakespeare we know nothing or next to nothing? They would find others like them to take the place of these. Always the identifications are demonstrated, for it would be strange indeed if characters in fiction had not some little trait or other in common with some person or other of the time. But if this was intended, what, then, becomes of our impression of Shakespeare as a rapid, prodigal playwright and free and careless poet? It's all wrong, if he trod as carefully as certain historical critics would have him do, following the data and documents, putting in the personalities and anxiously covering up his traces afterwards.

This business of identification goes on at a great rate. No philological journal or meeting would be complete without it, and the correspondence columns of the more tolerant periodicals provide space not only for the display of the discoveries but for their overthrow. Even foreigners engage in the sport on English ground. And other earls of late have been coming into their own — Oxford, Rutland, Derby — and I daresay there is scarcely an Elizabethan notable left who has not had his innings on the stage.

Sometimes the identifications assume an allegorical or symbolical cast, as in the *Tempest*, with the potent magician Prospero for Shakespeare, Ariel for genius, and the like. In this literature, though it is abundant enough, I am not well-read; but I feel safe in following Sir Edmund Chambers' account [4] of one of the latest specimens: " 'Shakespeare has employed Ophelia as a kind of Kathleen Ni Houlihan or symbol of the Irish nationality'; and in fact Ophelia was the Elizabethan name of King's county, although

[4] *Year's Work in English* (1926).

often . . . in the corrupted form of Offally. The Irish 'were daily found dead in bogs and woods with grass in their mouths.' Hence the picture of Ophelia's death. Or she may have been practising an Irish rite of well-worship. . . . She sang snatches of old tunes, 'a wonderful and strictly accurate symbol for the dying nationality of Ireland.' " And this un-Elizabethan literary and dramatic procedure was, it seems, inspired by Shakespeare's interest (once again!) in Essex. *Credat Judaeus Apella!* cries Sir Edmund. What would he say to Bottom playing, not Pyramus, but, with his long ears, the Scottish king?

3

I should like to say something about another literal tendency of our research, whereby there is discovered in literature a reproduction not only of a particular event but of the life of the time in general, its customs and manners; and so is discovered many a mare's nest, in modern literature as well as the Elizabethan. But that subject I have discussed elsewhere.[5] And I should like also to say something of researches not so literal, of influences not so external and so similar to sources — the impress of one man's art and style upon another's. When they are of the same period, above all of the same circle of society, how can they be at all clearly discerned? Who can quite disentangle the filaments of Byron's influence upon Shelley from those of Shelley's influence upon Byron, or Coleridge's upon Wordsworth from Wordsworth's upon Coleridge, or trace the indebtedness to each other of the collaborating Elizabethans? Here are both action and reaction, primary and secondary. To be so precise and absolute is to take upon us the

---

[5] *Modern Language Review*, 1924; and, more fully, in the second chapter of *Shakespeare Studies*. A discussion, from the same point of view, of Spanish conjugal honor, which I regret not having seen sooner, is to be found in Professor W. L. Fichter's edition of *El Castigo del Discreto* (N. Y., 1925). In the chapter referred to above is discussed another fallacy, somewhat similar, that of drawing conclusions from his writings concerning the author's own experiences or his mood at the time.

mystery of things as if we were God's spies; and the value of such researches lies in the likenesses and unlikenesses thus laid bare rather than in the conclusions drawn.

Nor are our contemporaries spared — there are so many more facts to use! Round the Brontës, says Mr. J. C. Smith, hangs a low mist or fog, "the breath of that great public which takes gossip for literature. At one time it was the wretched Branwell through whose eyes the sisters were supposed to have seen life. Now it is all the Brussels episode and M. Heger. M. Heger is Paul Emmanuel; he is Crimsworth; he is Rochester; he is Heathcliffe. We have come to shudder at his name." "These questions," he continues, "have an interest of their own, no doubt. But the student of literature must protest that to the study of literature as such this insatiable quest for origins is at best irrelevant, at worst merely obstructive. It confuses our sense of values."

4

Before turning for further exemplification of the historical-un-historical process to Milton (though equally well we might turn to Chaucer), we may learn the causes of this and the other fallacies even from Shakespeare's own unhistorical age, from Bacon. The illusion these scholars follow, is it not one of the Idols of the Tribe? I quote from the translation:

1. The human understanding is of its own nature prone to suppose the existence of more order and regularity in the world than it finds.
2. The human understanding when it has once adopted an opinion . . . draws all things else to support and agree with it.
3. Besides, independently of that delight and vanity which I have described, it is the peculiar and perpetual error of the human intellect to be more moved and excited by affirmatives than by negatives.

The aptness of the three quotations is, I trust, without comment apparent. We crave order and connections, sources or influences, and we draw all things else to support or agree with these. Source, influence, or convention (my own particular hobby), or the notion of fiction fashioned upon an ascertainable reality — such is the form and pattern, so to speak, of our thought; and we impose it on the material of literature almost perforce. Only in such terms do some of us think or cerebrate. Why, by the way, has Shakespeare been identified with Bacon? Is it merely because men cannot conceive of a half-educated rustic writing so well? Is it not in part because, there being no discernible relation (personal or literary) between them, men's thought has in its natural bent been thwarted, and has therefore in sheer helplessness — or sheer self-assertion, perhaps — fallen back upon the conclusion that the two must be one and the same? A connection it must have. A source, an influence, a bare allusion, might have sufficed to preserve to Shakespeare his literary identity. But the fact that between the two master-spirits of the age such connections are wanting, how in our unifying tendencies it should make us pause!

Literary scholars are not the only offenders. The customs of the stage are not literature, and I remember talking with a clever investigator at the British Museum who had got to the point of thinking that the Blackfriars theater was the center of the universe or at least the umbilicus of European theatrical life. Not content with saying that the custom of sitting on the stage arose there and spread to the other London theaters, he declared that it was carried over to Paris; and when I asked him how the Spanish too came to have the custom, at least as early as 1630, he replied, with a rising inflection, as if it were a matter of course, and the question were superfluous, "From Blackfriars." After a few years of research, of probing and proving, our eyes get set in our heads, and our answers (and conclusions, too) become automatic. A professor of economic history told me, not long since, of attending, a year or so ago, a meeting of historians in New York at which they were discussing the rise of autocracy and tyranny in the Roman Empire. They too considered only the question of source or influence, arising in Egypt or the Orient, and not one voice was raised for the theory of an origin independent and internal, out of the conditions at home. Our thought demands a single origin, at one spot, ignoring the identity and the spontaneous and universal fecundity of nature.

On the other hand, I remember a pretty illustration of the disengaged and larger vision in our own ranks, a brief comment many years ago by Professor Belden in *Modern Language Notes*. It was a striking parallel between a lyric of Heine's and a legend of the Wyandot Indians, about the marriage of the Sun and the Moon and of the Stars as their children. An alienation followed, a desertion. And now she follows him, and pale and languishing she rises in the east, as he, flushing with anger, sets in the west. But Professor Belden deliberately and austerely denied himself any belief in Heine's having heard the Wyandot story, which only since his death, indeed, had been made known to literature; preferring no doubt to believe that all men have imaginations, and can think much the same simple poetic thoughts by the North Sea and by Lake Huron. Anthropologists know they can; though there are others that think similar designs on baskets and pottery, to be found in Mexico as in Asia, must be the result of communication. Indeed, it is direct and actual evidence for that original myth-making power, which the reader feels instinctively in Heine and in Shelley, too, and is a notable characteristic of their genius. To them by nature the world was still young, was "herrlich wie am ersten Tag." There is likewise a remarkable parallel between an ancient Babylonian myth recently discovered and a passage in Dante; and should not the parallels between Shakespeare and Greek tragedy be viewed in a similar light? Paths cross, collisions occur, not only on this wide-wayed earth but in mid-ocean and (nowadays) in mid-air. And what is the chief delight in reading the ancient poets but that of finding our thoughts to be their thoughts;

or what, for that matter, is the chief delight in learning to know a friend? At times his words are ours, and often (without borrowing) we take them, as we say, out of each other's mouths.

5

In Milton scholarship there are fallacies of the same sort, and others too. A new school of Milton criticism has in recent years arisen which, indeed, has made notable additions to our knowledge of the poet. Monsieur Saurat, perhaps, is the leader of it; his book on Milton has been translated into English and has been widely read; and he has with him a Swedish scholar, Professor Liljegren, one German, and many Americans. The chief fallacy that I discern in their procedure is the historical, again, coupled with that craving for a revolutionary conception which appears in most of our literary scholarship, but is here aided and abetted by the new psychology. They themselves say much of their new views — of the new school — somewhat as Mr. Babbitt and Mr. More call themselves the New Humanists; and they approve and compliment each other, and freely (though honestly) play into each other's hands. Truth is the end of criticism; and often a coterie is inimical to the search for truth as not to that for beauty.

The new school insist that Milton was not so much a Puritan as a humanist, a son of the Renaissance and of the classical world; and they minimize what Puritanism they find. So the New Humanists and their followers find Shelley and even Wordsworth vaguely or weakly emotional, and Wordsworth — of all men — even immoral or irreligious.[6] Now there is no doubt that these researches have laid bare in Milton a greater degree of indebtedness to contemporary and ancient philosophy than had been recognized; but again the value of the work resides in the material presented rather than in the conclusions drawn, in the exposition rather than in

[6] See the reply of Professor J. W. Beach to Professor B. Cerf, *Publications of the Modern Language Association of America*, 1925.

the argument. The study of literature, as Professor Frederick Tupper has said, is in large measure a study in emphasis; and the emphasis some of the new Miltonians have shifted and disturbed. And that is what the New Humanists, in the opinion of some of us, have done to Shelley and Wordsworth.

Controversy is often merely verbal, but surely Milton was a Puritan and (in so far as a poet can be) more a Puritan than anything else. The English have been, rather naïvely, reproached for taking so little part in the new critical movement, but they need not look to their laurels so long as they have Sir Walter Raleigh to their credit; and to me he seems, though I confess I have not an expert's right to speak, to keep the balance more nearly even. No one worth considering ever thought of Milton as a crop-haired Praise-God or Zeal-in-the-Land, singing through his nose, breaking organs and smashing glass, hostile or indifferent to nature, art, or woman. The new school emphasize what Milton says of temperance, the pagan virtue; but what Milton has most to say of is obedience and righteousness. The new school draw attention to his passionate and sensuous nature; but Milton scorned it, and never gave it the rein. The new school, some of them, make Milton out to have been a Puritan less and less as time went on and more of a freethinker and philosopher. But the course of his thought as it appears in his poetry and prose from first to last reveals him as more of a dissenter, to be sure, but unflinching in his belief in God and (if not in the church) in the Bible, and less and less indulgent to the senses and earthly pleasure. He is more of a Puritan than ever, though just as he had left the Presbyterian chapel he now leaves the meetinghouse. Extreme dissent may look a little like freethinking and paganism, but it is worlds away. The Bible is in between.

If one sort of scholarship is, as we have seen, too literal, deeming that what song the Sirens sang, though a puzzling question, is not beyond all conjecture, another is too dubious and devious. To it nothing — no poet, no poem — is what it seems. It has the eyes of

Lynceus and is not to be taken in. It wears the spectacles of Teutonic philosophy or psychology, and penetrates the universal illusion. But a poem appeals to our naked senses and sensibilities; it was not penned for the *Forscher*, who has neither, or has transcended both the one and the other; and our natural impression cannot lightly be set aside. Indeed, it should be set aside or modified only as we can be proved to have misinterpreted, to have misunderstood.[7] Now the immediate impression derived from Milton and from his poetry — and as is the case to the same degree with few men, this is one and the same — is that he was what we ordinarily know by the word Puritan, though in a noble sense of the word; and by study and analysis that impression is not lessened but deepened. And *Lycidas* is more, not less, Puritan than *L'Allegro*; *Paradise Lost* is much more Puritan than *Lycidas*; *Paradise Regained* than *Paradise Lost*; and *Samson* even more than *Paradise Regained*. Sir Richard Jebb insists that (though in form it is) this great drama is not Greek, for it involves no fate, no dark cloud of destiny; but is Hebraic, in the vein of Jeremiah and of Deborah and Barak. The spirit of the Puritans was Hebraic, we know. And though in the *Hymn on the Nativity* and even in *Lycidas* the poet commingles Christian imagery and pagan, in *Paradise Lost* he seldom permits himself a classical allusion without at the same time labeling the story "feigned," or "fabled," or "an idle dream"; and in *Paradise Regained* he frowns, like a prophet or apostle, upon Greek philosophy and culture. This disapproval is, in an article on Spenser's influence upon Milton (by an American scholar, but considered by M. Saurat one of the corner stones of the new theory), explained away. But the influence of the poet of the Renaissance, except such as was hitherto recognized, is, I think, by no

[7] This is true in art as not in history. As I have often endeavored to show, the figures in drama — particularly in popular drama — must be taken at their face value unless the author has given a clear hint that they are not to be. With the author himself, not a fiction, we may go farther, and psychoanalyze him — if we have sufficient data. It can be done, no doubt, with Byron and Poe.

means demonstrated;[8] and the disapproval of Greek philosophy in *Paradise Regained* is not owing to its being, like scholasticism, antiquated and played out, but to its being simply mortal and mundane, in contrast with the "light from above, from the fountain of light." And the facts, of course, and common sense itself are for us. Milton *was* a Puritan, both in creed and in party, and was not so much a son of the Renaissance as a grandson. It is when he gives the rein to his fancy that he shows his kinship with the Renaissance, not in morals or religion.

The new school point to the fact that in Michael's vision of the future at the end of *Paradise Lost* there is no mention of the Reformation. Has Milton become indifferent? He had hoped that his

[8] The received opinion is that Milton shows the influence of Spenser only in his earliest poems. "Milton acknowledged to me," says Dryden, "that Spenser was his original." To this word, interpreted by Professor Raleigh in the sense of "his earliest admiration, his poetic godfather who first won him to poetry," Professor Greenlaw ("Spenser's Influence on Paradise Lost," *Studies in Philology*, 1920) has given instead a precise and definite meaning, and in reference to his masterpiece. Some part of the spiritual and even of the physical philosophy of the poem is derived from the elder poet; as well as some matters of detail such as his particular use of Demogorgon, the Garden of Adonis, and the "apple" for the "fruit of the tree."

The mere fact that sensitive critics like Sir Walter Raleigh, led by Milton's words to look for this influence, have hitherto not found it, is proof presumptive that it is not there. An influence not discernible with the naked eye is no influence, or the word no longer has a meaning. And the resemblance between the poets actually discovered seems for the most part only the almost inevitable likeness of two Christian poets, living in the same age, breathing the same air, and reading the same books — practically all the classics of their time. Here is the "influence" — of seventeenth-century England, of Greece, Rome, and Judæa (which Mr. Greenlaw, to be sure, also recognizes) rather than of Spenser. Dryden's words, moreover, when viewed, without prejudice, in their context, seem to show that he and Milton had no thought of subject-matter, still less of the subject-matter of *Paradise Lost*, but of style and poetic spirit, even of things metrical. Spenser had fanned the poetic spark within the Puritan's bosom, that is all. In his earliest poems this is apparent. But surely Milton owed little or nothing to Spenser for his ideas of Chaos and the atomic philosophy, for scholasticism and Platonism, for classical mythology, or for the "apple," which, put in Adam's hand, is at least as old as Caedmon. To me, personally, the most apparent signs of Spenser's spirit (if there be any) in *Paradise Lost* are purely esthetic and scenic, as in such concepts as "darkness visible" and "lay floating many a rood."

party would bring about a real Reformation in England, Luther's and Calvin's and Cranmer's having failed. And what has now come of it? The Restoration, triumph of King and bishops. The Reformation, then, why mention it? He himself now is Orpheus overtaken by Bacchus and his revelers, or Samson fallen among the Philistines, and his only consolation is in a future far away. So shall the world go on, says Michael,

> To good malignant, to bad men benign,
> Under her own weight groaning till the day
> Appear of respiration to the just,
> And vengeance to the wicked . . .

But that deep tone of melancholy, and of a consolation too remote, is not one either of indifference or of despair. It is the note of faith, though at bay.

Moreover, the impression that we legitimately derive from *Paradise Lost*, whether directly or indirectly, is that the fault of Adam was not that of excess, of disturbing the balance of temperance, but of mere disobedience, of breaking the law, of sin, as the Christians call it. Milton says as much in the first line of the poem: God and His angels, Adam and Eve, say it afterwards. Temperance is touched on once or twice; but to a Puritan not of the strictest sect, as to the ancient Hebrew before him, such an idea was not alien. Like the ancient Hebrews, Christians in good standing since, and many of the Puritans of his time, Milton did not hate the senses or abhor reasonable and legitimate enjoyment. He played the organ and let his hair grow. He smoked, he drank — he was not a fanatic. But he was severe, austere, not mild or tolerant. And the attitude he took to life was not that of Sophocles or Pericles, of Socrates or Plato, of Zeno, even, or Epictetus, and still less that of Spenser, who took pleasure in writing of Phaedria and Acrasia, the Bower of Bliss and the Squire of Dames, but that of a quick and wholly awakened conscience. Every poem reveals it. Even the youthful Latin poems, where under the spell of the classical tra-

dition he gave himself freer rein, are chaste and modest; but to
him they later seemed too unrestrained, and he unsparingly
penned his palinode.

> Haec ego mente olim laeva, studioque supino,
> Nequitiae posui vana trophaea meae.

And Milton was a poet. Like most *Forscher*, the new school —
some of them — seem at times to forget this, in their historical and
philosophical prepossessions. They are bent on making him of the
Renaissance not only in spirit but in thought. His learning was indeed prodigious, but the transition to that from his poetry is a
ticklish and a dangerous thing. As a philosopher he may rightly be
called a materialist and pantheist — I am not prepared to contradict it; but I see little justification for drawing such conclusions
from his verse. To the exigencies of poetic narrative are often to
be attributed the materialistic conceptions that appear in *Paradise
Lost*. Eating and sleeping, singing and loving, sweet sights and
smells, are in Heaven indispensable if it is to be a Heaven at all.
The poet cannot present the angels and celestial sanctities in a
vacuum. Life there seems empty and jejune enough at best. To recall More or Boehme, Plato or Plotinus, philosophers ancient or
modern, seems here rather irrelevant and superfluous. And if
Milton's own poetic spirit did not suffice him, the example of
Homer did. In any case, conclusions touching doctrine cannot
legitimately be derived from the incidents of the fable. Only when
Milton is didactic should his text be treated as if it were that of
Lucretius. Only then are such conclusions more justifiably to be
derived from Milton's epic than from Wordsworth's lyrics.

It is particularly in Adam's fall that these scholars find the principle of temperance illustrated. Adam is uxorious, fondly over-
come by female charm. But he has done more than deviate from
the golden mean. It is, as we have seen, an offence; it is a heinous
sin; it is an act of disobedience even at this point as well as in the
consequent eating of the apple, against which, as well as against

that, he had been explicitly warned by the visiting angel. And that Milton has presented the offence at its origin somewhat in the light of a thing good in itself overdone, is surely owing not to principle but to his need for motivation. Adam is supposed to be as yet sinless, and for dramatic and poetic propriety and plausibility there must be a transition. Without flaw, he cannot, logically, be tempted; only through the excess of a good quality can he be conceived to sin. Yet the deed is not judged accordingly, whether by the Lord or by the poet. And even in the philosophy of sex relations, which M. Saurat discloses in Milton elsewhere, the mild doctrine of the golden mean I fail to find. Milton is not Greek but Hebrew — of the patriarchal days — or, we might say, a noble and poetical Mormon. He is nothing at all of a naturalist but a legalist. The one relation, of marriage, is proper and right, and even to the intemperate point of polygamy; the other, beyond the bounds of wedlock, is wholly wrong. It is a matter of obedience, again, not of temperance, of free indulgence in the one case, of total abstinence in the other, not of moderation or excess. The Mormons, we must remember, came of Puritan stock, and were of that tradition; the Mormons, like the Puritans, the ancient Hebrews and the Mohammedans, were legalists, self-indulgent in one regard, strong prohibitionists in others, and exemplars of temperance in none. And in all the chief poems — *Comus, Paradise Lost, Paradise Regained,* and *Samson Agonistes,* alike — there is, as one of the school has admirably shown, the same central situation. It is that of temptation. What could be more Puritan? What less Greek? In all four it is not a question of temperance, moderation, or the golden mean at all. The doctrine of temperance is presented — though speciously — by Comus, by the Devil.

6

Was Milton himself aware of his insidious humanism? M. Saurat speaks of Milton's "taking up Puritanism because it embodied his favorite virtues of fortitude and temperance [pagan virtues!] and because it was the only organized force in that age which, by overthrowing the old order, would offer a chance for the realization of his revolutionary ideals. He joined the party, made it serve his turn, but was at bottom inspired by intellectual pride and ambition and by sensuous passion." Here is the new psychology at work. But though most human motives and emotions are mixed, and Milton's here too (maybe) in some measure, the man is to me incomprehensible as he joins in the conflict and abandons his poetic dreams, leaves the Church for the Presbyterians, the Royalists for the Parliamentary party, and then the Presbyterians for the Independents, and writes *Lycidas*, the sonnets *On His Blindness* and on *Piedmont, Paradise Lost, Paradise Regained*, and *Samson*, save as he is animated by moral, religious, and patriotic ardor. If John Milton was not candid and in earnest, the ground gives way beneath me. If he wasn't, who, then, was? Is there a nigger in every woodpile, a wicked card up every sleeve? Not up *this* sleeve — we beseech thee, O Lord! "Everything is what it is," says Bishop Butler, "and not another thing." But that obvious though sage maxim is, it seems, not now regarded — not in Milton criticism, not in Shakespeare criticism, Heaven knows, nor even in history itself. Witness the recent discussion of responsibility for the war. From all appearances England did not desire war, but that only proves she did. Even our sober and solid citizens have been affected, in their remoter, more speculative reasonings. They too now bore and burrow, too cunning for common facts. Only yesterday there was in a newspaper a letter from one of them, English in name, American by birth, but bent upon exonerating the Germans and throwing the weight of the burden on — President McKinley and Mark Hanna. The man ought to be called to the bar, or to a chair.

By this interpretation is attributed to Milton, not hypocrisy, to be sure, but a sort of designing spirit or unconscious insincerity.

Some, however, go farther than that. In their historical intemper-
ance and zeal they make him out to be of the Renaissance not only
in spirit but in deed. Professor Liljegren thinks Milton did not see
Galileo but in his pride and egotism pretended that he did; both
Liljegren and Saurat think that (somewhat like the English we
used to hear of who sank the Lusitania) Milton fabricated evidence
against Charles I by having the Pamela prayer, the prayer of a
heathen woman to a heathen god, foisted into the *Eikon Basilike,*
and then, for such devotions, treacherously attacked the dead
king's memory; and Dr. Mutschmann, it seems, considers Milton
not only a hypocrite but half mad, and an Albino into the bargain.
A Pope and a Swift in one! But Monsieur Saurat outdoes even the
German, and bears away the bell, when he suspects that Milton
may have owed his blindness to inherited syphilis. Here are the
precious affirmatives of which Bacon, long before our own little
science was born, took due notice. But the reader they "move and
excite" rather differently from the author.

Not only the new psychology but the new physiology, as well as
history and *Culturgeschichte!* And it all comes into play in the
matter of the *Eikon Basilike.* Milton is concerned not only as a
propagandist — there he is Puritan enough — but also as a disciple
of Machiavelli. It is on this latter aspect, characteristically, that
they insist. But all these attacks upon Milton's integrity seem to
be based on flimsy evidence. The mountain of argument raised by
Liljegren to demonstrate the infernal perfidy of the *Eikon Basilike*
affair is founded, as Mr. Smart, an Englishman, has shown, on the
testimony of a man who in his own day was known to be a jailbird
and a perjurer. And the passion for affirmation (or contradiction)
in a scholar must be mighty if it can lead him the length of charg-
ing a great worthy with mendacity simply because, as we understand, Galileo was closely guarded by the Inquisition. For how
closely, who can at this distance tell?

7

Why have they interpreted Milton so far askew? I have called it an historical fallacy, a psychological one; but why not interpret him according to his actual environment as a product of Puritanism, and as a Puritan psychoanalyze him? Turn about is fair play, and I will psychoanalyze the critics. Is there not here the spirit of anachronism as well, and have they not, in making him a son of the Renaissance, seemingly satisfied their historical sense while they really circumvented it, assimilating him to themselves? They have gone behind the returns, have, so to speak, psychoanalyzed the very *Zeitgeist* — that is, as is commonly the case, revealed themselves:

> Was ihr den Geist der Zeiten heisst,
> Das ist im Grund der Herren *eigner* Geist,
> In dem die Zeiten sich bespiegeln.

Puritanism is nowadays not acceptable in literature — we are one and all for humanism. Even the New Humanists so designate themselves, though "New Puritans" might have been a better title. And a free-thinking Spartan, stern teacher of temperance rather than obedience and righteousness, and, perhaps, ruthless propagandist and scion of Machiavelli besides — how much more interesting, piquant, "intriguing" a conception! The more complicated the better, it would seem, today; but the truth, not what is more interesting or ingenious, is what some of us are seeking.

8

Whether ingenuity or dullness be the cause, the truth is too little revealed, for all the portentous appearance of disclosing it. So elaborate and ponderous an apparatus and procedure, with so meager a product or result! A winepress, to squeeze out a cupful! And such an array of problems, many of them far-fetched or fictitious, so seldom really solved! Truth? How often we are given but the myths of scholarship, the monstrous and spectral imaginations

(*vide passim supra*) of the *un*poetic mind. That, I think, is why we
are dissatisfied with literary scholarship, with historical criticism.
What a droll situation (upon which, nevertheless, our whole system of degree-winning and dissertation-writing depends) that we
should be so satisfied with our own! In *their* writing we seek the
truth at all events. But how ironical that we, who despise the
belletristic trifler, should, for all our labor and show of rigor, attain to it often no better than he! We too are trifling — not dealing
with substantial things but playing a game with counters — though
we do not know it. Or shall I say, we are bluffing, both ourselves
and some few readers, with our parade of evidence and serried
array of arguments, so many of which will not stand the test? Facts,
certainly, are important; criticism based on mere impressions is
flimsy. But in literary criticism mere industry — mere argument
and ingenuity and technical adroitness — does not much avail.
There a fact is not a fact, a truth not a truth, save in its right relations; and an upsetting of the proportion, a disturbance of the
emphasis, turns it to error. The new truth is in effect often farther
from the mark than the old. "Le vrai à l'état brut, est plus faux
que le faux." Why is it that often the best and the most readable
scientific criticism is not what affirms and asserts but what denies
and contradicts, and disproves what has been so hopefully proved? [9]

[9] The evidence and the logic being so frequently of the sort that would not
pass muster in a court of law, one is tempted again and again to undertake this
work of refutation. One does not, because it is the writing of a friend or (what
is more ticklish) of an enemy, or because to do so would be throwing time away.
Fortunately some scholars, seeing their error themselves, publicly recant it, like
Dryden and Lemaître, who had the heart to poke fun at their own youthful
verses; but seldom does it happen save when they are making room for a new
hypothesis, casting down one idol to set up another. The axe is to be laid to
the root — the main trouble is the premature bursting into print. The universities and the editors of the journals can, if they will, guard writers (as well as
readers) from youthful indiscretions. Would that I had been guarded, and
however they themselves may feel about it, a good many others I can think of,
besides. But some departments print (and often they do a little more than
print) even their Masters' theses. Their principal value, when they are the
students' own work, is as an indication of the standards of scholarship at the
institution concerned.

(Then we breathe again freely!) But that is a thankless (though daily demanded) labor; and a better sort than either is that which analyzes and compares, expounds and equably illumines (as only your true scholar, who knows and respects the facts, can do it), instead of arguing or controverting. Essentially, and as a whole, I think, the new Milton, so ingeniously reproportioned and readjusted, is, though more illuminated in detail, less the real Milton than is the one we know. And naturally. Though we are writing history, it is the history of a literature. And even less than the history of institutions can that of literature be written by the aid of science.[10] This is but a tool. Historical criticism, though it pretends to be a science, should rather, in its humble way, be an art; and that requires more than tools and a mere workman's skill — imagination, a sense of proportion, a true and faithful reading of both text and time. Without these, historical criticism may be, indeed, written for pleasure, but not read. So a man would write, however he may live, unto himself alone. So a man would be read, if ever, by

[10] Often the scientific, objective method, for all its corrective value, of itself quite fails, as in questions of authorship. We know, to be sure, that Ben Jonson wrote the additions to the *Spanish Tragedy*, not because these are like his other work in so far as it remains to us, but simply because of Henslowe's entries. Still they are not unworthy of him or incompatible with the bent of his imagination elsewhere. When, however, the external and the internal evidence clash, a fine ear is the safest guide. A good case was some years ago made out against Dryden's authorship of *MacFlecknoe* in favor of Oldham's (though in a following number of the *Modern Language Review* this was pretty well overthrown), but no one who then reread the poem should have been convinced. Every line and couplet ring of Dryden — Dryden — not Oldham or another. It is no parallelism of thought or wording — authors repeat themselves, indeed, no more necessarily than other writers repeat them — nor even a similar structure, turn of phrase, or trick of meter. It is the tone, which only in part can be thus analyzed. There undoubtedly are interpolated passages in *King Lear* and in the witch scenes of *Macbeth*, but texts and external clues help us little as compared with an ear like Coleridge's, Swinburne's, or Professor Child's. Certainly such spurious passages are *not* scene i and the beginning of scene iii in the latter play. No evidence, external or internal, no argument like Mr. Cuningham's about consistency of structure or quality of meter or style can prevail against them. They have the authentic tone, the unmistakable accent — "that is *Shakespeare* or the Devil."

his son. However little to our liking the thought may be, are we
not, most of us, coming to that, then to dry-rot at ease till the
Judgment Day?

And how about the *others*, who are doing that? What is to become of us if *they* go on writing? No man now, even in his own
field, can keep abreast of the output, and continue to read literature itself — and write. And is it not more important for us as
students rather to spend our time on literature — that of the ancients, that of other languages than our own? As students of English literature we can learn more from French, Spanish, Italian,
German, Scandinavian, and Slavic literature than we can from
the labored and abortive articles and dissertations which diurnally
appear. (And yet some generous, omnivorous souls complain that
certain universities do not print their theses, not realizing that
thus in part these institutions preserve the preëminent reputation
of their degrees.) The only remedy (apart from a more judicial
spirit in the editors) seems to be critical bibliographies or digests.
Most bibliographies are as undiscriminating and all-embracing as
Nature. And as for the digests, what has really been proved by the
immense output of dissertations and articles concerning English
literature, and has at the same time been worth the proving, could,
I daresay (though I am speaking rashly) be brought within the
compass of somewhat less than five hundred pages. What we need
most is an *index librorum*, not *prohibitorum* — not *mortalium* —
but *mortuorum*, even if our own dear names must be written there.
Why should we all, willy-nilly, follow the prescribed path, down
every blind alley and (perchance) to the dustbin, when the way to
the mountains is open? Life is fleeting; for most of us, maybe, it is
more than half over, much of it having been frittered (though not
idled) away on the dingy by-paths, and through the constantly
more bewildering mazes, of scholarship. What false trails have we
not followed, what have we not had to learn and to unlearn! But
none of it has been so wasted as that which we have spent in read-

ing what others like us have penned. Here for once the golden rule does not apply. We must write — nothing this side the grave or the crematory can now stop us; but we would fain — for our souls' health must needs — spend more of those numbered but unknown days which remain to us (whereon we ourselves are not writing) reading them that have written for the time to come. And then, who knows? we may write a little better, and ourselves be read.

IX

Milton, Puritan of the Seventeenth Century

This essay is a study of a poet's personality. Seldom has one of the highest order left its impress in verse so boldly and completely as John Milton's. He wrote about himself, but above all he continually revealed himself in his art and manner. Confessions say much but reveal little, and this indirect and unconscious self-disclosure is really the more direct. It is so in Dante, who though a Catholic is the poet nearest akin — the stamp of his personality means more than all he undertakes to tell.

Milton was, of course, a Puritan, though we are inclined of late to minimize it. He was a political partisan and religious reformer, a propagandist and pamphleteer; and when he wrote his greatest poetry the cause he had advocated was already lost. He was blind, his friends were mostly dead or turned renegade, and his daughters were undutiful. Life was bitter to him, his outlook upon it was severe, and he died in his enemies' day. Facts and circumstances such as these do not harmonize with our prevalent notions of the greatest poetry. Turning away from Dante, we conceive of it as born of a more genial blood or in a blander air. Homer and Virgil, Chaucer and Shakespeare, were not moralists, Dante himself was not of a sect; and since *Paradise Lost* is great and glorious poetry we are inclined to forget what Milton was.

Some critics, therefore, make him predominantly a humanist,[1] a product of the Renaissance and the ancient culture. They find him teaching not so much righteousness as temperance, and have a shrewd notion that his Adam was well content to get out of Paradise and take a look at the world.[2] Since he was an Independent and a heretic, they think they have warrant for making him something of a skeptic; since he frequently reflects the ancient philosophy, they hold it was in large part substituted for the Christian theology; since he was hard and ascetic as the Puritans were, they take him for a stoic: and since in Michael's vision of the future in *Paradise Lost* the Reformation is not mentioned they would have that event, all-important to a Protestant, play no part in Milton's religious and cosmical scheme. Indeed, they make him partly of the age of the Renaissance, partly of their own. Not that this last is anything novel or unusual. Like Shakespeare, like Dante before him, the poet has always been read in the light of the reader's time, not the poet's. The sentimental eighteenth century took him for a poet of "the tender." The romantic age delighted in him as a visionary and a religious and political rebel. And this present epoch of history and culture, of sweetness and light, of the "new humanism" as some people would call it, likewise turns and makes out of the grim and doughty old Puritan, by way of the Renaissance, something more like unto itself.

It is, therefore, more precisely, the purpose of this essay to make distinctions and insist on differences, to rescue if possible Milton from the sixteenth century, to which he was indebted, and from

[1] The word is, like most critical phrases, rather loosely used, particularly since the advent of the New Humanism of Messrs. Babbitt, More, and Sherman. That is really a Puritan variety of estheticism, in the style of Matthew Arnold. Here the word is used as it applies, say, to Spenser; not as it applies, more properly, to the apostles or exponents of the New Learning, such as Ficino and Ascham, Erasmus and Bruno, Rabelais and Montaigne. It is so, it would seem, that the word is used by the new school of Milton criticism (Saurat and others) at which I am glancing.

[2] See above, "Was Paradise Well Lost?"

the twentieth, which is indebted to him, and replace him in his own. I shall say little of the ideas and the doings of Milton thus contradicted — of them I have spoken elsewhere [3] — but of what is more important in a poet, his art, and tone, and manner, contradicted quite as much. The tone and manner of Milton are individual and unmistakable, and are, as I perceive them, in the main those of a Puritan hero, a great poetical prophet. A Puritan, a religious and political dissenter, may be a poet, for there is Dante — there is Milton himself. (As a moralist, an individualist, Dante is, though a Catholic, Puritan enough, though as we shall see he has the Catholic's concrete, not the Puritan's rationalized imagination.) The tone of a humanist,[4] as I imagine it, is widely different. As heard in the poetry of the Renaissance, it is such as that of Spenser and John Fletcher, Donne and Herrick, and though the word is hardly big enough for him, Shakespeare. A humanist is tolerant and genial, all-embracing and all-enjoying. A humanist has humor, takes his liberty and is not greatly troubled about consistency, and sets the spirit and the flesh, Christianity and paganism pretty much on a level. A humanist is all things to all men and their opinions, and his thoughts and feelings are not perfectly harmonized or rigorously ordered. A Puritan's are, and to that end part of human experience is excluded from their scope. They are centered, like Milton's, in the moral and religious sentiment.

1

THE PURITAN TONE   •

In Milton there is nothing naïve, irregular or unregulated, lax or remiss. In Spenser and Ariosto there is much. They will glow with enthusiasm for virtue one moment and delight in the naked-

---

[3] See the two preceding essays.

[4] See above, p. 222, note. The word is used somewhat differently by some Milton critics; but of this fact I cannot here take account. They fairly agree in making him a posthumous son of the Renaissance, minimizing though not ignoring his asceticism.

ness of a nymph the next. And Shakespeare sympathizes not only with the Duke and Isabella but with Pompey and Mrs. Overdone. That is humanism. Milton, of course, is guilty of no such indulgence to others or himself. He does not scorn pleasure but he is wary of it. His loins are girt, his lamp is lighted, and his eyes are lifted up to the hills, whence cometh his help. Not that he is rapt, ecstatic, or blindly confident. He is no visionary, no enthusiast; on the contrary he has a vein of melancholy in him. Yet it is not that of Spenser or Shakespeare, of Shelley or Byron; it is neither the lover's melancholy nor the poet's, half-sweet. It is no complaint to moon or stars, no invocation to death. It is rather the melancholy of one whose faith is strong but whose hope is remote; who has been through the war, and seen his own and others' high expectations defeated and their reforms thwarted, the righteous man put down and the wicked exalted in his place. His eye hath kept watch o'er man's mortality, and man's frailty as well. But his faith does not waver, his hope is not quenched. His spirit is steadfast, not bent upon the glorious but vain and fleeting shows of this world, like that of a humanist, but raised above them.

And this surely is the spirit of the Christian or Hebrew, and not of the Greek. It is recognizably that of *Paradise Lost, Paradise Regained,* and *Samson Agonistes*; and of the sonnets *On His Blindness, On the Massacre at Piedmont,* and *On His Deceased Wife,* as well as of some of the minor poems penned in his sequestered youth. No poet ever remained through life so perfectly poised and identical, so serenely and imperturbably conscious and strenuous. He did not indulge himself, we have seen, as poets do, in melancholy, in song and emotions, for their own sake; and his very relaxations are stately. He unbends austerely, like a man who has heard the call; and his sonnets to a Young Lady, to Skinner, Lawrence, and Lawes are gracious and affable, but decorous and discreet. He is never careless, seldom gay. And even before the war, in his earliest sonnets, in *Comus,* in *L'Allegro* and *Il Penseroso,* the youth is as the man. His pleasures are meditative and moderate, innocent and sedate. Only in the Latin poems is there a looser rein, as he dwells on the beauties he sees in the park or in imagination enters into the delights of dance and song enjoyed by Diodati at a country house. These divagations he afterwards regretted, but we find in them nothing blamable. He is there not yet so strict and circumspect but is far from audacious or libertine. In youth to have been altogether as he was in age would have stifled the poet in him.

There is nothing lax or latitudinarian in his faith, for all his heresy and independence. As time went on neither church nor meetinghouse could content him, but that does not mean that he turned to the philosophers and the God of Nature. In *Paradise Lost, Paradise Regained*, and *Samson* he is more ascetic or Puritan than in *Comus* and *Lycidas*; and less indulgent to human frailty and to paganism. He watches his words. He becomes precise and punctilious as he makes use of the pagan mythology, indispensable to a poet in his day. Even in *Lycidas*, where in general he uses extraordinary tact in infusing into the traditional form and phrase a Christian thought and feeling, so as to avoid impiety or anachronism, he refers to God as all-judging Jove. But in the later poems there is no more of this, though Dante (naïver spirit) had called God Jove before him. There is no mediation, no compromise. Every time a pagan god or myth is alluded to there is a saving phrase, such as "fabl'd," or "feigned," or "an empty dream." He does it all incredibly like a poet, though anxiously, like a Precisian.

And yet for all his circumspection and rigor he is not a prig and bore as Wordsworth, in the *Prelude* and elsewhere, sometimes is. He is not complacent, is not continually taking stock of himself or summing up his solitary joys and virtues. Methodism had not come and gone: his eye does not roll inward but rests on what is afar. He is no Bunyan or Baxter; nor is he an Isaiah or Jeremiah, either, being heir to all the Greek and Roman culture. He loves beauty and the solid refinements of life. But the Greek spirit, the spirit of the Renaissance, in so far as he has accepted it, has in him suffered a change. It is duly subordinated, and its frankness and indulgence are sternly curbed. Christ he sets far above Socrates and Plato, Dante (surely) above Sophocles. The beauty he courts is chaste and severe. Eve is naked and so is Adam, and though Milton is a little heavy-handed and protests too much, it is the nakedness of virtue. Here Spenser, though a little of a Puritan too, would certainly have melted, and his descriptions would have been warm and human, as they are at Phaedria's and Acrasia's bowers. But Milton remains uncompromised, unchanged.

2

How does the man reveal himself in *Paradise Lost*? Structure or plot in the larger sense does not here concern us. What does concern us is the intangible but pervading spirit of the poem — the style, the elements of structure, like the repeated *motifs*, which echo and resound through its ample spaces, the attitude to man and nature and the world beyond. Pursuing this inquiry, we shall perforce pick and choose a bit, somewhat arbitrarily, for in an essay we cannot cover the poem.

The proëmium announces the theme, and strikes the key, which, with only such variations and modulations as may preserve so long a poem from monotony, is fairly kept throughout.

> Of man's first disobedience, and the fruit
> Of that forbidden tree, whose mortal taste
> Brought Death into the world, and all our woe,
> With loss of Eden, till one greater Man
> Restore us, and regain the blissful seat,
> Sing, Heavenly Muse, that on the secret top
> Of Oreb, or of Sinai, didst inspire
> That shepherd, who first taught the chosen seed,
> In the beginning how the Heav'ns and Earth
> Rose out of chaos.

That is the subject, that is the tone. There is, so far, nothing necessarily Puritan about either, but still less is there of the humanist. Both are lofty and exalted, stern and severe.

Passing over the extraordinary — the sublime — energy of phrase and verse, which changes in movement with the sentiment or the vision, as in the soaring sweep of the close, simply consider the first three lines and a half. Here, and above all in the second and third, there is that note of high lamentation and prophetic mournfulness, characteristic of the later poet and this poem. No other of his is so distinguished by it save the sonnet *On the Massacre at Piedmont*; and in *Paradise Lost* it is fairly pervasive and dominant. These words, placed as they are in the meter and in the harmony of vowels and consonants (which are dependent on the sense but by their music vivify it) become, with their recurrent sounds and brooding movement, a sublime wail for the sin of the world:

> whose mortal taste
> Brought death into the world and all our woe.

And it echoes and reëchoes through the poem. The last phrase, by a fine musical stratagem, recurs at the great and momentous occasions in the story. It is a *leitmotiv*, so to speak. Sin takes the key of Hell from her girdle,

> sad instrument of all our woe;

the serpent leads Eve, our credulous mother,

> to the tree
> Of prohibition, root of all our woe;

and at other points there are variations upon it, such as "world of woe and sorrow," and "that brought into this world a world of woe." In Book Nine, that of the temptation, the phrase, with special appropriateness, recurs, in changing form, several times. Though a musician, though the greatest conscious metrist in English and one of the greatest in any tongue, Milton has not much of the musical principle or method in his rhetoric, of the lyrical repetition and eddying, dear to Spenser [5] as to Swinburne. The only other *leitmotiv* in the poem is used less musically than dramatically, the famous, reverberating line,

> Thrones, dominations, princedoms, virtues, powers,

spoken by God when he addresses the heavenly host, and by Satan, first when he addresses his fellow rebels, and then when he returns from the earth in triumph. Hence the conspicuousness of this solemn one, winding through his solid and serried lines.

Of such a character is the ground-tone or burden of the poem. There are now and then other tones in the air, or treble, but fitting into the harmony. *Paradise Lost* has many and varied movements; an epic, it therefore verges upon drama, with shifting parts and changing accents, though it is always the poet himself that is speaking. There is a great range, one voice but many tones and notes. The poem ends, indeed, on a note of reconciliation, as Adam and Eve

> hand in hand, with wandering steps and slow,
> Through Eden took their solitary way.

And this is one of its exquisite beauties. Such a close has been gradually but fully prepared for, as God and man are reconciled. Heaven and Hell give place to Earth; the exalted passions and unreal light or gloom of either yield to the twilight of human existence as we know it; and the ground-tone of prophetic lamentation dies away at last into a murmur of human regret.

Milton's large utterance and lofty melancholy appear in other connections than with the sin of the human race.

> Darkn'd so, yet shon
> Above them all the Archangel; but his face
> Deep scars of thunder had intrench't, and care
> Sat on his faded cheek.

[5] See above, p. 183.

There it is the prophet's sorrow for the Apostate. And it often takes a turn that is dramatic; again and again the melancholy note is differentiated to fit Satan's lips or Belial's, though always contemplative, always recognizable in the last analysis as Milton's own.

> If thou beest he; but O how fall'n, how chang'd
> From him who in the happy realms of light . . .

This is, perhaps, human rather than Puritan, but more like a Puritan than like a humanist.

3

A mood also prophetic, and surely Puritan enough, is that of scorn for the weak and foolish, of wrath and vindictive indignation against the wicked.

> Him the Almighty Power
> Hurl'd headlong flaming from the ethereal sky,
> With hideous ruin and combustion down
> To bottomless perdition, there to dwell
> In adamantine chains and penal fire,
> Who durst defy the omnipotent to arms.

That's what he got! The downpour of punishment, even like that of the verse, is overwhelming, relentless, grim. And the grim and ironical, the scornful and sardonic, appears frequently in the poem, particularly when the poet touches on Catholicism or prelacy, on women and their wiles.

> And they who, to be sure of Paradise,
> Dying put on the weeds of Dominic,
> Or in Franciscan think to pass disguised.

Since he is one of the greatest of poets the bitterness is not so much in what he says as in the way he says it — the alliteration and rhythm, the turn of the phrase and of the line — and these verses have the grand curl of Milton's Puritanic lips. Superb and splendid, they are those of a fighter and hater turned poet. And

though superstition is a grievous folly, a more grievous is that of
Adam, Samson, Solomon:

> he scrupled not to eat
> Against his better knowledge, not deceiv'd,
> But fondly overcome with female charm.

To be *weak* is miserable! There is little pity or indulgence in those
hard, harmonious lines. Imagine them in the mouth of Spenser
or Shakespeare, of Donne or even Dante, with their tender com-
passion for those thus vanquished!

And then there is the independent and partisan, the rebel and
regicide, the recusant in religion, morals, and politics. He is all of
that, as well as God's prophet, alone against the world. And so he is
Abdiel,

> Among the faithless, faithful only he;
> Among innumerable false, unmov'd . . .

So strong is dissent within him that he is at times almost Satan
himself. His hand warms to the work as he depicts the archangel
scorning sheer force, glorying in unconquerable will, immortal
hate, and considering

> What reinforcement we may gain from hope,
> If not, what resolution from despair.

And these redoubtable elements of character Milton could have
found in his own Puritan bosom. Bunyan's Christian had something of this desperate courage, admired by the free-thinking but
Puritan Shaw. Cromwell and his Ironsides had it. But the ancient
Anglo-Saxons had it too, and these characteristics could, of course,
have been presented by Milton or another even if a mellow humanist, if also a poet. Milton's imagination far outruns the man
himself, but certainly a humanist's would have had considerably more ground to cover. Imagination, indeed, subject and style,
are quite all that there is in the matter before us whereby to
judge.

4

THE DEVILS

The devils are the best-drawn characters in the poem, the devils
and the woman. Is this, then, a self-betrayal, and is at last the secret
out? Is here again Milton's heart not in the work or for the cause,
just as when Adam, according to one critic, went out of Paradise
"in excellent spirits"?[6] In the hands of almost any other believing
but enlightened poet of the time the situation would necessarily
have been much the same. Of God and Christ, the angels and
archangels, little could be made because of their exalted perfec-
tions. Adam, in his sinlessness, is such another; and only in his
evil hour can he touch us. But the devils and the woman have sins
and weaknesses, are of this world, fit for drama. In Dante Heaven
is not so far inferior to Hell as in Milton; but it is not because there
is in him more zeal or sanctity. There is more naïveté. Milton had
his Puritan and congenital spirit of contentiousness and rebelliousness, which permitted him to enter into the character of the devils,
though without approving them. So far, he is like Dante with
Francesca and Ulysses, like Marlowe with Faustus. But he had not
the simple spirit of love and happiness, which permitted the Florentine to enter into the hearts of the angels. Quite apart from his
Protestant prejudices, it was impossible for him so to conceive of
Gabriel, who, in the highest circle, with wings spread wide, stands
looking into the eyes of the Virgin, singing, Ave Maria, gratia
plena, so enamoured that he seems a-fire —

> che con tanto gioco
> Guarda negli occhi la nostra Regina
> Innamorato sì, che par di foco.

Milton, too, as we shall see, takes, for the sake of reality, plenty of
earth up into Heaven, but he cannot make it burst like that into
flower.

[6] See above, "Was Paradise Well Lost?"

A great Puritan if a poet is also still more a man (so far the critics are right), and it is the humanity of him (which is not the same as humanism)[7] rather than the Puritanism, that makes him a dramatic poet. And Milton's hard, bold, and not wholly regenerate human nature must have taken a solid satisfaction in portraying the devils. With them his hands are unfettered and free, in them he finds the elements of our human character. Satan's proud imaginations and audacious sarcasms, Moloch's unbending defiance, Beëlzebub's policy and Belial's melancholy, must have been a delight to him as they are to us. The devils are all eloquent, all poetical, and despite Milton's own moral disapprobation, depicted with gusto. And yet they are Puritanical devils too. Except in the story of the progeniture of Death, which is really no better than an allegory, there is little that is indecent or vicious about them. They have none of the naughty ways and indecorous demeanor of Dante's. They are heroes, archangels newly fallen, still severe. Mammon, the least erected spirit, whose eyes had been bent on the gold of the celestial pavement, proposes, like a statesman, when he takes the floor in the diabolical counsels, to found an empire in Hell to outrival the heavenly, and make the most of their defeat. He is almost as proud as the rest, and scorns the thought of returning to "warble hymns"

> and to his Godhead sing
> Forc't hallelujahs.

And Belial, like Modo, "is a gentleman." Slothful and deceitful, and, so far, with nothing whatever of Milton's private and personal nature in him, he speaks, after Satan, the best of all; and his bland and sinuous reasonings, his irony and raillery, his exquisite love of life and pleasure, would win any audience — but this.

> That must be our cure
> To be no more; sad cure; for who would lose,
> Though full of pain, this intellectual being,

[7] See below, p. 244.

> Those thoughts that wander through eternity,
> To perish rather, swallow'd up and lost
> In the wide womb of uncreated night?

His arguments are winding and insinuating — "Is this then worst?"
— "that, sure, was worse" — "this would be worse" — "better these
than worse" — and there are both a "dying fall" and an ironic curl
to the phrasing of his final one, "If we procure not to ourselves
more woe." But to his subtle siren voice these doughty and stalwart
spirits, these infernal Ironsides, will not lend an ear, any more
than they do in *Paradise Regained* — any more than the Long
Parliament itself would have done to a Son of Belial. Counseling
Satan in tempting the Son of God to "set women in his eye and in
his walk," he gets a rebuke for his pains almost as if it came from
Raphael. These devils are not without moral insight and dignity.
Satan envies Adam and Eve when he sees them amid their innocent Paradisiacal caresses, but the sentiment does him honor, and
a moment before that he pitied them. And Belial, as he proposes
the measure, is, in his opinions, as the sardonic sound of the verse
betrays, a follower of St. Paul, of Calvin and Knox.

> Skilled to retire, and in retiring draw
> *Hearts after them tangled in amorous nets.*
> . . . .   beguil'd the heart

> Of wisest Solomon, and *made him build,*
> *And made him bow, to the gods of his wives.*

For himself the devil would scorn it!

Even in their occupations and diversions, whilst Satan is on his
fateful voyage, the devils are exemplary. Unlike Dante's, who are
his own contemporaries, they have as yet, of course, no human
beings to torture, but now that they are released from the perpetual round of hallelujahs, they are neither at a loss nor on the
loose. They look before and after. They have a past to lament and
a future to speculate upon, the arts to cultivate and projects to
consider, something to think about, say, or do. Here again Milton

has a freer hand; and is more at home with the devils than with
the angels, not because they are wicked, but simply because they
are limited, and are within the bounds of his and our own comprehension, within those, that is to say, of art. Some indeed were
for Titanic games and sports or for military exercises; but

> Others, more mild,
> Retreated in a silent valley, sing
> With notes angelical to many a harp
> Their own heroic deeds and hapless fall
> By doom of battle.
>
> . . . .
>
> Others apart sat on a hill retir'd,
> In thoughts more elevate, and reason'd high
> Of Providence, foreknowledge, will, and fate,
> Fix'd fate, free will, foreknowledge absolute,
> And found no end, in wandering mazes lost.

These last take to the sober social delights of our great-grand-
fathers! To have given them ignoble pleasures would have been,
indeed, to do violence to the probabilities. They were so recently
from Heaven — their only sin (though a very grievous one in the
eyes of Milton and his age) being rebellion against God, apostasy.
And it is not only gallant and chivalrous in a poet who is of this
opinion, that in denying them one virtue he does not deny them
the others; it is also fair and true — it is drama. But with such warrant and opportunity before him to let himself go, and really play
the devil a bit, few but a Puritan would have refrained. With far
less, Shakespeare or Spenser would have not, like Dante before
them. Milton's procedure is in keeping with his plan; only as time
elapses, in the later books, do the devils degenerate. Now, in their
first respite and amid their pastimes, they are demigods, though
dethroned. They are such as shortly before, when mustered in his
presence, glorious but broken, Satan had wept to see. And they
preserve an academic interest in theology!

5

The most dramatic part of the story is the ninth book, where the Devil and the woman get together, and the man drops into the background. This is the *scène à faire*, to which we have been looking from the outset, but particularly from the first unsuccessful attempt in Book Four, across the edifying narratives of Raphael and his sacred conversations with Adam. And here again Milton, though dramatic, is still himself. He is human, but a Puritan far more than a son of the Renaissance.

The preparations for the scene have been otherwise appropriate and adequate. The Devil is not as he was. Time has told upon him, envy and malice have grown upon him, and he is not the grand and romantic figure he was before his hosts. *He* could hardly have condescended to the serpent or have picked upon so frail and defenceless a victim. Even in the fourth book, as we have already noticed, there are traces of this development, envy and malice supplanting pity, though not without provocation. He seeks a league with the pair against the Highest; he would have them share his lot and his hiding-place, which he did not choose. And there are reasons of state, which we do not quote, as well —

> That I with you must dwell, or you with me,
> Henceforth; my dwelling, haply, may not please,
> Like this fair Paradise, your sense, yet such
> Accept your Maker's work; he gave it me,
> Which I as freely give; Hell shall unfold,
> To entertain you two, her widest gates,
> And send forth all her kings; there will be room,
> Not like these narrow limits, to receive
> Your numerous offspring . . .

There will be room, i' faith. This sardonic vein is deepening, the well of bitterness in him is opening up. It appears again at the end of the book, when he is caught by Zephon and Ithuriel, who know him not — perhaps his greatest grievance.

"Know ye not then," said Satan, fill'd with scorn,
"Know ye not me? Ye knew me once no mate
For you, there sitting where ye durst not soar;
Not to know me argues yourselves unknown."

And now in Book Nine, having been brooded over, this project of malice and spite has become in his mind something fairly heroic. It is a mission, a cause. He will hurt also himself, but he recks not if only he can hurt his foe. He will become the god of destruction, *der Geist der stets verneint*, since he can be none other:

> and him destroy'd,
> Or won to what may work his utter loss,
> For whom all this was made, all this will soon
> Follow, as to him linkt in weal or woe,
> In woe then; that destruction wide may range:
> To me shall be the glory sole among
> The infernal Powers, in one day to have marr'd
> What he, almighty styl'd, six nights and days
> Continu'd making, and who knows how long
> Before had been contriving, though perhaps
> Not longer than since I in one night freed
> From servitude inglorious well nigh half
> Th' angelic name, and thinner left the throng
> Of his adorers.

Titanic blasphemy, gigantic jeer! And the throng he will make thinner still, being ripe and eager for the deed.

6

THE WOMAN

And Eve, against him she has only her innocence. But for such a combat that might be armor enough, were it not like that of Achilles and Siegfried, incomplete. Up to this book the weak spot has not appeared; but the method of portrayal has been rather indirect and negative. We have seen her with Milton's eyes or Adam's, a radiant, alluring vision —

> And sweet, reluctant, amorous delay.
>
> And from about her shot darts of desire
> Into all eyes to wish her still in sight.

When she does speak she shines only by contrast with him. She looks up, not down; she seeks wisdom, does not impart it. But now, in Book Nine, there is a difference of opinion, and she looks him straight in the eye. She would work in her garden alone. For the first time she is self-confident, self-sufficient, and that is to be her undoing. When Adam, after his fashion, argues the point, not only on the general grounds of domestic policy and conjugal propriety but on the special one of prudence, Eve takes it ill — not his manner but his matter — or as ill as a sinless woman can.

> But that thou shouldst my firmness therefore doubt
> To God or thee, because we have a Foe
> May tempt it, I expected not to hear.

She is well-nigh a woman already, in her pique! And though she ends the speech sweetly and appealingly —

> Thoughts, which how found they harbour in thy breast,
> Adam, misthought of her to thee so dear? —

it is with a reproach. She is, in her innocence a pretty fighter, with her woman's tongue.

Without a flaw in the metal temptation is impossible; and this is the least and the most fitting flaw to give her. She is a woman, from the first. She falls through self-confidence, wilfulness, conjugal insubordination. Not from principle but from instinct she chafes under the "absolute rule."[8] Here we can see Milton's Pauline and Hebraic attitude to woman, as in the divorce pamphlets, asserting itself, both in his depiction of her submissive perfection before this and in her faulty wilfulness now. And yet in part this is coincidence. In the Scriptures it is the woman who is tempted and is first to eat; and it is difficult to see how Milton

[8] iv, 300.

could have faithfully treated the difficult subject better in any
other way. And

> Eve
> Persisted, yet submiss, though last, replied.

The final, mellow but wilful, word is hers.

> Thus saying, from her husband's hand her hand
> Soft she withdrew, and like a wood-nymph light

she went her way to ruin.

On setting eyes upon her, Satan, now the Serpent, feels, as the
verse betrays, a thrill of delight —

> when to his wish,
> Beyond his hope, Eve separate he spies;

though in a moment this is lost in admiration and pity. Soon,
however, he collects himself, and approaches her. Flattery is his
method, variously applied. He sings the praises of her beauty,
which, here admired by one man only, is shut in a prison, when
rightly it should have angels in its train. (She would be seen, he
thinks, as he himself would be known; and Adam later flings it in
her teeth that she longed "to be seen, though by the Devil himself.") It was her beauty indeed that drew him to approach her —
once his eyes were opened, and his tongue loosened, by eating of
the fruit — as to the loveliest thing in the world. What fruit? she
asks.

> To whom the wily adder, blithe and glad,

[What a line, in its hard and snaky delight!]

> "Empress, the way is ready, and not long";

and he leads her to it, only to hear her cry out that it is forbidden.
"Indeed," he replies, metaphorically raising his eyebrows, and now
touching up her vanity instead of caressing it —

> Indeed, hath God then said that of the fruit
> Of all those trees ye shall not eat,
> Yet lords declared of all in earth or air?

No, of this only. Thereupon he waxes indignant. Look at me, and
the marvels it has worked! I have not died, but life more perfect
have attained. Knowledge is good in itself. I am as a man since
I ate; so ye, being men, shall be as gods. "For beasts reserved?" she
muses, piqued again, to herself —

> For beasts, it seems; yet that one beast which first
> Hath tasted, envies not . . .

She resents the partial and ungenerous prohibition. She is filled
with curiosity, the spirit of Pandora and Psyche, Fatima and Elsa.
And as the mother of all the women there are to be she has another traditional trait, which has already asserted itself, the desire
to have her way. "A woman will have her will," as the proverb
runs among all males.

> What fear I, then; rather, what know to fear
> Under this ignorance of good and evil?

7

This is well done; but what follows is better. The shackles are
now entirely off the poet's hands, and he is dealing with a mortal,
a woman such as his mortal readers know, though otherwise he
keeps her fairly the same. She tastes, delighted. For, with all his
biblical prepossessions Milton is aware that sin is sweet, not bitter,
is an apple not of Gomorrah, but of the Hesperides, of Eden;
and with dramatic propriety he takes the sinner's own happy point
of view. At once her wilfulness and audacity assume larger proportions. She resentfully and petulantly calls the Lord the "great
Forbidder," as Satan has called him "the Threatener," and waxes
frivolous, insolent, impious —

> Heav'n is high,
> High and remote .   .   .   .

> and other care perhaps
> May have diverted from continued watch

> Our great Forbidder, safe with all his spies
> About him.

And what is she now but a daughter of Tyre or Babylon, her God a Moloch or a Baal? Peradventure he sleepeth. Adam when he falls does not comfort himself so, is not deceived but sins deliberately. Yet her blasphemy, like her finding her sin to be sweet, is natural, arising out of the situation. Her thoughts are the offspring of her passion. Satan, before this, does not call himself wicked, as does Richard III or Iago, but dwells on his "injured merit," and makes God out to be a tyrant. Eve has a similar "defensive reaction."

As compared to Adam's, her speech has a turn more human and more womanish. "Safe with all his spies about him." "Safe" means harmless; and "his spies," of course, the angels. She calls names, considering herself the injured, as the guilty do. Both thought and expression are personal and resentful, petty and feminine. She was personal and resentful in her speech before she plucked the fruit, and now that she is in the wrong the spirit grows upon her, as upon Browning's Ottima after her husband is murdered. She would take his dead hands in hers, and say

> I hate you worse,
> Luca,

and that is the normal feeling when still in the flush and full exhilaration of sin. So Moll Flanders, having robbed the child of its necklace, and thought of killing it too, "conscious of the risk it has run, becomes indignant with the parents for 'leaving the poor little lamb to come home by itself, and it would teach them to take more care of it another time.' " [9] In Elizabethan drama the feeling is nearly always remorse or pity. But moral insight and imagination, not what we call "seeing life," are for the fundamentals of characterization all that is essential; and though people do not ordinarily say so, Milton had the root of the matter in him.

Her next thought is personal too — of Adam.

[9] E. M. Forster, *Aspects of the Novel*, p. 83.

> But to Adam in what sort
> Shall I appear?

Even then, that is the question for a woman. Shall she tell him
and let him share her happiness, or keep and establish her new
superiority? But what if God have seen, and death ensue, and
Adam be wedded to another?

> A death to think! Confirm'd, then, I resolve
> Adam shall share with me in bliss or woe.

Jealousy counts for still more with her than love of sovereignty.
But all her thoughts are personal or practical, definite and concrete; and she is as different from Adam after his sin as Lady Macbeth is from Macbeth.

She now approaches him, but not at all with her heart upon her
sleeve, her sin in her face. Her one thought is of winning him to
share her lot, and she takes to blandishments and wiles. She con-
fesses, indeed, to a fault — in leaving him! But she has missed him,
longed for him, and never again will she quit his side. That she
has eaten of the fruit was owing to her desire for godhead, which
to her, however, is nothing, "unshar'd with thee." Then Adam,
though with many misgivings, rises to the occasion, and nothing
in his life of virtue ever became him like his taking leave of it.
There is an unwonted throb in his utterance as he cries, "How
can I live without thee?" He is a man at last, in his weakness,
though she was a woman at her best.

Her delight hereupon is rapturous because of his love as well as
her fears. Her frivolous recklessness again asserts itself:

> On my experience, Adam, freely taste,
> And fear of death deliver to the winds.

Then she embraces him, and for joy tenderly weeps:

> Much won, that he his love
> Had so ennobl'd, as of choice to incur
> Divine displeasure for her sake, or death.

What could be more womanish, or more in keeping? It is love made precious by sin, more costly, like that of the famous lovers of all time. *Questi, che mai di me non fia diviso!* Or (to speak of lesser ones) it is like the joy of Aldous Huxley's Gioconda, who, hearing that her husband has been accused of poisoning his first wife, eagerly believes it, to his disgust, in the thought that he did it out of his infatuation for herself.

Adam too finds the fruit sweet, for all his virtuous enlightenment; and for a space they revel together. But this first glow of exuberance over, they are unhappy. With his spiritual vision, Adam feels remorse and bewails their error. He has been guilty of no impiety, yet now he has a sense of shame, and dreads the face of God or angel, erst with joy and rapture so oft beheld. He reproaches her, as the cause, with her wilfulness and wandering. She retorts, quite true to her character and to her sex:

> Was I to have never parted from thy side?
> As good have grown there still a lifeless rib.
> Being as I am, why dids't not thou, the head,
> Command me absolutely not to go?

'Tis the unkindest cut, the most womanish touch, of all; but though not so incisive, he is as crushing, as he comes to the natural conclusion, which is Milton's own,

> and perhaps
> I also err'd in overmuch admiring.

This, on one side or the other, is the error in all such situations; but his error was the thing about him that she liked best.

In the later developments Adam, like Macbeth, has far more of a sense of sin; and suffers more in imagination and the religious sentiment. Eve is still centered in her personal relations, lost in her feeling for Adam. He still reproaches her, even threatens her, but she has no reproaches for him. Her contrition is less rational than his, but far sweeter and more beautiful. *Gewissensbisse erziehn zum beissen*; remorse makes Adam "wicked and hateful," though in the end he is bettered by it. But Eve goes no such roundabout way to improvement, abides in her affections, and is above praise as she begs forgiveness and takes the whole fault upon herself:

> Forsake me not thus, Adam. . . .

His reply is not nearly so much of a surrender as it should be; his (and Milton's) sense of the wrong done sticks too much in his mind; and to the end the contrast is preserved between them. Eve, to save the day and retrieve their progeny from the curse, proposes suicide. Here again her woman's practical, impulsive, lawless nature asserts itself. She "takes the nearest way"; she thinks even to defeat the purposes of the Almighty. Adam, who sees more clearly, and remembers and regards the law, dissuades her; [10] and it is to him alone that the vision of the future is vouchsafed, though he is afterwards to report it. And she is true to her woman's instincts even in her attachment to things and places. Unlike the man, she is a child of nature, a grateful or resentful pagan. The tree she had fairly worshipped after she had eaten of the fruit; when she seeks forgiveness she would return to the place of judgment; and when she hears the sentence of expulsion pronounced, she laments the loss of Paradise, her flowers and her bower. And more a woman than ever, she has for a person an attachment still greater than this:

> With thee to go
> Is to stay here; without thee here to stay
> Is to go hence unwilling; thou to me
> Art all things under Heav'n . . .

8

Now Devil and woman, both, fairly take your breath away. And Milton a Puritan? He is a dramatist, if not a "naturalist" — he is a man of the world. But he is that almost despite himself. The

[10] Mr. Erskine, in the article discussed in the seventh essay, says Adam's "admiration for the advice is sincere and unorthodox" (p. 578). This, like many other statements in the article, seems to me little warranted by the text.

character meant to be superior turns out inferior — Adam to Eve, as God to Satan. The consequence of the Pauline and Hebraic doctrine,

> He for God only, she for God in him,

is, as Sir Walter Raleigh says, "that Adam's single impulse of unselfishness, whereby he elects to share the offence and punishment of Eve, is a vice in him, a bad compliance." [11] But the reader cannot think it so; and he is bored by Adam's self-righteousness and condescension, his lectures and admonitions, whether in theology or on woman's sphere and household good, and by his reproaches and his abuse of the sex in general. These traits are owing partly to Puritanism, partly to the poet's own bitter personal experiences,[12] but above all to the inevitable clash between the moral and the human point of view. A character that is a vehicle cannot be an imaginative success as one that is not; and Milton's Eve, like Spenser's Una and Britomart, outshines the man. It is really the same as with the devils; the effect upon us of Milton's own disparaging remarks, as about Satan and Belial, is at times almost swept away once they begin to speak.

In the woman as in the devils we see the poet's humanity asserting itself. Why then do I deny him the label of a humanist? One shouldn't quarrel about mere words; and I do not deny it if humanism means nothing that has to do with a movement or a school, a doctrine or program, nothing self-conscious as humanism ordinarily does. This before us is a matter fairly unconscious. The Puritanism is the conscious motive; in the spirit of Puritanism he attacks the subject; and it is to me fairly unthinkable that it should be another doctrine or principle that here gets the better of that. It is the man within him, the imagination, not the Ancient Cul-

---

[11] *Milton*, p. 148.
[12] Particularly as Adam goes out of his way to prophesy unhappy marriages in days to come, *P. L.*, x, 895–908. Cf. Raleigh, *Milton*, p. 148.

ture or the Renaissance, but Nature herself. Drive her out with a pitchfork —

> Naturam expellas furca tamen usque recurret,
> Et mala perrumpet furtim fastidia victrix.

We are a prey to our method and our formulas; finding school within school, like the waistcoat under waistcoat on Thackeray's George the Fourth, and then — nothing! Really it is only what we see — though less conspicuously because he is less moral in his purpose — in Shakespeare himself. It is no school or movement asserting itself within him as he makes Shylock, Richard III, and Iago speak so much better than they are. It is the sympathetic imagination that possesses him as he throws himself into the part, as it does Milton when he gives the floor to Belial or evokes the womanly, womanish presence of Eve. And then, between us and the critics it is also a question of proportion and emphasis. They have belittled Milton's Puritanism — I have endeavored to demonstrate its prominence and importance.

9

THE POET'S SEVENTEENTH-CENTURY CONCEPTION OF THE SPIRITUAL WORLD: MILTON AND DANTE

Hitherto in our discussion we have seen something of the Puritan pamphleteer and stern prophet, in the poet as in the dramatist, in the foreground as in the background. When we turn to his style and imagery, the Puritan is, of course, less clearly discernible. There is gloom, sublimity, moral rigor and austerity still, but these are Puritan only in comparison with the qualities of a humanist; and the feeling for time and space, for pictorial and spectacular effects, and legendary, historical, and romantic associations, though congenial enough to a humanist, are not necessarily of any creed or sect, church or party. In the eighteenth century Milton was, with Spenser and Shakespeare, a patron of the Romantic Revival. His style was in some ways a model for the neo-classicists before that; and the spirit of his imaginations enters into the poets from Thomson to Keats. It is here that he shows a kinship to Spenser, though he is of a loftier nature, a sterner stuff. But in his conception of spiritual things, as it appears in his descriptive method and imagery, Milton is advanced and progressive, certainly Puritan rather than Catholic or Anglican, and not a humanist if that means to have anything of the spirit of a Greek. He is rationalized and abstract; and though a poet, he strives, as he deals with the other world, to distinguish the immaterial from the material, the supersensuous from the sensuous, as Dante, Homer, and Virgil do not. He is enlightened, in that day of theology and philosophy. The anthropomorphic imagery ("Jocund Day stands tiptoe on the misty mountain-top") of the Renaissance and the Greeks now no longer visited men's thoughts. And as we consider the matter, there are still other distinctions to make, and other likenesses and unlikenesses to demonstrate, between Milton's style and imagery and those of the ancients, Dante, and the moderns.

10

One point is his use of dimensions and distance. As has long been noticed, Milton's conceptions are distinguished by what is vast and vague, lofty and remote. It is not only in the imagery but in the style and the very substance of the story and fable. It is in the similes, it is in the circumlocutions, it is in the scene that he pictures and the stage that he sets. He has a sense for the endless, in both time and space. This has, no doubt, something to do with the Copernican system which, already received into men's minds, had now begun to enter into the inner precinct of their imaginations. It was a little world that was comprehended by Dante, and from the mountain which in a day or so he had climbed afoot the stars looked larger. Now the garden walls of the Ptolemaic uni-

verse were shattered, and men like Milton and Pascal peered with
a shudder into the unending spaces beyond. But the deeper reason
for Milton's penetrating them lay not in the nature of the world
as he saw it but in the nature of the imagination wherewith he
conceived of it, in the subject he had chosen, and in the epic form.

Even in the minor poems, as we shall see, such as *L'Allegro* and
Il Penseroso, the *Hymn on the Nativity* and *Comus*, there are
evidences of his delight in what is spacious and afar, shadowy and
dim. If it were not for Spenser, he might seem to us a romantic
poet before his day. Still, there is nothing of the vast and vague as
we find it in *Paradise Lost*; and this is owing partly to the prodigious dilatation, during twenty years, of his genius, partly to the
demands of his lofty theme. He was dealing with Heaven and Hell,
with the Creation and the Fall, and the scene must be commen-
surate with the new notions of such things now borne into the
minds of men. Dante's terrestrial and celestial system would have
seemed petty and puerile, and so would the beings that inhabit it.
These must be on a corresponding scale. They were spiritual, and
Milton's way to make them such was to make them vast and undefined. Moreover, he was thus following and further developing the
epic principle as it was then understood. The ancients, particularly Virgil and his followers, had sought, not for the vast and vague,
but for the lofty and sublime. Gods and heroes, great deeds and
great scenes were their subjects, and the style and imagery were
chosen to suit.

In the effort to attain the effect of the great or exalted, or at least
avoid the commonplace and humble, they had recourse to circumlocutions. "Where the might of Gabriel fought," is the way Milton
puts it, but the phrase is modeled on the Homeric "might of Hercules" for "Hercules the mighty"; and certainly it magnifies his
strength.[13] So Milton has "from off the tossing of these fiery waves"

[13] See Verity on *P. L.*, vi, 355. The verbal noun instead of the participial
adjective ("the tossing," above, "far off his coming shon," vi, 768) is another

and "overhead the dismal hiss of fiery darts in flaming vollies flew"; as Virgil has *minae murorum* for "threatening walls," *rotarum lapsus* for "gliding wheels." But this rhetorical artifice particularly fell in with Milton's spiritual, metaphysical purpose, and he makes more of it. The world which he is presenting is a world of shades and specters, and it serves rightly to dim the lights, to draw the veil. It lends itself to the effect of distance or uncertainty, which he is seeking; it disguises things humble and familiar, which he would avoid.

> Four speedy cherubim
> Put to their mouths the sounding alchymy

instead of trumpets. And instead of the presence of the figure himself we have but his shadow —

> and by them stood
> Orcus and Ades, and the dreaded name
> Of Demogorgon.

For the same reason the poet makes particular use of the epic device of less familiar and more resounding personal appellations — *Alcides* for *Hercules, Mæonides* for *Homer, Mulciber* for *Vulcan*. More melodious, they are also more remote.

As we have seen, Milton was writing in an age of greater intellectual enlightenment. There was now both a natural body and a spiritual body, as to Dante and Virgil there hardly were. With them nearly everything in the other world is solid and substantial, except the shades themselves; and these in turn have every quality and aspect of the flesh save that of suffering a touch or an embrace. But such materialism Milton endeavors to avoid. He cannot entirely, if he is to remain interesting, but by vastness of dimensions and indistinctness of outline, and by remote and

variety of classical circumlocution, another abstraction, for the same purpose. To those of either sort no modern English poet is so addicted as Swinburne:

> Come with bows bent and with emptying of quivers. . . .
> Over the splendour and speed of thy feet. . . .

roundabout phrases, which replace the common word, and repel the common world, he goes far toward doing this. And he has still other ways and means.

11

Chief of these is his suggestive portraiture and imagery. It is unnecessary to rehearse what Macaulay and Raleigh have said about his dim intimations as contrasted with Dante's precise and intense delineation. That (externally) Milton is mysterious, Dante picturesque, every one now knows. What we shall dwell on is Milton's more sophisticated, seventeenth-century conception and purpose, and I know no better way of demonstrating it than by a comparison of his and Dante's methods.

The Florentine, of course, is telling what he would have us consider a true story, of what he saw and what befell him. The Englishman is repeating sacred hearsays, adumbrating mysteries, in parables and the incompetent language of men. The one has all the vividness and circumstantiality of the traveler; the other has the remoteness and clouded grandeur of the seer or prophet. The one is bent upon making the spiritual world real, with just a touch of the unreal to establish a difference, as when he describes the angel flying over the sea, "beating the air with his eternal feathers, which are not changed like mortal hair." The other is bent upon making the spiritual world unreal, with just a touch of the real to serve as a point of departure. Death snuffs the smell of mortal change on earth —

> So scented the grim Feature, and upturn'd
> His nostril wide into the murky air —

and the rest is left wholly and utterly to the reader's excited imagination.

For, as Dante did not, Milton sees between the two worlds a great gulf fixed; and therefore he draws upon the imagery, not of the world about him, of nature and common life, of craftsmen or husbandmen, at Florence or at Pisa, but of history, legend, and superstition; not upon what he and we have seen, but upon what he and we have read of or heard. He conjures up, not the images of actuality, but mere memories and associations, as less definite and distinct, shadowy as the spirit. When he does make use of natural objects and phenomena, he chooses them from far away — the vulture on Imaus bred, the icebergs of Petsora, a fleet close sailing from Bengala or the isles of Ternate or Tidore. Or if they be near at hand, still he flings over them a veil or mist of superstitious or legendary association. The archangel's face is compared to the sun when it

> from behind the moon
> In dim eclipse disastrous twilight sheds
> On half the nations, and with fear of change
> Perplexes monarchs.

Only when colored and darkened, or far removed, by superstitious, legendary, or remotely historical associations, does Nature well serve his turn. How much dimmer then and unsubstantial! And thus he can lend his subject something even of a moral turn. When Raphael is winging his way through the sky,

> to all the fowls
> He seems a phoenix, gaz'd by all, as that sole bird
> When to enshrine his reliques in the Sun's
> Bright temple, to Egyptian Thebes he flies.

A holy bird, aloof and on a mission, not as others are!

Another device which Milton freely employs to adumbrate the spiritual, in its infinity and its shadowy terrors, is that of paradox or oxymoron. "Darkness visible" is an example. Satan in his infernal exaltation is another —

> by merit rais'd
> To that bad eminence; and from despair
> Thus high uplifted beyond hope, aspires
> Beyond thus high.

And above all, the figure of Death:

> The other shape,
> If shape it might be call'd that shape had none . . .

When the limitations of the natural are thus contradicted and
overridden, the presence of the supernatural is borne in upon us.
But it is an intellectual rather than a sensuous figure, characteristic
of the seventeenth century as not of the thirteenth.

And as a matter of course a more obvious device is employed,
of which in the circumlocutions we have seen examples already,
the use of abstractions. Milton touches them finely. "If shape it
might be called that shape had none." "So spake the grisly Terror."
"And on his crest sat Horror plum'd." "So spake the Son, and into
terror chang'd His countenance." "While I abroad through all the
coasts of dark destruction seek deliverance for us all." This is a
device of the ancient poets and of Spenser as well. But probably no
other poet has made so sublime a use of it, for none ever found it
so wholly to his purpose. In Dante's solid world it had little place.
Science has refined upon faith and in the end dissolved it away. In
the vast phantasm of the modern world, where what is material
becomes fairly spiritual, and what seems dead is alive, and what is
solid and concrete is fired by energies, impelled by affinities, and
governed by laws and forces — where the range of man's vision is
so wide and of his continuance and enjoyment comparatively so
narrow — there is still ampler scope than ever for the use of abstractions and circumlocutions, paradoxes and oxymorons, as in
the poetry of Swinburne and Hugo. Of this world — of this thought
which breaks over the confines of expression — Milton witnessed
the beginnings.

All these devices save that of abstractions are roundabout, or as
Macaulay says of the imagery, circuitous. The poet wheels and
circles round the subject instead of attacking it; and in this way a
vague impression is made upon us instead of the figure itself being
seized. Our emotions are aroused, though little by the most immediate route. Our intellectual prepossessions are respected, our

prejudices spared, but the primary power within us is too little touched. It is through the intellect, indeed, that Milton approaches the subject. The associations are conjured up out of our reading; and these circumlocutions and veiled proper names, these paradoxes and abstractions, all in the first instance depend upon it. Dante at his best presupposes nothing but human nature, and approaches the subject by the unaided imagination. He proceeds from the familiar to the unfamiliar, from the known to the unknown. Milton depends on allusion; Dante, on the visual or auditory image. Milton draws upon legend and history; Dante, upon the present. And how expensive and wasteful is Milton's method in comparison! How many grandiose words and rolling periods, where Dante contents himself, and the ages, with a phrase. Milton takes to simile; Dante to the concentrated metaphor. And Milton's similes are the epical, ample sort of Homer and Virgil, which produce an impression on us as they illustrate the subject by bringing in at the end a picture, indeed, though one which only indirectly concerns it; and which then, oftentimes, with the formula "or like," "or as when," sweep on to another. The poet blurs the outline, intent not upon it but upon the impression alone. An example is the comparison of the angel forms on the fiery pool in number to the

> autumnal leaves that strow the brooks
> In Vallombrosa, where th' Etrurian shades
> High over-arch't imbow'r; or scatter'd sedge
> Afloat, when with fierce winds Orion arm'd
> Hath vext the Red-Sea coast, whose waves o'erthrew
> Busiris and his Memphian chivalry
> While with perfidious hatred they pursu'd
> The sojourners of Goshen, who beheld
> From the same shore their floating carcasses
> And broken chariot-wheels.

And thus one vision succeeds another and only the indefinite notion of innumerableness remains. Dante keeps to one image, his

piercing eye upon it. It is not the impression that concerns him
but the thing itself.

12

Yet in some respects Milton bears the palm away. His devils, as
Macaulay rightly observes, are a far greater imaginative success,
and so (in itself) is his Hell. Dante's devils are gross and fantastic
gargoyles; and the pit and prison which they inhabit, with its close
confines and material horrors, often oppresses and sickens us. It
is all too real. He dwells on the stench, in true medieval fashion;
and the various ingenious tortures are so exactly and relentlessly
described as often to be grotesque or revolting. There is little of
Milton's grand spaciousness and Tintorettesque chiaroscuro.
Often only the human figures give us the necessary poetical eleva-
tion and relief, like Farinata holding Hell in great disdain.

The punishments in Milton's Hell are vague and undefined as
the figures in it. They are spoken of, or referred to, but save the
flames of the pool whereon to lie, and the burning marle whereon
to tread, or the darkness to look not through but upon, they are
scarcely presented. The poet takes refuge in generic or abstract
terms, in wide and shadowy prospects of woe rather than particular
spectacles of torment, and gives to the whole a spiritual turn:

> he with his horrid crew
> Lay vanquisht, rolling in the fiery gulf,
> Confounded though immortal; but his doom
> Reserv'd him to more wrath; for now the thought
> Both of lost happiness and lasting pain
> Torments him: round he throws his baleful eyes
> That witness'd huge affliction and dismay
> Mixt with obdurate pride and steadfast hate:
> At once as far as angels ken he views
> The dismal situation waste and wild . . .

And the same style is used as he describes the overthrow of the
angels in Book vi (860–867), when

> eternal wrath
> Burnt after them to the bottomless pit.

How different from the horrible and unsparing exactitude of many a passage in Dante: "Forth from the mouth of each protruded the feet of a sinner, and his legs up to the calf, and the rest was within. The soles of all were both on fire, wherefore their joints quivered so violently that they would have snapped withes and bands. As the flaming of things oiled is wont to move only on the outer surface, so was it there from the heels to the toes." And yet, no question, this flame scorches, as Milton's cannot. Just as it does in the *Purgatorio*, in the passage where Dante, coming between the setting sun and the fire of purification, makes it ruddy with his shadow:

> Ed io facea con l'ombra più rovente
> Parer la fiamma.

Ruskin compares Milton when Satan rises from the pool:

> On each hand the flames,
> Driven backward, slope their pointing spires, and, rolled
> In billows, leave in the midst a horrid vale. . . .

Here, and in the passage above, about "the dismal situation waste and wild," and in the "darkness visible," there is much that is sublime and picturesque, but not the "intense essence of flame." "Pure, white, hurtling, formless flame," says Ruskin of the passage from Dante; "very fire crystal; we cannot make spires nor waves of it, nor walk on it, there is no question about singeing soles of feet.[14] It is lambent annihilation." And there is intense essence of imagination, also, with no merely picturesque by-product. It is the flame of the Faith, quite as Dante's demons are the devils of Gehenna. "Take heed, take heed," cries Virgil. "Then I turned as one who is slow to see what it behooves him to fly, and whom a sudden fear unnerves, and delays not to depart in order to see.

[14] In the passage from which are quoted the three lines above is the expression "Such resting found the soles of unblest feet," I, 237.

And I saw behind us a black devil come running up along the crag. Ah! how fell he was in aspect, and how rough he seemed to me in action, with wings open, and light upon his feet" —

    Con l'ale aperte, e sovra i piè leggiero.

It scares you even in the verse! It is the sort of devil that may catch and carry you off, in a heedless carnal last moment, any day. *Quaerit quem devoret.*

For if Milton uses popular superstition to make the other world unreal and remote, Dante does this to bring it nearer home. Like Shakespeare with his witches and ghosts, fairies and mooncalves, he develops the notions, and fulfils the expectations, of his public. Like the greatest of poets, he speaks what the people feel and think, bodies forth what they believe in and fear. He avails himself of what is already in their minds, and gives it scope. But Milton, himself past believing in the devils of fable, in eclipses as omens, diverts these living interests from their primary course somewhat to an esthetic end.

13

To the medieval mind, still believing, Dante's Hell is certainly truer and more terrible than Milton's; and even to ours, unbelieving, the Terrestrial Paradise is sweeter than Eden, the Celestial, for all the prim and fantastic precision of its design, more like a heaven. In Milton the externals and the setting are nobler, but for all his enlightenment and his jealous care there is less of a sense of the spiritual world. For though it is well to appease and content the intellect it is better to set a-fire the imagination. The real alone can do this, and of it Milton has given us too little. Macaulay half acknowledges this to be the case: in speaking of Dante's accuracy of description, he says that though a fault it is on the right side. It unquestionably is. No doubt Dante often offends with his crass materialism, particularly in Hell. His spirits at times are as solid and substantial as those which in the semblance of chubby babies issue forth from the mouths of the dying in the Triumph of Death in the Pisan Campo Santo. One of the damned lays hold of the boat of Phlegyas to stop it and has to be flung off by sheer force. Others, prone on the ground, are trod upon by Dante and Virgil as they proceed. Virgil, though himself a shade, repeatedly carries his corporeal disciple in his arm; and they both ride on the back of Geryon, a spirit or demon. The two worlds are in Dante often somewhat confused or confounded, but the one enjoys all the vitality of the other — they are merged. The spiritual is that implied in the dogmas of the Conception, the Incarnation, and the Real Presence, the Resurrection of the Deity and of the Body. It is almost that of his pupil and namesake, Rossetti, where the dying maiden leaves word for her lover, gone on a pilgrimage —

> Say, I'm looking in his eyes,
> Though my eyes are dim.

The chief trouble with Milton is that having successfully created vast immaterial powers, omnipotent and omniscient or nearly so, he turns about and puts them — into a story. It is a contradiction in terms — a story implies limits in knowledge and power. The infinite playing a part, which is necessarily finite! The all-but-infinite, leader of a third part of the heavenly host, plotting and intriguing — the infinite countering him in turn! If God be, how can the angels make shift to rebel against him? It would be utterly silly, if indeed it were possible. And if he be altogether good and just, how in Heaven, where is no sin, could the idea of rebellion enter into the angels' minds? In a story there must be a motive, and they are provoked by God's publicly and formally designating his Son as Vice-gerent, whom this day he has also begotten, and "whom ye now behold at my right hand." All this together is almost as dismaying to the reader as to the future devils themselves. Satan in the epic is provoked like Macbeth in the play, though here by a *coup d'état* that is rather a *coup de théâtre*. Obedience is enjoined under the direst threatenings, but rebellion breaks out immediately and at first enjoys a success. The only explanation is that this is by God's permission, and the only explanation of that in turn is the highly unsatisfactory one that it is a demonstration of his power, for his "glory." The word is fitting in our mouths, even as applied to the motive of a God, but hardly in his own. So he and his immaterial angels become finite and material, as he, for his part, explains and argues, boasts and threatens, contrives and conquers; and they, for their part, quarrel and harangue, fling insults and defiance, arm and muster, march and countermarch, wield the spear and the falchion, fire cannon or hurl mountains in reply — and all this in Heaven, the ineffable Empyrean! The regal pomp and circumstance, the military parade and tumult — despite the sublime description, was it, as Taine questions, worth while leaving earth to find these? And as in a long story it must be, all sorts of subsidiary details, hard to accept imaginatively, then enter in. Eating, drinking, sleeping, loving, and various diversions or pastimes, must be allowed for and alluded to if the story is to be a story; but the presence of them and the lack of them are almost equally disconcerting. The devils, indeed, seem not to eat, drink, or sleep — that may be one of their punishments — though the angels do. But still they have their diversions, as we have seen; the angels can but sing and play on their harps — once only, upon a great occasion, do they dance; [15] and God — infinite, eternal boredom — can do none of these. Both angels and also devils may be wounded and suffer pain, in Heaven itself; and though in dealing with these material details Milton characteristically and felicitously avoids definiteness and precision, he cannot avoid continually raising awkward questions in our minds and difficulties in our path. The story thus contradicts and well-nigh destroys the immaterial effect which Milton has so painstakingly and skilfully

---

[15] v, 620. It is on the occasion of the begetting, and the designation as Vicegerent, of the Son. The dance was "mystical"; hence, for once, permissible in a Puritan poem. Dante is more tolerant.

produced. In Homer it does not do this, the gods being only in the background, and being but mortals made immortal.

14

Dante's story is different. It is not a history of origins and causes, or a justification of the divine polity and governance — things important to the rationalizing seventeenth century as not to the Middle Ages, and the one incredible, the other futile, for us today. It is a voyage, a successive panorama; the actors (whether in the body or in the spirit) being finite, with angels or devils (almost as finite) only at moments intervening. These are beheld but in passing; and the question whether they eat, drink, or digest, sleep or divert themselves, does not arise. The Infinite keeps in the background altogether; and in so far as there is a story, it is that of one soul, what it sees, and hears, and feels. And while the structure of the *Divine Comedy* is by no means so firm and logical, compact and architectural, as that of *Paradise Lost*, which begins well in the middle of things, and, from the fall of the angels leads rationally and directly to the fall of man, nevertheless, in its looseness and consecutiveness, it offers ampler imaginative opportunities, which are deftly employed for the presentation of the world of the spirit. By the very nature of the scheme (as not of Milton's) there are four planes or distances in the picture, which throw one another into relief. There is that of Dante, the living one, that of the dead who are being punished or purified, that of Virgil, dead but neither purified nor punished, and that of the angels and devils. Thus there are various contrasts possible, whether implicit or explicit. By the latter sort the diverse natures of these beings are presented through the simple but concrete method of their effect one upon another, their remarking of differences, their exaltation and condescension, their wonder and amazement, their envy, resentment, or fear. The angel coming over the waves to Purgatory, whose feathers are not changed like mortal hair, is thus described by Virgil, who knows their like, to Dante, who doesn't. Dante himself, within his range, remarks upon the bearing of the Heavenly Messenger, who comes to open the gates of Dis. "The destroyed souls scattered before him like frogs before a snake in the water, as he passed over the Styx with dry feet; and from his face he removed the thick air, waving his left hand oft before him, and only with that anguish seemed he weary. Ah! how full of disdain he seemed to me!"

The main method, however, is by registering the effect of Dante's own presence on the spirits and devils. Hell and Purgatory regard him. They notice the pebbles he stirs with his foot as he walks, the shadow he casts, the movement of his throat as he converses. *He* is the strange one, in this other world. And the spirits cry out upon him, or shrink away from before him, as he speaks or goes. How much more convincing is this — the effect of the real upon the unreal, the real and the unreal changing places — than any possible effect of the spirits on Dante himself! That would be the method of the negative, the unreal and abstract, the method, however subtly and mysteriously touched, of Milton. And it would be less suggestive and startling — why shouldn't the man's throat move, or his body cast a shadow? Where, pray, is he? [16] It is the question before all others that he, as he reports, would hear us ask.

And yet of necessity must be registered at the beginning the effect of the supernatural upon the visitor himself, and this is done with the greatest tact. As Dante, in the wilderness, was falling

[16] The effect on the traveler himself is rightly reserved, not for distinctions between soul and body, but for pity and horror, as evidences of the truth of his story. "Which still makes me shudder," "still it grieves me for them but to remember it," "of such redness that the memory still curdles my blood," and (of the frozen pools)

onde mi vien riprezzo
E verrà sempre, de' gelati guazzi.

Shakespeare, indeed, with his ghosts, Coleridge, in the *Ancient Mariner*, with his spirits, gives the effect of the supernatural on mortals; but the scene is in this world.

back from before the ferocious beasts to ruin, there appeared to him one who through long silence seemed hoarse. That is, he did not speak, though with urgent reason to do so. "When I saw him in the great desert, 'Have pity on me,' I cried to him, 'what so thou art, or shade or real man.'" Like the ghosts of folklore and of Shakespeare, only then does he speak when "spoke to." [17] Then

Risposemi: 'Non uomo, uomo già fui.'

It is all done indirectly, dramatically, by his silence and his speech and by the effect of both. There is no attempt to picture his shadowy, transparent form. Dante thought him a spirit, possibly a man: "No man, a man I was," is (in the original) the eerie and penetrating reply. But the most convincing thing is the question "or shade or real man" — *od ombra od uomo certo*. The order is unusual — his first thought is of a shade, he is in the land of shades already.

In both instances, the effect upon Dante and the effect of Dante as well, there is involved, as I have presented it, a skilful method of assumptions; and assumptions (with preparations, indeed, but no explanations) are the best means of producing that willing suspension of disbelief which constitutes poetic faith. The method of effects and contrasts, sketched above, is that in Shakespeare. After the fitful talk and troubled questioning on the platform, "What," says Horatio, "has *this thing* appear'd again tonight?" He does not mention it by name, for that would be to summon it; they expect it, for they have seen it before this; and the fundamental premise is assumed. It is not yet established. That is done, not by explanations or proofs, but by Horatio's doubt being overthrown. "Horatio says 'tis but our fantasy'," mutters Marcellus. "Tush, tush," he rejoins, "'twill not appear." But appear it does, and the effect upon him convinces us spectators in the house. "Most like," whispers Horatio, and in his very words is the shudder of conviction; "it harrows me with fear and wonder."

[17] Cf. the chapter on the ghosts in my *Shakespeare Studies* (1927), especially pp. 193–194.

Dante's method of contrast, Milton, to be sure, could not employ in Hell, there being as yet no human beings in it. In Eden only Eve sees Satan, and then as a serpent; and Raphael and Gabriel can make no particular impression upon either her or her husband, since they are an everyday occurrence. And on Satan the only effect the immortal human pair can produce is that of enviable loveliness and happiness. Until the fall, when his story is almost over, Milton has not at his disposal these resources of contrast and interplay, of the mortal as a means of approach to the immortal; and he must depend on his great but unaided powers of circuitous description.

15

And there is a general contrast, also, which, as Dante employs it, is only in part at Milton's disposal, but of which even so he but meagerly avails himself. I mean that between this mortal life as we know it, on the one hand, and that in Hell, Paradise, and Heaven, which we know not, on the other. Dante's Hell, Purgatory, and Paradise differ not only from each other as Milton's three worlds do, but from the green Earth as Milton's do less clearly. They are continually flung up against it in relief. All Hell yearns for it or cries out upon it. Purgatory tenderly remembers it. Heaven looks down upon it with a smile. For Earth, though not described or presented, is continually the *point de repère* of the story. The souls in the beyond recall their terrestrial joys and sorrows, their deeds and their misdeeds, their friends and their enemies, and are concerned either to preserve or to obliterate themselves in human remembrance. Among the most thrilling touches in the *Inferno* are those of Farinata's desperate interest in his party at Florence and of Guido Cavalcanti's father's outcry at the thought that his son is no longer alive. Amid all their horror and torment they find it in their hearts to think of these things, indeed it is *because* of them that they do. They are human still, though damned. Indeed, the punishment meted out to them is their earthly passion intensified and (so to speak) inverted. What was their meat is now their poison. The illicit lovers are still locked in each other's arms, tossed and buffeted by the tempest of passion; the hypocrites are still hypocrites, bowed down under their mantles of lead, which are coated with gold.

In all these ways the likeness only brings home to us the difference: the contrast is thus only accentuated and concentrated. It is the principle of many of Dante's comparisons with familiar objects — of the falling flakes of fire with snow on Alps without a wind, or of the beings under them peering at him, with those who look at each other in the evening under the new moon, sharpening their eyebrows at him like an old tailor as he threads a needle. The familiarity and materiality of the figure does not really bring the two worlds together. For an instant it does, but only to fling them emphatically apart: Hell is to Earth as the dropping flakes of fire to — snowfall without a wind. And nowhere does Dante show his instinctive tact better than in the *Purgatorio*, where the scene being in the open, on the mountain, and there being no longer any horrors for a contrast, he is at the pains to remind us of the difference between this and mortal life by multiplying the signs of immateriality, less frequent in the *Inferno*, such as the wonder and fear of the spirits on beholding Dante and such as the empty embraces of Casella. Even in the *Paradiso* there are marvelous glimpses and thrilling reminders of the Earth. In the twenty-second canto the hero, so near to ultimate salvation, looks, at Beatrice's bidding, down through all the heavenly spheres to the world set at their focus, and sees this globe to be such that he smiles at its mean semblance — "and the little threshing-floor, which makes us so fierce, all appeared to me, from its hills to its harbors." And so, from a point still higher, in the twenty-seventh canto, while all the heavenly sanctities blush for shame, Saint Peter declares his seat on earth vacant in the eyes of God. His heart remembers it. Though a saint, he is still the pope, a man.

There is also a great vision of the new world and earth in the
third and fourth books of *Paradise Lost*, as Satan discovers them;
but these are a sinless world and earth, with which ours have little
in common, and the life that we know does not directly appear
in the poem, as we have seen, till towards the end, after the fall,
as Adam and Eve sorrowing but in peace leave Eden hand in hand.
This is beautifully ordered, and is essential to the balanced and
harmonious effect of the poem; but there is lacking the close and
continual interrelation and various contrast to be found in Dante,
in particular, his plastic or dramatic method. There is in *Paradise
Lost*, as we have seen, plenty of drama; and the dramatic form is
throughout finely developed, in so far that, as Addison long ago
observed, "there is scarce a third part of [the fable] which comes
from the poet." But if in *Paradise Lost* we are reminded of everyday life, we are not by the imagery, for there, as we have seen, it
is avoided; nor by the utterances of the characters, for as yet there
are none who can know of it; but simply by Milton's own comment
or allusion. This is proper and permissible enough in a narrative
when it does not jar upon the prevailing tone, or is not off the
subject, as it is when Milton gibes at prelacy or Catholicism; but
structurally it is not interesting. Narrative, in its perfection, approaches the dramatic; does not suffer the author to speak for
himself but only for others; does not tell a thing but presents or
suggests it. Hence, taken as a whole, Milton's epic, while logically,
formally more compact, and far better as a story, with effects of
suspense and dénouement which in Dante are somewhat lacking,
is less compact in its very spirit and essence. It is not held together
by Dante's continual use of interplay and interpenetration, suggestion and complication, parallel and contrast. And so here, as
otherwise, it does not lend itself so well to the main purpose of
bodying forth the spiritual world. It serves for narrative rather
than presentation.

Or (to put it otherwise) it has not so much the effect of the
plastic. Rightly Milton seeks to make the spiritual different and

remote. But his method as we have seen it — of elevated and unfamiliar words and imagery, of circumlocutions and abstractions
— is not the most telling method. It is really simple rather than
subtle, direct rather than indirect, narrative and descriptive rather
than dramatic, graphic rather than plastic. The best approach to
the unfamiliar is from the familiar, is to the new from the old, is
to the ghostly and spiritual from the solid and real. This lends
vividness, and if there be a cunning juxtaposition and contrast,
as we have seen, it lends the illusion of distance too. There is in
Dante something like the perspective of cubist or neoimpression-
ist painting, secured not by shading and gradation but by the apposition of contrasting colors. The perspective is suggested rather
than depicted. And the spiritual world is brought before us, as
we have seen, not warily and remotely, philosophically and explicitly, but boldly and implicitly, by means of the structure and
an art of projection, by skilful adjustments and assumptions. And
in the *Ancient Mariner* Coleridge, though he has Milton's discre-
tion, too, and none of Dante's naïveté, uses much the same method
that here and there we have been tracing — simple and familiar
language (with only a suggestion of the archaic), simple and concrete comparisons drawn from the Mariner's memory of experiences previous to the voyage — which throws the strangeness and
weirdness of this later experience into relief, as do also the inter-
ruptions of the wedding, with its homely traditional merriment,
and of the Wedding Guest, fearful yet spell-bound.[18]

What above all contributes to Dante's purpose is the greater
wealth of emotion that he can bring to bear. He has the immense
advantage of a time that is present, and of the Earth at the center
of the story, though not within the field of vision. Milton, on the
other hand, must lay his scene now in Hell, now in Heaven, before
Earth was. He has therefore no store of experience, no magazine
of emotional energy, on which to draw. His place and his time are

[18] Cf. Mr. Lowes' *Road to Xanadu*.

too distant and dim to touch us. He must needs (or at any rate does) speak the language of the intellect. Heaven, at this early time, at the beginning of things, before human passions have been generated, means law, and Hell rebellion, and Earth obedience and disobedience. But to Dante, passing, amid his hopes and fears, from the Earth and the mortal life he knows of, Hell means horror and despair, Purgatory love and aspiration, Heaven ecstasy and rapture. Thus each of the supernatural domains is charged and colored with passion; and thereby ample amends are made to us for the grotesqueness of Hell and the quaintness of Paradise. Milton's scenery is far vaster and grander, but it is in comparison a little vacant and cold.

In all these respects, then — his abstract conception and clear discernment of the natural body and the spiritual, his interest in the problem of evil and his enlarged notions of time and space, Milton is in sympathy with the Puritan theology and the seventeenth-century science of his time. Though a poet, he is consistent, logical, and analytical, like a Calvinist; not naïve, not hesitating between two worlds — paganism and hebraism, happiness and holiness — like a humanist. Classical in structure and (at bottom) in his style and rhetoric, he develops the old epical artifices to produce effects of vagueness and immateriality which they had never before been made to serve. In form he is classical, in spirit he is ascetic. And the difference between him and Dante in general is, as should be expected, that between the Middle Ages and the Secondary Reformation, not the Middle Ages and the Renaissance.

16

HIS SEVENTEENTH-CENTURY ROMANTICISM

The grandiose and sublime devices and inventions, discussed above, have also a picturesque and romantic[19] aspect, already

[19] For a further discussion of Milton's romanticism, I beg to refer the reader to the essay on Spenser, pp. 174 ff.

touched upon, which is not, of course, specifically Puritan, and brings the poet nearer us today. They serve the purpose of presentation but they also adorn and beautify. To Milton himself no doubt his imagery and ambient method were not the esthetic affairs they are to us and were to Keats. "Darkness visible" is a spiritual torment, not merely a Rembrandtian study in light and shade. Though in it, as in tragic poetry, there is an element of beauty, the emphasis is on the dread and horror. And yet far less, as we have seen, than in Dante. And we cannot but remember that this and other instances were probably inspired by Spenser, as in the Cave of Error:

> his glistring armor made
> A litle glooming light, much like a shade;

or as in the Cave of Mammon:

> a faint shadow of uncertain light
> Such as a lamp, whose life does fade away,
> Or as the Moone, cloathed with clowdy night,
> Does shew to him that walkes in feare and sad affright.

Here the esthetic intention and pictorial relish are apparent. Yet they are, too, in similar passages of Milton's minor poems, though they did not grow upon him, but, as he developed, were subordinated and subdued —

> Where glowing embers through the room
> Teach light to counterfeit a gloom . . .

> Casting a dim religious light.

Even in his Horton period, to be sure, Milton was no Keats or Coleridge, just as the melancholy of *Il Penseroso* is not that of Keats's ode; yet most of these interests in the vast and the mysterious already appear, and for their own sake, with something of a romantic delight:

> To behold the wand'ring Moon
> Riding near her highest noon,
> Like one that had been led astray

> Through the Heav'ns wide pathless way;
> And oft, as if her head she bowed,
> Stooping through a fleecy cloud.
> Oft on a plat of rising ground,
> I hear the far-off curfew sound,
> Over some wide-water'd shore,
> Swinging slow with sullen roar . . .

There the sense of space and distance, with a sight or a sound to lure the imagination on, is quite in the vein of the Romantic poets, from Collins to Keats and Shelley. In *Comus* the mere movement of the third line below, after the tripping ones for the Spirit's flight, suggests the endless expanse of the dome of heaven:

> I can fly or I can run
> Quickly to the green earth's end,
> Where the bow'd welkin slow doth bend.

And in the same poem is the delight in the mystery of space and shadow, fanciful or supernatural shapes and voices, things "weird" and "forlorn," which we find before this in the *Hymn*:

> calling shapes, and beckoning shadows dire
> And airy tongues, that syllable men's names
> On sands, and shores, and desert wildernesses.

> No nightly trance, or breathed spell,
> Inspires the pale-ey'd priest from the prophetic cell.

> The lonely mountains o'er,
> And the resounding shore,
>   A voice of weeping heard, and loud lament;
> From haunted spring, and dale
> Edg'd with poplar pale,
>   The parting genius is with sighing sent.
> With flower-inwov'n tresses torn
> The nymphs in twilight shade of tangled thickets mourn.
> . . . .

> Peor, and Baalim,
> Forsake their temples dim,
>   With that twice-batter'd god of Palestine;

And mooned Ashtaroth,
Heav'ns queen and mother both,
    Now sits not girt with tapers' holy shine;
The Libyc Hammon shrinks his horn,
In vain the Tyrian maids their wounded Thammuz mourn.

As Mr. Bailey suggests, Keats undoubtedly had the first lines in mind as he wrote:

No shrine, no grove, no oracle, no heat
Of pale-mouth'd prophet dreaming.

And in the *Hymn to Christ* and in the *Ode to Psyche* there is the same pleasure, for their own sake, in pagan mysteries and ceremonies, in dreams and trances, in a spiritual moaning and sighing and the glimmering of tapers in the gloom, which we call romantic now. In both there is the right dusky air. Milton, though with greater reserve and continence, began somewhat like Keats — and did not Keats bid fair to end like Milton?

The moving waters at their priest-like task,
Of pure ablution round Earth's human shores.

He had farther to go to attain

To something like prophetic strain,

but he would have arrived.

17

Yet Milton, of course, was not a Keats. This romantic turn, which in his later period he subordinated and subdued, may be conceded to humanism, but a humanism, then, unlike our own. How unlike, appears when we consider this very matter of the infinite, over which his imagination played — was not by it played upon, as is that of our recent poets! In that last figure Keats is in this respect far in advance of Milton; as also are Carlyle, Hugo, and Swinburne. To Milton the vast and spacious is rather actual and physical; in this later day it has entered into the very web of men's imaginations, and has attained to the perfection of expression, which is metaphor. Milton's inward eye reaches

> to the green earth's end
> Where the bow'd welkin slow doth bend,

or beholds the throne
> Of Chaos, and his dark pavilion spread
> Wide on the wasteful deep.

And these visions are sublime. Yet they are, in a measure, scenic, spectacular. They are like those of Tintoretto, of Claude Lorraine and Turner, or the vast landscapes of Byron and Shelley, and are for the space, the vista itself. They are not philosophical, not symbolical. Those qualities are to be found in Keats' lines above, in Swinburne's *Hertha*, with its figure of the Life-Tree, in his *Hymn to Proserpine*, with its figure of the Wave of the World, and in his *Tristram*, with its figure of "Time's pauseless feet and world-wide wings," as in Hugo's figures of the stars as pebbles in the grave of Eternity and of Pegasus winging his way to make a

> brèche au firmament
> Pour que l'esprit humain s'évade.

Of the infinite these poets have ventured to make new imaginative wholes.

And as for the sentiment of time, it plays in Milton comparatively little part. Carlyle's and Arnold's, Hugo's, Swinburne's, and Hardy's constant sense of man's life as a drop or mote in the abyss of eternity, is fairly foreign to him. The sentiment of time is a subtler thing than that of space: it affords a finer ironical contrast, size being a less momentous matter than permanence; and Milton shows a sense of irony in connection with neither. He did not brood; life to him was not much of a mystery; and what sense of mystery we have found in him is for the most part external.[20] It

---

[20] Sir Walter Raleigh finds in him even less mystery than I do: "the fierce simplicity of his processes of thought" (p. 128); "had no deep sense of mystery" (pp. 113, 128, 184); "his clear and positive imagination" (p. 87, etc.).

is scenic, spatial, and a matter of light and shade and a devious description. It does not lie at the heart of things. The irony he feels, as in *Samson*, is like that in the Greek tragedies or the Hebrew prophets, the contrast between man's purposes and Fate's; not between what man seems, or would be, and what he is. It is He that hath made us and not we ourselves, are the words on Fitzgerald's tombstone; and the difference between the meaning of them there and in the ancient psalm is somewhat the difference between Milton and us. He and the Hebrew would not have us glory! For both, the opposition between man and God is not bitter and abysmal. Man to him is immortal, is not, with his belongings, to be swallowed up in what is no better than an instant, in the gulf. He has a place in the sun. Over the Puritan poet's eyes Eternity does not hang, as it does over ours today, like the night. With scarcely a hint in preparation, Conrad can write of Daudet's characters and be at once understood: "They are very near the truth of our common destiny: their fate is poignant, it is intensely interesting, and of not the slightest consequence." What is in the back of his mind and of ours here furnishes the transition; indeed, it is upon this dark ground-work that is spread the whole intricate texture of our poetic thought. We write, we may speak, in symbols, as Milton did not; and it is a mingled web we weave, good and ill together, the individual being merged and tangled in the whole:

> Puisqu' à la voix de ceux qu' on aime
> Ceux qu' on aima mêlent leurs voix;
> Puisque nos illusions même
> Sont pleines d'ombres d'autrefois;
>
> Puisqu' à l'heure où l'on boit l'extase
> On sent la douleur déborder;
> Puisque la vie est comme un vase
> Qu' on ne peut emplir ni vider. . . .

By these dissolving visions and troubled meditations, though of a Christian poet, a poet of the infinite, how he would have been baffled! In no case could he have uttered the like. His imaginations were grander and more passionate, but comparatively a little hard; vaster and more vivid, but comparatively a little simple and bare. He was a reformer, a warrior, though with the pen, the lyre. For he was of the seventeenth century, not of ours; and he believed, as really Cromwell did, that the race was to the swift, the battle to the strong.

INDEX

Index to Proper Names